THE CATHOLIC UNIVERSITY OF AMERICA
CANON LAW STUDIES
Number 57

PAPAL RESCRIPTS OF FAVOR

A DISSERTATION

Submitted to the Faculty of Canon Law of the Catholic University of America in Partial Fulfilment of the Requirements for the Degree of

DOCTOR OF CANON LAW

BY THE

REVEREND WILLIAM H. O'NEILL, J.C.L.
Priest of the Diocese of Seattle

THE CATHOLIC UNIVERSITY OF AMERICA
WASHINGTON, D. C.
1930

Nihil Obstat:

JACOBUS HUGO RYAN, Ph.D., S.T.D.,
Rector Magnificus Universitatis,
Censor Deputatus.
Washingtonii, D. C., die xiv Aprilis, 1930.

Imprimatur:

EDUARDUS JOANNES O'DEA, D.D.,
Episcopus Seattlensis.
Seattli, die xxv Aprilis, 1930.

COMPOSED BY
MONOTYPE COMPOSITION CO., INC.
BALTIMORE, MD.

TABLE OF CONTENTS

PART III

PART IV

FOREWORD

To the Apostolic See, the central authority of His Church, Christ has entrusted the task of distributing many temporal and spiritual favors. These favors are of a varied nature:—some connected with the Church's purely spiritual mission, others with her administrative work, while still others are honorary in character granted in recognition of services rendered to the Church's cause. Time and changing circumstances have affected their number and character. In distributing these favors the Popes, at times, have acted on their own initiative, but oftener in answer to the petitions of their subjects. Papal favors granted in writing in answer to petitions form the subject matter of this treatise.

In the historical introduction, attention has been confined to the discussion of the origin and general development of the papal institution of Rescripts of Favor, with special reference made to the different historical factors that have retarded or accelerated its progress. A brief historical outline of the progress of Papal Rescripts of Justice has been made merely to show forth in bold relief the place that Rescripts of Favor have occupied in the general system of Papal Rescripts. Even for Rescripts of Favor only a general historical outline has been attempted. No attempt has been made to trace the history of each one of the numerous favors that, in the course of time, have been granted through Papal Rescripts, since such a study would lead far beyond the scope of this present work. Instead, the two kinds of papal favors, Benefices and Dispensations, that have exerted the greatest influence on the history of Papal Rescripts have been accorded particular attention in the historical introduction, and in the second part, the efforts of the Roman Pontiffs to develop an adequate system to care for the distribution of their favors have been described. In a general way, the gradual unfolding of papal powers had much to do with the development of Papal Rescripts of Favor. With the growth of the Church came the gradual unfolding of the powers of its central authority, followed, in turn, by continued and persistent efforts on the part of the Church to perfect a system capable of caring for the petitions for favors that came pouring into Rome from all parts of the world. With this progress are connected many important historical factors that have been taken into consideration in explaining the Church's changes of policy in granting different kinds of favors, changes of policy that required her gradually to perfect and accommodate to her own needs a system borrowed from civil law.

The present law has a special title, Title IV in the First Book of the Code, on Rescripts in general, including Papal Rescripts and Rescripts of Bishops and other Ordinaries, Rescripts of Justice and Rescripts of Favor, in which the underlying principles that govern their petition, granting, interpretation and duration are concisely set forth. These principles, in so far as they concern Papal Rescripts of Favor, are explained under their respective headings in the last two parts of this treatise. In this explanation usually a comparison has been established between the present and past attitudes of the Church towards these principles.

At present, the occasion for seeking Papal Rescripts of Favor is not of so frequent occurrence as it was in former times, since the faculties connected by the Code with different ecclesiastical offices, as well as the delegated faculties granted to Ordinaries, have obviated the necessity of much of the direct recourse to Rome for papal favors, but, nevertheless, the principles regarding Papal Rescripts of Favor have not lost their practical importance. Even now occasionally petitions must be sent to Rome for favors either of the external or internal forum, and when such occasions arise it is vitally important that one should know exactly how and where to send the petitions and how to interpret the papal mandate and grant. Moreover, knowledge of the principles that govern the petition, granting, interpretation and duration of Papal Rescripts of Favor is useful for those who must petition for rescripts of Bishops and other Ordinaries, since practically all the principles that apply to the former also apply to the latter.

The writer takes this occasion to express grateful acknowledgment to the Right Reverend Monsignor Filippo Bernardini, S.T.D., J.U.D., Dean of the School of Canon Law, to the Reverend Hubert L. Motry, S.T.D., J.C.D., the Reverend Valentine Schaaf, O.F.M., J.C.D., and the Reverend Francis J. Lardone, S.T.D., J.U.D., members of the Faculty of the School of Canon Law of the Catholic University, for their assistance and direction in the preparation of this dissertation.

PART I

Historical Introduction

CHAPTER I

Preliminary Notions About Rescripts

Article I.—Definition

Rescript was defined by pre-Code Canonists as "a written reply given by the Pope," [1] or, in a somewhat more complete form, as "a written reply given by the Pope to someone's consultation, report or petition." [2] Rescripts, at that time, only applied to Papal documents.[3] Can. 36, §1, however, has extended the meaning of Rescript so as to include similar documents of other Ordinaries. Taking cognizance of this change in meaning, introduced by the present law, canonists writing since the publication of the Code, define Rescript as "a written reply of the Roman Pontiff or other Ordinaries," or as "a written reply of the Roman Pontiff or other Ordinaries to someone's consultation, report or petition."[4]

Article II.—Divisions

This treatise is concerned exclusively with *Papal Rescripts. Episcopal Rescripts* are mentioned merely to note their canonical existence and to refer to the new division of Rescripts that have arisen since the Code. The definition

---

[1] Verani, *Juris Canonici Commentarius*, lib. I, tit. III, n. 1.

[2] Reiffenstuel, *Jus Canonicum*, lib. I, tit. III, n. 2; Pirhing, *Jus Canonicum*, lib. I, tit. III, n. 2; Ferraris, *Bibliotheca*, v. Rescriptum, n. 2.

[3] Reiffenstuel, *Jus Canonicum*, lib. I, tit. III, n. 3; Maroto, *Institutiones*, I, p. 309, nota (1).

[4] Maroto, *Institutiones*, n. 278; Ayrinhac, *General Legislation*, p. 143.

given by pre-Code Canonists for *Rescripts* may be accepted now as the proper definition of *Papal Rescripts.*

The most important, as well as the most ancient, division considers Rescripts from the point of view of their subject-matter, distinguishing between *Rescripts of Justice, Rescripts of Favor* and *Mixed Rescripts. Rescripts of Justice* contain provisions pertaining to legal suits and the administration of justice, e.g., the appointment of judges, determination of kinds of trials, explanations of obscurities in law, and the like. They are called Rescripts of Justice because they refer to matters connected with courts of justice.[5] *Rescripts of Favor* grant favors in no way connected with judicial contentions, e.g., dispensations, privileges, indulgences, honors, and the like. Dispensations from Vindicative, not Medicinal, Penalties are included in this class. They are called Rescripts of Favor because they contain things to which the recipient has no legal title, powers, permissions, etc., because they contain things that are granted as a result of the free choice and generosity of the Roman Pontiff.[6] *Mixed Rescripts* contain at the same time provisions pertaining to the administration of justice and favors not connected with judicial affairs.[7]

Another division that considers Rescripts from the point of view of their subject-matter, distinguishes between those that are *in conformity with (secundum), contrary to (contra),* and *beside (praeter ius)* the Common Law. *Rescripts in conformity with the Law* are those which tend to promote its execution, e.g., designation of a special judge to decide a certain case. *Rescripts contrary to the Law* are those which either relax the law for a person in a particular case or a limited number of cases, e.g., dispensations, or relax it permanently for an individual person or group of persons, as in the case of certain privileges. *Rescripts beside the law* are those which confer favors or

---

[5] Reiffenstuel, *Jus Canonicum,* lib. I, tit. III, n. 28; Maroto, *Institutiones,* n. 278; Ojetti, *Commentarium,* I, p. 208.

[6] Reiffenstuel, *Jus anonicum,* lib. I, tit. III, n. 29, 30; De Meester, *Compendium,* I, n. 290; Vermeersch-Creusen, *Epitome,* III, n. 429.

[7] Verani, *Commentarius,* lib. I, tit. III, § 2, n. 2; Wernz, *Jus Decretalium,* I, n. 149; Cocchi, *Commentarium,* I, p. 158.

powers which neither come under any provision of law nor are opposed to any of its enactments, e.g., indulgences, faculties and certain privileges.[8]

From the point of view of their extension, Rescripts are classified as *General* and *Special.* When all the cases of a certain class, all the persons of a certain place, or all the cases at issue between two persons are dealt with, the Rescript is called *General;* when only certain persons or cases are affected, it is called *Special.*[9]

When the phrase "*motu proprio*" appears in the rescript, the rescript is classified as "*Motu Proprio;*" when the clause is missing, the rescript is said to be given "*Ad Instantiam.*" The presence or absence of this phrase, "*motu proprio,*" in the rescript is significant. When present, it means that the favor is granted, not because of the reasons set forth in the petition, but on account of the free choice and liberality of the Pope, who acts, as it were, spontaneously, without being prompted to grant the favor merely on account of the reasons presented by the petitioner, and without being concerned about the circumstances mentioned in the petition. When the phrase is absent, it means that the Pope, after examining the petition, has granted the favor on account of the motives therein proposed. This distinction has its foundation in the Corpus Juris Canonici.[10]

An equally important distinction is made between Rescripts granted "*in forma gratiosa*" and those granted "*in forma commissoria.*" In the former, no intermediary is used to execute the rescript, the favor is granted by the rescriptor himself directly to the person named in the rescript; in the latter, the favor is granted through the medium of an executor, i.e. through someone commissioned by the Pope to execute the rescript or empowered by him to grant the favor.[11]

---

8 De Meester, *Compendium,* I, n. 290.

9 Maroto, *Institutiones,* n. 278.

10 C. 23, *de praebendis et dignitatibus,* III, 4, in VI°; D'Annibale, *Summula,* I, 222, nota (1); Maroto, *Institutiones,* n. 278.

11 Prummer, *Manuale,* p. 38. Cf. Part III, Chapt. III, Art. III, for the subdivisions of rescripts granted "*in forma commissoria.*"

Article III.—Comparison with other Papal Documents

A comparison with other Papal pronouncements and documents will help to further clarify the concept of Rescript. A Rescript differs, first of all, from an *"Oraculum Vivae Vocis,"* inasmuch as a Rescript is a written concession or declaration of the Roman Pontiff, while an *"Oraculum Vivae Vocis"* is an oral Papal concession or declaration, which may afterwards be put in writing, but only for the sake of proof.[12] A Rescript is intended for the good of private individuals and needs no promulgation, while a *Law* is intended for the common good and requires promulgation to be effective.[13] A Rescript is concerned primarily with a particular personal affair and very frequently is given in simple form, whereas a *Constitution* is a Papal document in which a law is solemnly declared.[14] A Rescript differs from an *Encyclical* which is a solemn letter sent by the Pope to all the Bishops of the Catholic world, or at least to all those of a certain country.[15] A Rescript is a direct answer to a previous petition or inquiry, whereas a *Decree* is not an answer to a specific inquiry, but a letter sent entirely on the initiative of the Pope, usually through the medium of a Congregation that has legislative as well as administrative power.[16] Finally, a Rescript differs from a *Decretal* as a genus differs from its species, because a Rescript may be concerned either with the concession of a favor or the declaration of a right or course of action, whereas a Decretal is concerned only with the latter.[17] Some authors,[18] it must be admitted, contend that Rescripts differ from Decretals because Rescripts have always been sent in answer to an inquiry or petition, while some Decretals

---

[12] Wernz, *Jus Decretalium,* I, n. 149; Ojetti, *Commentarium in Codicem,* I, p. 207.

[13] Sanguinetti, *Institutiones,* p. 68; Ojetti, *Commentarium,* I, p. 207.

[14] Cocchi, *Commentarium,* I, p. 158.

[15] Ayrinhac, *General Legislation,* p. 143.

[16] Smith, *Elements of Ecclesiastical Law,* p. 27; Maroto, *Institutiones,* n. 278; Coronata, *Institutiones,* I, n. 57.

[17] Laurin, *Introductio in Corpus Juris Canonici,* p. 15; Maroto, *Institutiones,* n. 278; Coronata, *Institutiones,* I, n. 57.

[18] Wernz, *Jus Decretalium,* I, n. 149; Cocchi, *Commentarium,* I, p. 158.

were issued by the Pope when no previous inquiry has been made. Such an opinion, however, is inadmissible since the Decretals have for centuries been looked upon as letters sent by the Pope in response to consultations, as the glossators to the dict. grat., dist. III, voc. "*Omnes,*" and to the bull "*Rex Pacificus,*" voc. *Constitutiones,*" clearly testify.[19] The real and only difference, then, between Rescripts and Decretals is that the former is more comprehensive than the latter.

[19] Reiffenstuel, *Jus Canonicum,* lib. I, tit. II, n. 10; Ponsius, *Jus Canonicum,* I, p. 180; Schulte, *Geschichte der Quellen,* I, p. 42; Laurin, *Introductio in Corpus Juris Canonici,* p. 15.

CHAPTER II

Rescripts in Roman Law

Rescripts were first used by the Roman Emperors towards the close of the First Century of the Christian era in the form of written replies to the inquiries of judges and other public officials. These answers were written either on a separate document from the inquiry in a brief and informal manner, or on the side or bottom of the application itself. The former, known as *"Epistolae,"* existed during the reign of Trajan (98-117), while the latter, the *"Subscriptiones"* or *"Adnotationes,"* appeared under Hadrian (117-138).[1] A special form of Rescripts, the *"Pragmaticae Sanctiones,"* was issued by the Emperor in matters of great importance, when, e.g., the inquiry was made by a school, a city or a province. From the fifth century, however, these *Pragmaticae Sanctiones* were called *Constitutions* and ceased to have the character and nature of Rescripts.[2]

History suggests this classification of Rescripts taken from the point of view of both the form of the documents and the class of people to whom they were addressed, but there is another division of more interest to us, namely, the one that differentiates Rescripts of *Justice* from those of *Favor.*

Rescripts of Justice were the first to appear in Roman Law. Originally, Rescripts were not intended to change the law or grant exceptions to it but rather to explain it

---

[1] C. I. 23. 7; Buckland, *Text-Book of Roman Law,* pp. 19, 20; Cicognani, *Jus Canonicum,* II, p. 202; Savigny, *System of Modern Roman Law,* I, p. 103; Maroto, *Institutiones,* n. 279, nota (1); Sohm, *The Institutes of Roman Law,* p. 105.

[2] C. I. 23. 7. 2; Cicognani, *Jus Canonicum,* II, p. 202; Savigny, *System of Modern Roman Law,* p. 103; Morey, *Outlines of Roman Law,* p. 106.

to the inquirer. In their original form, they were granted by the Emperor to protect the process of justice in different parts of the Empire and hence were called Rescripts of Justice.[3] From the time of Hadrian, judges were wont to ask advice from the Emperors about trials that were extremely difficult of solution. They informed the parties involved in the litigation that an appeal for advice was being sent to Rome and invited them to add documentary proofs to their explanation of the case to the Emperor. The reply of the Emperor, the Rescript, contained either the decision that the Judge was to render or else the principle on which the final decision was to be made—provided, of course, that the Emperor recognized the need of interposing his authority in the matter.[4] Rescripts of Justice were also issued to private individuals. During the reign of Hadrian, parties involved in litigations or impending litigations were permitted to direct personal inquiries about their cases to the Emperor. They were prompted to appeal to the Emperor for a decision either because they feared that the Judge before whom they were to appear was prejudiced against them, or because their rank and dignity restrained them from appearing before an ordinary Judge. If the Emperor decided to answer their inquiry instead of allowing the matter to go through the ordinary process of law, he sent his decision to the petitioner, leaving him free, however, to disregard or take advantage of the rescript, as he saw fit.[5]

Some letters, however, were sent to the Emperor, not to inquire about the law but to seek exceptions from it, to petition favors from the Emperor. As a result, the Emperors, in the course of time, granted different kinds of favors and privileges to their subjects. They granted dispensations from tutorship;[6] privileges to creditors in case of bankruptcy;[7] and legitimation of children, whereby natural children were placed under the power of their father. In

[3] Buckland, *Text-Book of Roman Law,* p. 20.

[4] Buckland, *Text-Book of Roman Law,* pp. 665, 666.

[5] Radin, *Handbook of Roman Law,* pp. 76, 77; Buckland, *Text-Book of Roman Law,* p. 666; Sohm, *Institutes of Roman Law,* p. 105.

[6] D. XXVII. 1. 30. 2.

[7] D. XLII. 5. 24. 2. 3; D. XLII. 5. 32.

order to take care of cases in which the father, during his lifetime, neglected to petition the Emperor for the legitimation of his children, it was specially provided by law that the children themselves could obtain it, on condition that their father intimated in his will a desire that they be legitimated.[8] The answers of the Emperors to these petitions for favors were commonly known as "*Personales Constitutiones,*" but despite the fact that some authors, who contend that Rescripts were always in accordance with the law, are unwilling to classify the "*Personales Constitutiones*" as Rescripts, many modern authors feel no hesitancy in designating them as *Rescripts of Favor.*[9]

Not all imperial letters in answer to particular inquiries or petitions can be classified as Rescripts. Occasionally, the Emperor, in response to an inquiry concerning some disputed point in a trial, issued a letter formulating a rule intended for general application. The letter would be occasioned by an inquiry about a particular case, but it was the intention of the Emperor that the answer should be applied not only to the case in question but to all similar cases. Accordingly, means would be taken to have the rule promulgated:—sometimes provision for the method of promulgation would be made in the letter itself, but oftener it would be carried out in accordance with previous directions given to the functionaries to whom the letters were addressed. In earlier times these letters were called *General Letters* or *General Rescripts;* [10] later, when the Emperors began to issue them more frequently, they were known as *Laws, Edicts,* and *Constitutions.* In the Theodosian Code, which is in the main, a compilation of such enactments, they are referred to as constitutions and general edicts.[11] Despite the fact that in earlier times they appeared in the sources as Rescripts, these letters really cannot be classed as Rescripts, properly so-called, because

[8] N. LXXXIX. 9. 10; Leage, *Roman Private Law,* p. 71; Hunter, *Introduction to Roman Law,* p. 203.

[9] Hunter, *Introduction to Roman Law,* p. 203; Leage, *Roman Private Law,* p. 71; cf. Savigny, *System of Modern Roman Law,* p. 104, nota (c).

[10] D. XI. 4. 1. 2; D. XLVII. 12. 3. 5.

[11] C. Th. I. 1. 6.

they were intended for general application:—they are better assimilated to Edicts or Mandates.[12]

Rescripts in Roman Law were distinguished from *Imperial Decrees, Mandates,* and *Edicts. Decrees* were final decisions rendered by the Emperor in cases tried before him. Before Justinian's time they had value only for the particular cases for which they were granted, but Justinian ordained that they were to have force of law for all similar cases and obliged judges to use them as guides in rendering their decisions.[13] *Mandates* were Imperial instructions addressed to certain officials, e.g., Provincial Governors, Judges or Legates, concerning work connected with their official duties. They had the force of law in the provinces for which they were issued. *Edicts* were solemn ordinances issued by the Emperor by virtue of his supreme magisterial power, communicated first to the Senate and then promulgated by the Provincial Governors. They had the force of universal law.[14].

In estimating the value of Rescripts in Roman Law distinction must be made between Rescripts of Favor and Rescripts of Justice.

Rescripts of Favor had a very limited value. They bestowed upon the individual a certain right to a particular object or power to which previously he had no claim, e.g., dispensations, pecuniary assistance or legitimation of children; as soon as the rescript became actually effective, however, it ceased to have any further value than of insuring possession of the newly attained power or object.

Rescripts of Justice had a far greater legal value than did Rescripts of Favor. Whether they contained a rule already existing in law or an extensive interpretation of a previous law, Rescripts of Justice had full legal value for the particular cases that occasioned their issuance. Whether the rescript was addressed to the Judge or to one of the litigants, the Judge was no longer permitted to decide the

---

[12] Savigny, *System of Modern Roman Law,* pp. 105, 106.

[13] C. I. 14. 12 pr; Maroto, *Institutiones,* n. 272; Savigny, *System of Modern Roman Law,* pp. 100-102; Sohm, *Institutes of Roman Law,* p. 105.

[14] Savigny, *System of Modern Roman Law,* pp. 98, 99, 113, 114; Sohm, *Institutes of Roman Law,* p. 105.

case according to his own convictions but was bound to decide it in accordance with the rule contained in the rescript. Moreover, if one of the litigants received the Rescript he could use it even after a long lapse of time: in fact it had such a value that his heirs could use it in case the recipient of the Rescript did not avail himself of its benefits during his lifetime.[15]

Unfortunately the great legal value of these Rescripts exposed trials to the danger of miscarriage of justice. When the parties themselvés appealed to the Emperor, it was very easy for them either to falsify facts and give a rather one-sided view of the case in their petitions, or to tamper with the Rescripts. The Emperors resorted to various means to lessen this danger of fraud and falsification. They gave precise and specific directions regarding the form of rescripts so that any tampering with the documents might easily be detected;[16] they allowed the opposing parties to have recourse to special procedure, even appeal, whenever falsehood or fraud was suspected, and instructed Judges to investigate and punish such frauds;[17] they even declared that all rescripts contrary to recognized laws or to the interest of the State were to be considered null and void.[18] Finally, when all remedies failed to correct the abuses, Justinian forbade Judges to take cognizance of any private rescripts:—thereafter, only the rescripts that were sent directly to the Judges had any legal value.[19]

Provided that its authenticity or validity was not questioned, a Rescript of Justice had a real legal value for the particular case in question, but a limited value, nevertheless: limited, as far as law was concerned, to that specific case.[20] That such a limitation was intended by the Emperors is confirmed by the fact that no provision was made for the promulgation of Rescripts of Justice, something absolutely necessary in order that any pronouncement of

---

[15] C. Th. I. 2. 4. 2; C. Th. 1. 2. 12; Savigny, *System of Modern Roman Law*, p. 107.

[16] C. I. 23. 3. 4. 6.

[17] C. I. 23. 7; C. I. 22. 2-5.

[18] C. I. 22. 6; C. I. 19. 3. 7; C. Th. I. 2. 2. 1; N. LXXXII. 13.

[19] N. CXIII. 1.

[20] C. I. 14. 2; C. Th. I. 2. 11.

the legislator be recognized as having full force of law.[21] This limitation of legal value was established either because there was no necessity of giving rescripts any greater value or because the Emperors feared that if rescripts were given wider application, erroneous and false principles of law might arise from falsified petitions or from cases in which special circumstances were involved.

While Rescripts of Justice were not given full legal value for other similar cases, they were not devoid of all authority. As decisions of the Emperor, they enjoyed a special importance, and indirectly influenced other trials and subsequent legislation. But, at the same time, inasmuch as their authority was of such a nature that they were open to criticism and rejection by the jurists, there was no great danger that false principles of law would arise from fraudulent petitions.

Judges presiding over trials were influenced directly and indirectly by these Rescripts of Justice: directly, if they were personally acquainted with the Emperor's decision in a similar case; indirectly, by the Jurists. The Jurists lived near the Emperor, frequently assisted him in the compilation of the Rescripts, and had fairly free access to the archives. Naturally they were influenced by the decisions contained in the Rescripts and, in turn, influenced the Judges who consulted them during litigations. Moreover, some of their works which were considered to have great value, seem to be, in part, at least, collections of Rescripts. The "*Papirii Justi Libri XX Constitutionum,*" judging from the fragments that have been preserved, was a compilation of Rescripts; so also, for the most part, were the Gregorian and Hermogian Codes. These compilations of Rescripts were bound to influence the decisions of Judges and even to affect the trend of subsequent legislation.[22]

When the inquiries and petitions sent to the Emperor became very numerous, a regular office was established to care for them and a learned legal council was formed to decide upon the questions at issue. Until the time of

---

[21] Savigny, *System of Modern Roman Law*, pp. 109, 110.

[22] Savigny, *System of Modern Roman Law*, p. 110; Sohm, *Institutes of Roman Law*, p. 107.

Hadrian this council was more or less casual and changing, but thereafter it became a more permanent organization. Thus the decision, although given in the Emperor's name and invested with his authority, was usually the decision of a highly competent privy council that had judicial as well as professional experience to assist the Emperor in such technical work.[23]

In Roman Law, therefore, Rescripts, properly so called, as distinct from General Rescripts, were clearly distinguished from Edicts, Mandates, and Decrees, inasmuch as they had legal value only for a specific case; and Rescripts of Justice, by far more numerous and more important than Rescripts of Favor, were a potent factor in influencing contemporary and succeeding processes of justice.

---

[23] Radin, *Handbook of Roman Law*, p. 77.

CHAPTER III

Historical Development of Papal Rescripts of Favor

Article I.—Summary History of Papal Rescripts in General

The historical development of Papal Rescripts of Favor is best comprehended in its true significance when viewed in the light of the development that, in the course of time, has also attended Rescripts of Justice.

§1. *Before the Twelfth Century*

Authors are fairly well agreed that the Church has adopted her institution of Rescripts from Roman Law.[1] No servile attitude toward Roman Law, however, prompted her in this:—it was but a natural outcome of her own development. Possessing powers in ecclesiastical matters even greater than those exercised by the Emperors in civil affairs, and with a kingdom spread throughout the world, it was to be expected that the Pope would receive and answer, in writing, many inquiries and petitions of his subjects. If there had been no civil law with available methods and institutions, undoubtedly the Church would have, on her own initiative, evolved a system somewhat similar to the Roman institutions of Rescripts to care for the inquiries and petitions she received. As a matter of fact the Church found in Roman Law an institution that suited her purpose and she adopted it.[2]

Authors likewise agree that Rescripts are a very ancient institution in the Church, that the Popes from the earliest times, when petitioned by Bishops or faithful for favors

[1] Wernz, *Jus Decretalium*, I, n. 149; Chelodi, *Jus De Personis*, n. 75; Cicognani, *Commentarium*, p. 202; Ojetti, *Commentarium*, I, p. 207, nota (3); Vermeersch-Creusen, *Epitome*, I, n. 123.

[2] Wernz, *Jus Decretalium*, I, n. 149.

or for the solution of doubts about law, were wont to reply by means of Rescripts.[3] It is regarding the determination of the exact time when the Popes first issued Rescripts that authors seem to disagree. Some[4] say that the first Rescript was granted by Pope Siricius to Bishop Himerius in 385; while others[5] insist that there were earlier ones granted by the Popes. Although apparently at disagreement, these two opinions are not irreconcilable. The oldest Rescript actually known to us is the one of Pope Siricius, but it cannot be said, with certitude, that Popes did not grant them before that time. Rescripts, being of a private character, would not be accorded the same attention as other Papal documents and consequently would not have the same chance of being preserved. While there is no positive evidence on which to base a certain conclusion, it is at least probable that the Rescript of Pope Siricius was not the first Papal Rescript.

Unquestionably the letter of Pope Siricius must be classed as a Rescript.[6] The words of the letter itself, *"ut ad ea, quae ad consulta, rescripsimus,"*[7] show that it was written in response to a petition or inquiry of Bishop Himerius. The contents of the letter are varied:—granting permission to lapsed clerics to exercise their orders, giving the solution of many questions regarding the administration of the Sacraments of Baptism, Penance, and Orders, determining the proper tribunal for disputes among churches, the attitude Bishops should take towards condemned clerics, etc. Unfortunately, the petition of Bishop Himerius is not extant and we are unable to say positively whether or not all that is found in the rescript of the Pope was in answer to the inquiry of the Bishop, but since the Pope towards the end of the letter refers to a previous consultation it is

---

[3] Wernz, *Jus Decretalium,* I, n. 149; Ojetti, *Commentarium,* I, p. 207, nota (3); Chelodi, *Jus De Personis,* n. 75; Vermeersch-Creusen, *Epitome,* I, n. 123; Maroto, *Institutiones,* n. 279; Cicognani, *Commentarium,* p. 203.

[4] Chelodi, *Jus De Personis,* n. 75.

[5] Wernz, *Jus Decretalium,* I, n. 149, nota (14).

[6] Wernz, *Jus Decretalium,* I, n. 149; Cicognani, *Commentarium,* p. 204; Chelodi, *Jus De Personis,* n. 75.

[7] Coustant, *Epistolae Romanorum Pontificum,* I, p. 631, n. 11; Amort, *Elementa Juris Canonici,* I, p. 221.

certain that at least some of it was in answer to a previous petition. The letter may be classified as a mixed Rescript since it not only grants favors but also settles judicial disputes, e.g., by determining the proper tribunal for disputes among churches. Moreover it was a General Rescript (in the sense given in Chapter I), i.e. a rescript not intended for a physical or moral person but for all those of a certain district, since at the end of the letter Bishop Himerius was instructed to acquaint not only those of his own diocese but also those of the dioceses of Gaul and Africa with the contents of the letter.[8]

Between the time of Pope Siricius and Pope Alexander III (1159-1181), Rescripts were granted rather frequently by the Popes. As early as the Fifth Century, judging from the words of the Popes, Rome was often consulted by Bishops from all portions of the Christian world.[9] During this period, Rescripts of Justice occupied a place of importance in Church affairs similar to that which they held in Roman Law. They were granted more frequently than Rescripts of Favor and exercised a very important part in the development of the disciplinary law of the Church. Many of the Decretal Letters, which were Rescripts of Justice, found their way into the older collections of Canon Law, and through them, into the *Decree of Gratian* and the other books of the *Corpus Juris Canonici.* These Decretal Letters were written by the Popes to different bishops, abbots, and other ecclesiastics concerning disciplinary matters, and the fact that they commence with such words as *consulisti, consuluit, insinuante, insinuatum est, significasti,* and *postulasti* is sufficient evidence to classify them as Rescripts.[10]

---

[8] Coustant, *Epistolae Romanorum Pontificum,* I, p. 631, n. 11; Amort, *Elementa Juris Canonici,* I, p. 221.

[9] Pope Innocent I (399-402), writing to the Council of Milevitanus, states that "replies to petitions go forth from the Apostolic fountain throughout all the provinces."—M. P. L., 20, 589; Pope Leo the Great (440-461), in a letter to the bishops of the province of Vienna, says "The Apostolic See is consulted by innumerable reports."—M. P. L., 54, 630.

[10] Reiffenstuel, *Jus Canonicum,* lib. I, tit. III, n. 1.

§2. *After the Twelfth Century.*

The twelfth century marks the turning point in the development of Rescripts—as far as their use and theory were concerned.

From the time of Pope Alexander III (1159-1181), Rescripts of Justice as well as Rescripts of Favor were granted more frequently. The Popes reserved more benefices and dispensations to themselves and granted dispensations more freely; they delegated judicial cases oftener, and increased the formalities in judicial processes, with the natural result that the work of granting Papal Rescripts assumed a place of importance in the ecclesiastical life of Rome. This naturally drew the attention of canonists to the study of the theory of Rescripts, and under the influence of the attendant study of Roman Law, the theory of Rescripts enjoyed its first real important development.

The compilation of Bernard of Pavia (1189-1191) known as the *Compilatio prima,* was the first to contain a special title on Rescripts. Thereafter all the canonical collections, including those of the *Corpus Juris Canonici,* followed his example. The attention and concern of the Popes to develop the theory of Rescripts is clearly evidenced by the increasing number of Decretal Letters referring to the canonical doctrine of Rescripts that each succeeding canonical collection contained. By the time the *Corpus Juris Canonici* was closed, the doctrine of Rescripts was in many points identical with the law now contained in the Code.[11]

In the fourteenth century, the publication of the Rules of the Apostolic Chancery which contained many regulations regarding the issuance, execution and use of Rescripts, helped considerably to develop the theory of Rescripts.[12]

Progress and change continued to mark the history of Rescripts. Rescripts of Justice and, among Rescripts of Favor, those granting Benefices decreased rapidly, while those granting Dispensations became more frequent. The

---

[11] Wernz, *Jus Decretalium,* I, n. 149; Maroto, *Institutiones,* n. 279; Vermeersch-Creusen, *Epitome,* I, n. 123; Cocchi, *Commentarium,* I, p. 147; Ojetti, *Commentarium,* I, p. 207, nota (3). Cf. Part III, IV, where comparison is frequently established between Decretal Law and the Law of the Code.

[12] Wernz, *Jus Decretalium,* I, n. 149.

present stage in the process of the evolution of Rescripts finds dispensations, especially matrimonial dispensations, constituting the major portion of Papal Rescripts.[13]

To trace historically, one by one, the development of the various kinds of Papal Rescripts of Favor, benefices, dispensations, privileges, indulgences, honors, degrees, etc., would tend towards repetition and tediousness. Benefices and Dispensations stand out prominently as having real historical value. The following two articles of this chapter will trace summarily their development in history with particular attention given to the external influences that have effected their canonical status and importance.

Article II.—Development of Papal Rescripts of Benefices

An ecclesiastical *Office*, in the broad sense, is "a function exercised for a spiritual end in conformity with canonical rules," as, e.g., the office of chaplain; in the strict sense, it is "a function established by divine or ecclesiastical authority, permanent in character, to be conferred in the form prescribed by the canons, and implying some participation of ecclesiastical power, either of order or jurisdiction," [14] e.g., the office of pastor or bishop.

An ecclesiastical *Benefice* is a "juridical entity, established or erected in perpetuity by competent ecclesiastical authority, consisting of a sacred office and the right to receive the revenues connected with the office." [15] Papal benefices are consistorial if conferred in the Consistory, otherwise non-consistorial. The major benefices which have complete and perfect jurisdiction, legislative, judicial, and coercive, as the Bishopric, are usually conferred in the Consistory.[16]

Papal reservation of benefices are papal acts removing from the jurisdiction of bishops certain benefices that are to become vacant in the future. At first the Popes by individual acts, by "*Mandata de providendo*" and by "*Litterae*

[13] Wernz, *Jus Decretalium*, I, n. 149; Chelodi, *Jus De Personis*, n. 75.
[14] Can. 145, §1; Ayrinhac, *General Legislation*, p. 316.
[15] Can. 1409.
[16] Golden, *Parochial Benefices*, p. 12.

Expectativae," interposed their authority in the conferring of benefices outside of Rome. They issued mandates to Bishops recommending certain clerics for benefices vacant in their dioceses, or expectative letters designating certain clerics for benefices that would become vacant in the future, either particular benefices or the first benefices to become vacant. Later, by general acts, they removed all benefices of certain characteristics from the jurisdiction of bishops and personally cared for the appointment to the benefices by means of mandates and expectative letters.[17]

When issued in answer to petitions, these Mandates and Expectative Letters became Papal Rescripts of Favor. Actually many of them were issued in response to petitions, and as has already been mentioned in the preceding article, towards the end of the Middle Ages, Rescripts of Benefices shared with Rescripts of Justice the place of prominence among Papal Rescripts.

§1. *Papal Reservation of Benefices before the Twelfth Century*

The history of Papal Rescripts of Benefices is intimately connected with the history of papal reservation of benefices, since the number of papal rescripts of benefices increased when more benefices were reserved by the Popes.

The Popes, like other Bishops, from earliest times, conferred the benefices of their own diocese, but long before the twelfth century they began occasionally, though not regularly, to take some part in the appointment of ecclesiastical benefices outside the diocese of Rome.[18] As early as the time of Gregory the Great (590-604), Popes issued occasional mandates for benefices, even abbacies, in Italy and its adjacent territory, when necessity or the lack of fit candidates required it. This practice continued until the twelfth century.[19]

---

[17] Golden, *Parochial Benefices*, pp. 40, 41.

[18] Thomassinus, *Ecclesiae Disciplina*, pars II, lib. I, cap. XLI, n. 2-22; cap. XLII, n. 1-5; Wernz-Vidal, *Jus Canonicum*, II, n. 228; Ojetti, "Roman Curia," *Catholic Encyclopedia*, XIII, 152; Golden, *Parochial Benefices*, p. 39.

[19] Thomassinus, *Ecclesiae Disciplina*, pars II, lib. I, cap. XLI, XLII, n. 1-5.

§2. *Papal Reservation of Benefices after the Twelfth Century*

The twelfth century marks a decided change in the policy of the Popes regarding the appointment to benefices outside the diocese of Rome. From that time onward, the Popes became more and more active in the disposal of ecclesiastical benefices throughout the world, at first by commanding that certain benefices be granted to particular individuals, and later by taking from the individuals who had been appointing to certain ecclesiastical benefices the power to continue to fill the benefices, and reserving the power to themselves. Before the Holy See had reserved to itself the actual granting of a great number of benefices it had asserted its innate right to dispose of all the benefices and offices in the entire church.[19a]

To understand the motives that prompted the Popes to take a more active part in the disposal of ecclesiastical benefices throughout the world, one must take into account the conditions of the times. In the eleventh and twelfth centuries, simony and laxity among the clergy were the two great evils that the Popes had to contend with in their endeavors to reform the Church. Civil interference with canonical appointments and lay investiture were largely responsible for the presence of these evils in the Church. Gradually, the civil rulers had been able to gain control of the appointment of the more important benefices in their domains; bishops and abbots, owners of large tracts of land, came to be looked upon by them practically in the same light as the secular nobility, and the civil rulers in appointing or influencing the appointment of these officials looked for individuals that would be suitable from their own point of view. All this naturally resulted in the appointment of many ecclesiastics who were undeserving of the benefices entrusted to them. The Popes in seeking to reform conditions in the Church saw the necessity of severing the connection of the civil power from the appointment to ecclesiastical benefices:—hence the untiring zeal displayed especially by Gregory VII and Innocent III in destroying the

[19a] Implicitly contained in decretal of Nicholas I (858-867)—c. 1, D. XXII, explicitly stated by Clement IV (1265-1268)—c. 2, *de praebendis et dignitatibus*, III, 4 in VI°.

institution of lay investiture.[19b] But even when the Church finally succeeded in 1122 to obtain recognition of the principle of the freedom of the Church in ecclesiastical appointments, the interference of civil authority in appointments to the benefices of the Church did not cease.[19c] Moreover, although the elections to the important benefices were restored to ecclesiastical personages, e.g., elections of Bishops gradually came into the control of the canons of the cathedral chapters with confirmation by the Metropolitan, the negligence of the electors, dissentions in their ranks, and unreasonable delays in the filling of important ecclesiastical benefices [19d] caused the Popes to exercise more and more their prerogative of disposing of ecclesiastical benefices throughout the Church by individual appointments or by reservations of different kinds of benefices. Always their purpose, as expressed in various documents, which are referred to later, was to provide the ecclesiastical benefices with suitable officials and to provide means of sustenance for deserving poor clerics.

Beginning with the twelfth century, when ordination and the granting of benefices became distinct,[20] the Popes issued mandates and expectative letters more frequently, even outside the territory of Italy. They were prompted to do so by a desire to supply support for clerics who, contrary to the canons, were ordained without title, or for clerics who had proved themselves especially deserving of reward.[21] Innocent III (1130-1143), Eugene III (1145-

---

[19b] Munro, *The Middle Ages*, pp. 165, 168-169; Mann, *Lives of the Popes*, VII, pp. 35, 36, 77, 88, 210; *Cambridge Medieval History*, V, p. 99; VI, pp. 38, 40, 60, 99; Hulme, *The Middle Ages*, pp. 402, 403; Coronata, *Institutiones*, n. 393; Thomassinus, *Ecclesiae Disciplina*, pars II, lib. III, cap. XXVII, n. 4; pars III, lib. II, cap. XII; Stiegler, *Dispensation*, p. 316.

[19c] *Cambridge Medieval History*, V, p. 99.

[19d] Ayrinhac, *Constitution of the Church*, p. 148; Coronata, *Institutiones*, n. 393.

[20] Golden, *Parochial Benefices*, p. 40.

[21] Thomassinus, *Ecclesiae Disciplina*, pars II, lib. I, cap. XLIII, n. 1-6.

1153), Adrian IV (1154-1159), and Alexander III (1159-1181) granted Mandates and Expectative Letters.[22]

By the time that the Decretals of Gregory IX were published in 1234, the practice of issuing Mandates and Expectative Letters had become common enough to have some of them included among the decretals of the Church's first official canonical collection.[23] Among them was a Mandate [24] and an Expectative Letter concerning Canonries.[25]

During the twelfth century, the Popes received the disposal of many Bishoprics and Abbacies that were resigned "*in favorem.*" Even in the two preceding centuries instances of this had occurred, but in the twelfth century the number of resignations was greatly increased due to the fact that so many synods were held to eradicate the evils of simony, incontinence, and lay investiture. When the bishoprics and abbacies were resigned "*in favorem,*" their disposal became reserved to the Pope, who usually conferred them on their original possessors, provided, of course, that they had repented of their crimes.[26]

Clement IV (1265-1268) was the first Pope to promulgate a general reservation of benefices. He reserved to himself all benefices that became vacant in the Curia, i.e., that became vacant on account of the death of the beneficiary at Rome. He insisted, however, that although this reservation had not been explicitly defined by his predecessors, it had existed as a custom, and, moreover, declared in clear and unmistakable terms that although the Roman Pontiffs had not reserved the appointment of all ecclesiastical benefices to themselves, they had, nevertheless, the right to dispose of all the benefices and offices of the entire Church.[27] This marked a new period in Papal reservation of bene-

---

[22] Thomassinus, *Ecclesiae Disciplina,* pars II, lib. I, cap. XLIII, n. 2, 3; Leurenius, *Forum Beneficiale,* II, q. 526; Wernz-Vidal, *Jus Canonicum,* II, n. 228.

[23] C. 6, 37, 38, X, *de praebendis et dignitatibus,* III, 5; c. 4, X, *de concessione praebendae,* III, 8; c. 30, 37, 38, 40, X, *de rescriptis,* 1, 3.

[24] C. 6, X, *de praebendis et dignitatibus,* III, 5.

[25] C. 4, X, *de concessione praebendae,* III, 8.

[26] Thomassinus, *Ecclesiae Disciplina,* pars II, lib. I, cap. L, n. 1-12.

[27] C. 2, *de praebendis et dignitatibus,* III, 4, in VI°; Thomassinus, *Ecclesiae Disciplina,* pars II, lib. I, cap. XLVIII, n. 1; Reiffenstuel, *Jus Canonicum,* lib. III, tit. V, par. XV.

fices. Boniface VIII (1294-1303) extended this reservation so as to include all the benefices of Legates, Nuntios, and other beneficiaries who were accustomed to go to Rome and who died within two legal *"diaetae"* of Rome. Exception was made only for parochial benefices that became vacant during the vacancy of the Holy See, and benefices that had not been granted before the death of the Pope.[28]

During the Avignon Period (1309-1376) and the Great Western Schism that followed (1378-1417), the Papal reservations were greatly increased. Clement V (1305-1314), the first Avignon Pope, extended the reservation of Clement IV to include Cathedral Churches that became vacant at the Apostolic See.[29] John XXII (1316-1334) added all dignities, personatus, benefices, monasteries, priories, administrations, and offices that became vacant in the Holy See in any way whatsoever, whether by death, deposition, privation of office, cessation of elections, refusal of postulations, renunciation, or by any provision, transfer or acceptance of a work of Consecration or Blessing.[30] In his Constitution *"Exsecrabilis"* issued in 1317,[31] he reserved all benefices that were resigned by those who had been granted permission to resign in order to obtain other benefices. Benedict XII (1334-1342) in his Constitution *"Ad Regimen,"*[32] Clement VI (1342-1352) and Urban V (1360-1370) increased the number of reserved Cathedral Churches.[33]

The fourteenth century witnessed the beginning of general Papal reservation of Bishoprics.[34] Clement V (1305-1314) and Benedict XII (1334-1342) were the first Popes to reserve to themselves the appointment of Bishoprics. Their example was followed by Gregory XI (1370-1378),

---

[28] C. 34, *de praebendis et dignitatibus*, III, 4, in. VI°.

[29] C. 3, *de praebendis et dignitatibus*, III, 2, in Extrav. Comm.

[30] C. 4, *de electione*, 1, 3, in Extrav. Comm.

[31] C. 4, *de praebendis et dignitatibus*, III, 2, in Extrav. Comm.

[32] C. 13, *de praebendis et dignitatibus*, III, 2, in Extrav. Comm.

[33] Wernz-Vidal, *Jus Canonicum*, II, n. 229.

[34] Thomassinus, *Ecclesiae Disciplina*, pars II, lib. I, cap. XLIV, n. 1, 2; Riganti, *Commentarium in Regulas*, Reg. II, par. 1; Phillips, *Kirchenrecht*, tit. V, p. 388 ff.; Wernz-Vidal, *Jus Canonicum*, II, n. 187, 227, 592; Chelodi, *Jus De Personis*, n. 188.

who reserved all patriarchal, archiepiscopal and episcopal sees, no matter in what way they became vacant.[35]

During the fourteenth century, an institution arose that was to prove itself of utmost importance in the evolution of reservations of benefices, namely, the *Rules of the Apostolic Chancery*. These Rules, which contained a list of reserved benefices, were put into written form for the first time by John XXII, in his Constitution "*Exsecrabilis.*"[36] These Rules were subject to many changes and modifications because of the reservations of succeeding Popes, but Nicholas V (1447-1455) gave them a more stable form that has remained practically unchanged until the time of the Code. At first, the Rules were temporary in character, i.e., each succeeding Pope had to promulgate them by a special act upon taking office, but Urban VIII (1623-1644) remedied this defect by deciding that they would, *ipso facto*, go into effect on the day after the Pope took office.[37]

Among the reservations added to the Rules of the Apostolic Chancery, one of the most important was the reservation contained in the Ninth Rule, enacted by Nicholas V (1447-1455), whereby all the benefices that would become vacant during eight months of the year, designated as the Papal Months, would forthwith become reserved to the Holy See. In the very beginning of the Ninth Rule the Pope set forth his reason for reserving these benefices, namely, that he could provide poor and deserving clerics with benefices. Leo IX (1513-1521) modified this rule somewhat in regard to Patriarchs, Archbishops and Bishops by the so-called concession of alternative months, whereby only every other month was reserved to the Holy See.[38]

Besides the reservations contained in the *Corpus Juris Canonici* and the *Rules of the Apostolic Chancery* there are others found in the *Constitutions* and *Motu Proprios* of the

[35] Thomassinus, *Ecclesiae Disciplina*, pars II, lib. I, cap. XLIV, n. 4; Riganti, *Commentarium in Regulas*, Reg. II, p. 203; Mollat, *Les Papes d'Avignon*, III, c. III, p. 388; Ayrinhac, *Constitution of the Church*, p. 148; Wernz-Vidal, *Jus Canonicum*, II, n. 227.

[36] C. 4, *de praebendis et dignitatibus*, III, 2 in Extrav. Comm.

[37] Urban VIII, const., "*Sanctissimus in Christo Pater*," 21 Oct. 1623, *Bullarum . . . Taurinensis* editio, XIII, 9; Wernz, *Jus Decretalium*, I, n. 252; Ojetti, *Commentarium*, I, p. 24.

[38] Riganti, *Commentarium in Regulas*, Reg. IX.

Popes of the fifteenth and sixteenth centuries. These reservations were principally in the nature of punishments for crimes committed by the beneficiaries. Alexander VI, in his Constitution *"In Eminenti,"* 13 April 1502,[39] reserved the benefices of persons guilty of attacking any person taking part in litigations in the Roman Curia. Paul IV, in his Motu Proprio *"Inter Caeteras,"* 27 May 1557,[40] reserved the benefices of those who took an examination for another person who was seeking a benefice, and of those who promised annual pensions in order to obtain a benefice; and in his Constitution *"Romanum Pontificem,"* 17 Oct. 1564,[41] he reserved all benefices obtained through simony. Pius V, in his Constitution *"Cum ex Apostolatus,"* 27 Jan. 1567,[42] reserved all benefices that became vacant on account of the crime of heresy, and all parish churches that had not been erected according to the form of the Council of Trent. Gregory XIII, in his Constitution *"Humano Vix Judicio,"* 5 Jan. 1584,[43] reserved the benefices of those who did not comply with the regulations about publication of resignations. Thus different crimes, committed by ecclesiastics in acquiring benefices, caused the above mentioned as well as many other kinds of benefices to come within the sphere of Papal disposition.

§3. *Benefices Actually Conferred by the Popes*

From the fact that, *in principle and by law,* benefices were reserved to the Pope, one is not justified in concluding that all reserved benefices were *actually granted* by the Roman Pontiffs. Other elements must be taken into consideration in estimating the number of benefices granted by the Popes, namely, the resistance and opposition of certain nations to the claims of the Pope, the Concordats entered into with different nations, and the special Indults that were granted.

As early as the thirteenth century France and England showed resentment toward the Papal Mandates and Expec-

[39] Fontes, n. 61.
[40] Fontes, n. 92.
[41] Fontes, n. 106.
[42] Fontes, n. 117.
[43] Fontes, n. 152.

tative Letters and complained about the number of foreigners who were gaining possession of their benefices.[44] In the fourteenth and fifteenth centuries, especially during the Avignon period and the ensuing schism when benefices, even major benefices, were granted more freely by the Popes, this resentment grew into open refusal and revolt.

In England, the Kings periodically condemned the reservations of the Popes and commanded that the benefices be granted according to the ancient custom of freedom. They defended their action by saying that the foreigners who were taking possession of the benefices did not have the interests of the Church in England at heart. In France the trouble arose after the return of the Popes from Avignon to Rome. During the major portion of the fifteenth century, France refused to receive the mandates and expectative letters of the Popes or, at most, accepted only a small proportion of them. In 1399, the Council of the Gallican Church decided to provide all benefices by free election and the appointment of bishops and patrons. In the Council of Basle (1433-1436), the French agreed to allow the Pope to grant one benefice, if the Ordinary had ten at his disposal; two, if he had fifty or more. These provisions, with slight modifications, found their way into the famous "*Pragmatica Sanctio.*" Although the "*Pragmatica Sanctio*" was not strictly observed everywhere in France, it was the law of the country, and each succeeding King endeavored to have it strictly enforced. Nor were England and France the only ones who opposed the Papal reservations:—in varying degrees Germany, Spain, and Poland also refused the appointees of the Pope.[45]

Germany was the first country to enter into an agreement or Concordat with the Pope regarding the provision of benefices. Confusion and trouble arose when the Popes and the ordinary grantors disposed of the same benefices, and it was to remedy that disagreeable condition that Nicholas V (1447-1455) and Emperor Frederick in 1447

---

[44] Thomassinus, *Ecclesiae Disciplina,* pars II, lib. I, cap. XLIII, n. 7-9.

[45] Thomassinus, *Ecclesiae Disciplina,* pars II, lib. I, caps. XLIV, XLV; Reiffenstuel, *Jus Canonicum,* lib. III, tit. V, cap. XVIII.

entered into the Viennese Concordat.[46] In 1516, Leo X succeeded in negotiating the *Gallican Concordat* with France.[46a] According to its provisions expectative letters and mandates were allowed for benefices that became vacant in the Curia; also for Abbatial, Episcopal, and Primatial benefices, but with the provision that they would await presentation by the King. For all other benefices, expectative letters were ruled out, and only one mandate was permitted when the grantor had ten benefices at his disposal; two, if he had fifty or more.[47] Many other Concordats were subsequently entered into by the Pope with different civil rulers. These Concordats considerably altered the character of mandates and expectative letters that contained Episcopal appointments by requiring the Popes, before issuing them, to await the presentation of candidates by civil rulers.[48] They affected also the granting of other benefices, by limiting their number, as e.g., the dignities and offices in chapters;[49] or by limiting the Papal months.[50]

Moreover, during the Avignon period and the troubled times that followed, Indults were issued to Bishops and other dignitaries, empowering them to grant certain benefices that the Pope had reserved to himself.[51]

Finally the Council of Trent, greatly disturbed by the many grave abuses that accompanied the granting of expectative letters, e.g., the false allegations in the petitions, simony, etc., forbade them for all future time.[52]

The Reservation of Benefices, greatly limited by Concordats and Indults, gradually decreased in importance.

---

[46] Reiffenstuel, *Jus Canonicum,* lib. III, tit. V, caps. XVIII, XIX; Wernz-Vidal, *Jus Canonicum,* II, n. 229; *Raccolta di Concordati,* pp. 168-177.

[46a] *Raccolta di Concordati,* pp. 233-251.

[47] Thomassinus, *Ecclesiae Disciplina,* pars II, lib. I, cap. XLV, n. 8, 9.

[48] Vermeersch-Creusen, *Epitome,* II, n. 767; Chelodi, *Jus De Personis,* n. 188; Ayrinhac, *Constitution of the Church,* p. 149; Cocchi, *Commentarium,* III, n. 252; Wernz-Vidal, *Jus Canonicum,* n. 227, 229, 231.

[49] Wernz-Vidal, *Jus Canonicum,* II, n. 232, 664.

[50] Vermeersch-Creusen, *Epitome,* II, n. 767.

[51] Thomassinus, *Ecclesiae Disciplina,* pars II, lib. I, cap. XLIX, n. 1-12; Wernz-Vidal, *Jus Canonicum,* II, n. 229.

[52] Conc. Trident., Sess. XXIV, *de Ref.,* c. 8, 19.

The Code has further diminished the importance of beneficial rescripts by eliminating many of the ancient reservations. At present, the only benefices, outside of the diocese of Rome, that are reserved to the Pope are the following:—consistorial benefices and all dignities of cathedral and collegiate churches; benefices that become vacant by the death, promotion, resignation or transfer of Cardinals or Papal Legates, major officials of the Sacred Congregations, Tribunals and Offices of the Roman Curia, and those who are "*Familiares*" of the Pope, even if merely honorary, at the time of the vacancy of the benefice; benefices, even outside of Rome, that become vacant by the death of the beneficiary at Rome; benefices invalidly granted on account of simony; and benefices in which the Pope personally or through a delegate interposed his authority by declaring the election to the benefice invalid by forbidding the electors to proceed to the election, by admitting resignation, by promoting, transferring or depriving the beneficiary of his benefits, or by granting a benefice "*in commendam.*"[53] Can. 1435, §1, explicitly states that only the above-mentioned reservations are now in force, and so the Reservation of Papal Months, among others, has ceased.[54]

Rescripts of Benefices, of such vast importance towards the end of the Middle Ages, gradually decreased in number, but their fate did not materially affect the status of Rescripts of Favor because all the time the popes were granting dispensations in ever increasing numbers, as shall be seen in the following article.

Article III.—Development of Papal Rescripts of Dispensations

§1. *Definition of Terms.*

Dispensation is defined as "a relaxation of a law in a particular case for a sufficient reason by competent authority."[55] *Matrimonial Dispensation* is defined as "a

[53] Can. 1435.

[54] Vermeersch-Creusen, *Epitome*, II, n. 767.

[55] Can. 80, 84; Wernz, *Jus Decretalium*, I, n. 120; Maroto, *Institutiones*, n. 302.

legitimate act of a superior, by which the obligation forbidding marriage with or without the nullification of the contract, is relaxed in a particular case;" [56] or as "an act of legitimate power by which, in a particular case or for a particular person, the law is relaxed in so far as its effect of rendering a marriage illicit or invalid is concerned, the force of law remaining, however, for the other members of the community and other cases." [57]

A dispensation merely suspends a law in a particular case:—the law remains in force, but is relaxed by competent authority in a particular case, i.e., in favor of an individual person, moral or physical, or of a whole community but only for one act or for a fixed determined time.[58] It is essentially an act of jurisdiction requiring the intervention of a lawful superior.[59] This act of jurisdiction suspends the law for a particular case in such a way that in case of, e.g., a marriage impediment, one who could not otherwise licitly, or licitly or validly contract matrimony, is freed from that obligation so completely that once the dispensation is effectively and unconditionally granted the impediment which first existed never revives.[60]

At present, *Dispensations* are distinguished from *Privileges*. *Privilege* is "a special favor or right of a somewhat permanent character and not intended for a mere transitory act, contrary to or beside the common law, granted by a special act of the proper ecclesiastical power to a physical or moral person." [61] The word Privilege, derived from "*privata lex*," means literally a private law. It is a law not in the sense that it imposes any obligation on the person receiving it, but in the sense that it forbids others from interfering with the proper use of the right or favor. It has the character of a law also inasmuch as it is somewhat stable and permanent. Its private character distinguishes it from laws, properly so called, since it is intended

---

[56] Vermeersch-Creusen, *Epitome*, II, n. 301.

[57] De Smet, *De Sponsalibus et Matrimonio*, n. 732; O'Keefe, *Matrimonial Dispensations*, p. 3.

[58] Ayrinhac, *General Legislation*, p. 177.

[59] Can. 80; Suarez, *De Legibus*, VI, c. 10, n. 6; c. 12, n. 7.

[60] Vlaming, *Praelectiones*, n. 392.

[61] Maroto, *Institutiones*, n. 291.

for the good of a particular person, physical or moral, and they are intended for the common good.[62] There are at present three main differences between Dispensations and Privileges. Dispensations are always contrary to the common law, while Privileges may be either contrary to the law or beside the law; Dispensations are very frequently given for a transitory act, while Privileges ordinarily have a more stable and permanent character; Dispensations concern a fact, while a Privilege is a norm of action.[63]

The word "*Dispensation*" did not always have, however, the limited meaning it now possesses, nor was it always distinguished from a Privilege contrary to the law. Until the twelfth century, by Dispensation was meant any mitigation or relaxation of the law done for the good of the Church, whether it was a derogation or abrogation of the law, a change of law or an excuse from the law, a remission of a penalty or a legitimation of an act performed against the law. It had a wide comprehensive meaning which included privileges contrary to the law.[64] Rufinus (1157-1159) and Huguccio (1188) were the first to use Dispensation in the restricted sense of a relaxation of a law in a particular case. Their example was afterwards followed by other Decretists.[65] This modification of meaning in the term Dispensation is of great importance in the study of the history of dispensations. In this Article, however, unless otherwise stated, "*Dispensation*" will be taken in the strict sense of today.

The history of Dispensations is marked by change and development. Varying circumstances of time and place caused the Popes to grant dispensations with greater or lesser liberality; different motives prompted them to change their practical attitude toward the relaxation of law. Directly these factors concern the history of dispen-

---

[62] Wernz, *Jus Decretalium*, I, n. 158; Cocchi, *Commentarium*, I, n. 128.

[63] Roelker, *Principles of Privilege*, p. 21; Herinx, *Summa Theologica*, n. 54; Humphrey, *Conscience and Law*, p. 164; Zallinger, *Institutiones*, lib. V, tit. XXXIII, par. 263.

[64] Brys, *De Dispensatione*, pp. 3, 16, 74; Stiegler, *Dispensation*, pp. 24, 40, 70.

[65] Brys, *De Dispensatione*, pp. 95, 99, 147, 164.

sations, indirectly, the history of Rescripts of Favor, inasmuch as they affected the development and progress of the Rescripts that contained dispensations.

The history of Dispensations divides itself naturally into three main periods; before the tenth century, from the tenth century until the middle of the twelfth century, and from the middle of the twelfth century until the present day. The Popes before as well as after the tenth century granted real dispensations in the strict sense in which they are understood today; they not only granted *"ex post"* dispensations which relaxed the law after it had been broken, but also *"ad faciendum"* dispensations which gave a person the power and right to act contrary to the law. The main difference between the first two periods is that before the tenth century the Popes were prompted to grant dispensations rather by the motive of the common good of the Church, while afterwards they granted them even for the private good of individuals, with the natural consequence that in the first period dispensations were granted only at rare intervals, while in the second period they gradually increased in frequency. The third period witnessed the further growth of dispensations and, in particular, matrimonial dispensations.

§2. *Before the Tenth Century*

Despite the fact that many documents pertaining to the dispensational activities of the Popes are lost, there are enough records extant to prove that real dispensations were granted before the tenth century. The following are the most certain instances. Melchiadis (311-314) dispensed the Donatist Bishops from an irregularity they had incurred. Damasus (366-384) dispensed Flavianus from an irregularity that prevented him from being promoted to the See of Antioch.[66] Siricius, in 385, dispensed the lapsed clerics from the irregularity that prevented them from exercising their orders. This is the first papal dispensation which can be proved by direct and positive evidence to have been granted in the form of a rescript, i.e., as a written

[66] Thomassinus, *Ecclesiae Disciplina*, pars II, lib. III, cap. XXIV, n. 7; Stiegler, *Dispensation*, pp. 85 ff.; Brys, *De Dispensatione*, p. 38.

reply to a particular petition. Innocent I, in 414, dispensed from the law that prevented those who were ordained by the heretic Bonosus from exercising their orders.[67] Boniface I, in 422, dispensed from the law forbidding the transfer of Bishops. Celestine I, in 426, granted a dispensation to the converts from Nestorianism.[68] Leo I, in 440, dispensed from the law concerning transfer of Bishops.[69] Pelagius I, in 559, granted a dispensation to a bigamist so that he could be ordained to the diaconate. Hadrian I, in 794, gave to Alginamus, Bishop of Messin, and Hetelbaldus, Bishop of Cologne, a dispensation from the law of residence so that they might live in the palace of the Emperor.[70]

Esmein[71] contends that absolutions, not real dispensations, were granted during this period. Such was not the case. In the early church a public penance entailing exclusion from ecclesiastical communion was imposed on those who confessed serious sins, an exclusion that continued in force until reinstatement was brought about, after public penance had been performed, by the absolution of the Bishop.[72] The cases quoted above do not fall in the class of absolutions. Whether or not the clerics concerned were excluded from the communion of the faithful, they were also, because of the crimes committed, forbidden to exercise their orders or to advance to higher orders. The absolution of the Bishop alone did not bestow on them the right to exercise their orders or to be advanced, but a law had to be suspended, a dispensation granted in order that

---

[67] Coustant, *Epistolae Romanorum Pontificum,* I, p. 631, n. 11; p. 385; Thomassinus, *Ecclesiae Disciplina,* pars II, lib. III, cap. XXIV, n. 3, 8; Stiegler, *Dispensation,* pp. 85 ff.; Brys, *De Dispensatione,* pp. 14, 38.

[68] Stiegler, *Dispensation,* pp. 85 ff.; Brys, *De Dispensatione,* p. 38.

[69] Jaffe-Loewenfeld, *Regesta Pontificum Romanorum,* I, n. 410; Thomassinus, *Ecclesiae Disciplina,* pars II, lib. III, cap. XXIV, n. 11; Stiegler, *Dispensation,* p. 85 ff.; Brys, *De Dispensatione,* p. 38.

[70] Mont. Germ. Hist., *Capitularia Regum Francorum,* I, cap. LV, p. 68; Stiegler, *Dispensation,* p. 49; Brys. *De Dispensatione,* p. 27, 15.

[71] *Le Mariage En droit Canonique,* II, p. 317 ff.

[72] Vacandard, *Dictionnaire de Théologie Catholique,* v. Absolution, t. I, col. 160; Stiegler, *Dispensation,* p. 43; Brys, *De Dispensatione,* p. 17; Ojetti, *Commentarium,* I, p. 326, nota (7).

they might take part in clerical activities.[73] Moreover, the above-mentioned actions of the Popes were real dispensations regarding future actions:—the Pope did not intervene to legalize the criminal actions of others but to absolve them from their sins and censures, and to relax the law that forbade them to perform certain future actions on account of the irregularities that they had incurred. Finally, the cases of Boniface I and Leo I in the fifth century and Hadrian I in the eighth were manifestly dispensations *"ad faciendum"* that relaxed the law so that persons guilty of no crime or violation of law were permitted to act contrary to the common law regarding residence and transfer of Bishops.[74]

It seems well established that the Popes between the fourth and tenth centuries granted dispensations, but at the same time it must be admitted that the number of dispensations that were granted, although not as small as contended by some, was nevertheless comparatively small. The Popes regarded themselves as the divinely appointed guardians of the law and held fast to its rigorous enforcement except when the necessity or good of the Church demanded that an exception be made. They insisted repeatedly that they had a divine commission to guard the Canons, but did not consider themselves bound in such a way that they never could or would relax the law, because in many of the letters in which they insisted that they were guardians of the law, they also either actually granted dispensations or referred to their right to relax the law when the necessity or good of the Church demanded it.[75]

Another fact that must be taken into consideration in explaining the small number of dispensations granted dur-

---

[73] Vacandard, *Dictionnaire de Théologie Catholique*, v. Absolution, I, col. 159 ff.; Stiegler, *Dispensation*, pp. 43, 44; Brys, *De Dispensatione*, pp. 18, 19; Ojetti, *Commentarium*, I, p. 326, nota (7).

[74] Stiegler, *Dispensation*, pp. 45, 46, 49; Brys, *De Dispensatione*, pp. 27, 28.

[75] Innocent I (410-417), Jaffe-Loewenfeld, *Regesta Romanorum Pontificum*, I, n. 363; Leo I (440-461), Jaffe-Loewenfeld, *o. c.*, I, n. 410; Gelasius I (492-496), C. I, D. LV; Symmachus (498-514), Thiel, *Epistolae Romanorum Pontificum*, I, p. 362; Martin I (649-655), ep. X ad Pantaleonem—M. P. L., 87, 172; John VIII (872-882), ep. CCXLIII ad Basilium . . .—M. P. L., 126, 854.

ing this period is that although the Popes ascribed to themselves the universal right of dispensing from the common law of the Church, they had not yet claimed the exclusive power of dispensation. Nicholas I (858-867) expressly claimed universal power of dispensation,[76] and his claim was recognized by the Ecumenical Council of Constantinople in 869:[77] but exclusive power was claimed only in certain matters. Instances are found of Popes condemning synods for granting permission to bishops to name their successors;[78] forbidding particular bishops and synods to dispense in certain matters, e.g., Siricius and Innocent I; threatening those who presumed to dispense, e.g., Leo I; and even explicitly and openly claiming exclusive right to dispense in certain matters, e.g., Gelasius I. But nowhere can there be found any explicit claim on the part of the Popes to *exclusive* power of dispensation in *all* matters of common law, and even when exclusive power was claimed in certain matters, it was not always respected by bishops and synods.[79]

The fact that the Popes, as guardians of the Canons, were loath to dispense unless the necessity or good of the Church required it, combined with the fact that they had not claimed exclusive power of dispensation in the entire common law, nor even obtained general obedience regarding matters that they reserved to themselves, explains why Papal Dispensations were so few during the first nine centuries.

§3. *Tenth Century to the Middle of the Twelfth Century*

During this period a radical change took place regarding Papal dispensations.. The Popes began to grant even "*ad faciendum*" dispensations more freely, not only for reasons affecting the common good of the Church, but also for those

---

76 M. P. L., 119, 889-973; Brys, *De Dispensatione*, p. 41, nota (4).

77 Phillips, *Kirchenrecht*, t. V., p. 972; Stiegler, *Dispensation*, p. 169; Brys, *De Dispensatione*, p. 41, nota (4).

78 Thomassinus, *Ecclesiae Disciplina*, pars II, lib. III, cap. XXIV, n. 13, regarding the African Church; Brys, *De Dispensatione*, p. 39, regarding the Spanish Church.

79 Stiegler, *Dispensation*, pp. 90-93; Brys, *De Dispensatione*, pp. 39, 40, 66.

of a private nature.[80] They began to dispense from laws that previously had not been dispensed from, e.g., the law requiring that the pallium be given at Rome.[81]

Two important facts help to explain this unusual change. First, the bishops' powers became greatly limited, especially in regard to the Sacrament of Holy Orders. Bishops exercised only a limited power over those whose ordination was unlawful on account of simony, those irregular on account of physical defects or private or occult faults, those who disregarded the law about cumulation of benefices or the law of residence, and the like; they were denied all power to dispense from irregularities incurred by lack of knowledge or by bigamy; finally they were forbidden to allow ordinations *"per saltum."* [82] Even though the Bishops did not always abide by these limitations and denials of power, nevertheless this reservation of power by the Pope tended to increase the number of papal dispensations.

Moreover, the conditions of the times practically forced the Popes to be more liberal in granting dispensations. A large number of unlawful ordinations and irregularities resulted from simony either on the part of the one ordaining or the one ordained,[83] from lay investiture,[84] or from the crime of concubinage,[85] and the Popes found it necessary to grant dispensations to remedy such deplorable conditions. And in their efforts to extirpate the abuses of bishops in dispensational matters, to correct the evils of the times and to promote unity in the Church, the Popes were gradually being led to proclaim their own exclusive power to dispense from the common law of the Church; [86] and the closer they approached to the position of being the sole dispenser of church law, the greater became the number of Dispensational Rescripts.

---

[80] Brys, *De Dispensatione*, pp. 42, 43.

[81] Urban II, ep. XXVII—M. P. L., 151, 310; Jaffe-Loewenfeld, *Regesta Pontificum Romanorum*, n. 5359, 5538, 5540.

[82] Stiegler, *Dispensation*, pp. 149-305, 336 ff.; Brys, *De Dispensatione*, pp. 59, 60, 64.

[83] Thomassinus, *Ecclesiae Disciplina*, pars II, lib. III, cap. XXVII, n. 4; Fournier, *Yves de Chartres et le droit canonique*, p. 1 ff.

[84] Stiegler, *Dispensation*, p. 316.

[85] Thomassinus, *Ecclesiae Disciplina*, pars III, lib. II, cap. XII.

[86] Brys, *De Dispensatione*, pp. 63, 66.

It was also during this period that the first matrimonial dispensations were granted. There had been no matrimonial dispensations, in the strict sense, in the previous period, and only a very small number of matrimonial privileges contrary to the law:—in fact only two that are known. Gregory the Great (590-604), according to the narration of Venerable Bede, granted to the English converts a privilege permitting those who were married to retain their wives although related in the third or fourth degree, and permitting those who were single to marry relatives within the same degrees. More than a century later Gregory II (713-731) granted a similar privilege to the Germans.[87]

These are the only recorded exceptions made from the general law of matrimony before the tenth century, while there is abundant proof to show that the Popes ordinarily were unwilling to grant such favors. When Gregory the Great granted the privilege to the English, he deemed it advisable to write to Bishop Felix to explain his reason for doing so. He explained that he had been forced to make an exception to the law since a strict adherence to the law would have easily deterred many from conversion, and reassured the Bishop that no harm was to be feared, because his action was not to be taken as a rule or precedent.[88] The reaction of astonishment and incredulity manifested by the people, clergy and Bishops alike, when a dispensation was claimed by a certain noble on his return from Rome, as we find reported by St. Boniface to Pope Zachary (741-752),[89] strengthens the opinion that before the eleventh century only in very exceptional cases was the matrimonial law relaxed even by the granting of privileges.

In the eleventh century, however, the Popes in a few instances, for very weighty reasons, granted real matri-

---

87 Stiegler, *Dispensation*, p. 256; Rigantius, *Commentarium in Regulas*, Reg. XLIX, n. 8 sq.; Wernz, *Jus Decretalium*, V, n. 610; De Smet, *De Sponsalibus et Matrimonio*, n. 743; Capello, *De Sacramentis*, III, n. 221; Chelodi, *Jus Matrimoniale*, n. 38.

88 Gregory VII, ep. XVII, ad Felicem Messianensem Episcopum—M. P. L., 77, 1323.

89 Thomassinus, *Ecclesiae Disciplina*, pars II, lib. III, cap. XXV, n. 6-8; Rigantius, *Commentarium in Regulas*, Reg. XLIX, n. 5; Wernz-Vidal, *Jus Canonicum*, V, n. 405.

monial dispensations. There is divergence of opinion among authors as to the time when the first dispensation was granted. Some authors [90] thought that the first one was granted by Paschal II (1099-1118) to Philip I, King of France, and his cousin Bertha, who had entered into a union despite the impediment of consanguinity and had remained together despite the anathemas and interdicts of Urban II, predecessor of Paschal II. Whereas most authors look upon this as a real matrimonial dispensation, Stiegler [91] and De Smet [92] correctly point out that it was merely a permission granted to the parties to live together as brother and sister. Most authors [93] contend that the first matrimonial dispensation was granted in 1059 by Nicholas II to William, Duke of Normandy, and his cousin, validating the union they had entered into against the laws of the Church. This exception was made in order to avert war between Flanders and Normandy.[94]

The first *"ad faciendum"* matrimonial dispensation was granted in the twelfth century. Some authors [95] say the first one was granted by Innocent III in 1209 to Otho IV, King of Germany, and his cousin Beatrice after the combined pleas of people, clergy, and papal legates had convinced the Pope that the dispensation was necessary to avert war between Otho IV and Philip, the father of Beatrice. There was certainly, however, an earlier dispensation granted by Alexander III (1159-1181) to John, son of

---

[90] Thomassinus, *Ecclesiae Disciplina*, pars II, lib. III, cap. XXIX, n. 10; Heiss, *De Matrimonio*, par. 47, n. 3.

[91] *Dispensation*, p. 265.

[92] *De Sponsalibus et Matrimonio*, n. 743.

[93] Rigantius, *Commentarium in Regulas*, Reg. XLIX, n. 639; Scherer, *Handbuch des Kirchenrecht*, p. 454; Stiegler, *Dispensation*, p. 265; Wernz, *Jus Decretalium*, V, n. 610; Wernz-Vidal, *Jus Canonicum*, V, n. 405; Chelodi, *Jus Matrimoniale*, n. 38; De Smet, *De Sponsalibus et Matrimonio*, n. 743; Capello, *De Sacramentis*, III, n. 221.

[94] Jaffe-Loewenfeld, *Regesta Pontificum Romanorum*, n. 3671.

[95] Thomassinus, *Ecclesiae Disciplina*, pars II, lib. III, cap. XXIX, n. 10; Heiss, *De Matrimonio*, par. 47, n. 3; Vlaming, *Praelectiones*, n. 393; Chelodi, *Jus Matrimoniale*, n. 38.

King Henry II of England, and his cousin;[96] and very probably one granted as early as 1100 by Urban II.[97]

But matrimonial dispensations, during this period, were granted only on extremely rare occasions. Many petitions, even of Kings who had invalidly contracted marriage, were refused.[98]

§4. *Middle of the Twelfth Century until the Present*

The pontificates of Alexander III (1159-1181) and Innocent III (1198-1216) mark a further step in the progress of Papal Rescripts of Dispensation. Thereafter, the power of dispensing was more openly and expressly given as one of the prerogatives in perfect accord with the power of pontifical jurisdiction;[99] the power of dispensation was extended not only to the Pope's own laws but to those of his predecessors and of General Councils;[100] and finally the plentitude of Papal jurisdiction was the reason that was presented by the Popes for their claim to such great power.[101] During their Pontificates, Alexander III published at least twenty-two, and Innocent III, thirty-two letters containing dispensations from their own laws and the laws of General Councils.[102]

---

96 Rigantius, *Commentarium in Regulas*, Reg. XLIX, n. 9; Wernz, *Jus Decretalium*, V, n. 610; Wernz-Vidal, *Jus Canonicum*, V, n. 405; Capello, *De Sacramentis*, III, n. 221.

97 Stiegler, *Dispensation*, p. 278; De Smet, *De Sponsalibus et Matrimonio*, n. 743.

98 Rigantius, *Commentarium in Regulas*, Reg. XLIX, n. 5—refusal by Gregory VII of petition of King Robert of France; Stiegler, *Dispensation*, p. 259—refusal by Leo IX and Gregory VIII; De Smet, *De Sponsalibus et Matrimonio*, n. 743.

99 Innocent III, ". . . we according to the plentitude of our power have the right to dispense from the law,"—c. 4, X, *de concessione praebendae*, III, 8; Innocent III, "The Supreme Pontiff is lifted up to the plenitude of power and since he is the moderator of the canons he does not inflict any injury on the law by dispensing, especially since dispensation relaxes the bond of law for one in such a way that it does not dissolve it for others and so brings about the benefit of special favor without destroying the rigor of the general constitution,"—M. P. L., 216, 943.

100 C. 20, X, *de electione*, 1, 6.

101 C. 4, X, *de concessione praebendae*, III, 8; Inn. III, ep. CLI—M. P. L., 216, 943.

102 Stiegler, "Dispensation," Ak K R, 78 (1898), p. 665; Brys, *De Dispensatione*, p. 238.

This claim of exclusive power by the Popes was interpreted, however, by the Decretalists in such a way as to permit the bishops to dispense whenever the power was explicitly or implicitly granted to them, when legitimate custom arose, or when the urgent necessity or good of the Church demanded it.[103] This naturally allowed the bishops to interpret favorably their power of dispensing, but, nevertheless, once the principle of the exclusiveness of papal power was clearly formulated and recognized, the number of Papal dispensations increased rapidly; all the more so, since about the same time the good of a private person was recognized as sufficient cause for making an exception to the law.[104]

The increasing number of dispensations caused the Pope to establish permanent departments in the Roman Curia to take care of the different kinds of dispensations; and it also caused the Council of Trent[105] to define more clearly the reasons that would be considered as sufficient for the valid and licit granting of dispensations.

In the thirteenth century, the power to dispense from matrimonial dispensations was reserved to the Holy See, and subsequently matrimonial dispensations increased to such an extent that different departments in the Roman Curia began to take charge of the issuance of matrimonial rescripts.[106] In fact, matrimonial dispensations became so frequent toward the end of the Middle Ages, and were granted for such light reasons, that the Council of Trent felt it necessary to make special provisions concerning them.[107]

This strict attitude of the Church was short lived. With heresy rampant and faith greatly weakened, the Church was compelled to grant dispensations, especially matrimonial dispensations, more freely in order to prevent greater evils. As a result, dispensations were granted even

---

[103] Brys, *De Dispensatione*, pp. 248-253, 272.

[104] Brys, *De Dispensatione*, p. 189.

[105] Sess. XXIV, *de Ref.*, c. 5; Sess. XXV, *de Ref.*, c. 18.

[106] Wernz-Vidal, *Jus Canonicum*, V, n. 405.

[107] Conc. Trident, Sess. XXIV, *de Ref.*, c. 5.

from the closer degrees of matrimonial impediments, and the number of dispensations grew apace.[108]

Beginning with the sixteenth century, however, certain delegated powers in matrimonial affairs were granted to Bishops and Apostolic Missionaries in remote regions through the "*quinquenial*" and "*triennial*" faculties for the external and internal forum respectively.[109] This lessened somewhat the number of dispensations granted directly by the Popes through Rescripts.

Another factor that diminished somewhat the number of Papal dispensational rescripts was the teaching, gradually accepted by theologians and canonists, which attributed to bishops, in case of necessity, the power to dispense from occult diriment impediments of the ecclesiastical law for marriages invalidly contracted or to be contracted in the future. It was claimed that Bishops had the power to grant dispensations for marriages invalidly contracted, when at one and the same time the solemnities of the Church had been observed, the marriage had been contracted in good faith through ignorance of law or fact of an occult impediment, the marriage had been consummated, a separation could not be brought about without scandal arising, and the Holy See could not be petitioned for the dispensation, without great difficulty, because of the distance, poverty of the parties, etc.[110] It was also commonly taught that Bishops could dispense "*ad contrahendum,*" in cases of urgent necessity, from an impediment of the ecclesiastical law, provided that the impediment was occult and one from which the Holy See was accustomed to dispense, and that the dispensation could not be obtained from the Holy See or from one with delegated power without great difficulty.[111]

---

[108] Heiss, *De Matrimonio*, par. 47, n. 4; Vlaming, *Praelectiones*, n. 393; Chelodi, *Jus Matrimoniale*, n. 38.

[109] Wernz, *Jus Decretalium*, V, n. 610; O'Keeffe, *Matrimonial Dispensations*, p. 13.

[110] O'Keeffe, *Matrimonial Dispensations*, p. 15, where he quotes such authors as Reiffenstuel, Corradus, Van de Burgt, De Becker, Aichner, Dens, Wernz, Gasparri and Feije.

[111] O'Keeffe, *Matrimonial Dispensations*, p. 29, where such authors as Reiffenstuel, Santi, Gasparri, Wernz, Aichner, Van de Burgt, Benedict XIV, Dens and Scavini are quoted.

No power, however, was ascribed to bishops in case of *public* impediments for *urgent cases.* In fact, a decision of the Sacred Congregation of the Interpretation of the Council of Trent in 1660, confirmed by the Sacred Congregation of the Council in 1661, denied that they had such power for marriages to be contracted; [112] and an instruction of the Holy Office of June 8, 1756, denied all power to them in case of public impediments, whether for marriages invalidly contracted or to be contracted.[113] In the latter part of the nineteenth century, however, the Holy Office [114] conferred on local Ordinaries the power to dispense, in *very grave danger of death,* those who had contracted a civil marriage or had otherwise lived in concubinage [115] from all *public* or *occult* [116] impediments except those resulting from Priesthood or from Affinity in the direct line *"ex copula licita,"* or those which were merely impediment,[117] whether the impediment directly affected the sick party or not.[118] On July 8, 1903, the Holy Office also conferred on local Ordinaries [119] the power of legitimating offspring provided they were neither adulterous progeny or children born of a sacriligious union. On May 14, 1909, the Sacred Congregation of the Sacraments granted the same power of dispensing from all diriment impediments to priests assisting, in the absence of the Bishop, pastor or delegate of either of them, at marriages of parties who, in imminent danger of death, desired to be married *"ad consulendum conscientiae, et si casus ferat, ad legitimationem prolis."* [120] Later, it was definitely decided that this power could be exercised also by pastors,[121] and was applicable even to parties who had not lived in concubinage.[122] The fact that the above-mentioned powers granted to local Ordinaries

---

[112] *Coll. de Prop. Fide,* n. 399.
[113] *Coll. de Prop. Fide,* n. 399.
[114] S. C. S. Off., 20 Febr. 1888—Fontes, n. 1109.
[115] S. C. S. Off., 1 Julii 1891—*Coll. de Prop. Fide,* n. 1741.
[116] S. C. S. Off., 23 Aprilis 1890—*Coll. de Prop. Fide,* n. 1728.
[117] S. C. S. Off., 18 Martii 1891—*Coll. de Prop. Fide,* n. 1750.
[118] S. C. S. Off., 1 Julii 1891—*Coll. de Prop. Fide,* n. 1758.
[119] *Coll. de Prop. Fide,* n. 2071.
[120] AAS, I (1909), 468, 469.
[121] S. C. S. Off., 29 Julii 1910—AAS, II (1910) 650.
[122] S. C. S. Off., 16 Aug. 1909—AAS, I (1909) 656.

and priests could be exercised only in serious danger of death prevented them from making a very appreciable difference in the number of matrimonial dispensations granted directly by the Roman Curia. Their importance as far as diminishing papal rescripts was concerned is scarcely comparable to the powers exercised by Bishops in the internal forum in cases of urgency.

Another source of restriction of dispensations, granted by Papal Rescripts, is found in the powers granted by the Popes to their Nuncios, Internuncios, and Apostolic Delegates in the last centuries.[123]

Finally the Code has restricted the impediments and enlarged and clarified the dispensational powers of bishops so that now many more dispensations can be obtained without recourse to Rome.[124]

But despite all restrictions, papal dispensations, especially matrimonial dispensations, have continued to multiply until today they constitute the major portion of the Rescripts granted by the Holy See.[125]

---

[123] Wernz-Vidal, *Jus Canonicum,* II, n. 512, 513, 515; Vermeersch-Creusen, *Epitome,* I, n. 813 sq., where faculties now granted to them by the Holy See are given.

[124] Wernz-Vidal, *Jus Canonicum,* V, n. 405.

[125] Wernz, *Jus Decretalium,* I, n. 149; Chelodi, *Jus De Personis,* n. 75.

PART II

The Granting of Papal Rescripts of Favor

CHAPTER I

DEVELOPMENT OF THE ROMAN CURIA IN RELATION TO PAPAL RESCRIPTS OF FAVOR

At present, the task of granting, composing, and dispatching papal favors through Rescripts is handled in an orderly systematic way by different departments of the Roman Curia, but the present systematic arrangement has been attained only after repeated changes and reforms. In studying the progress of the Roman Curia in its relation to papal favors, distinction must be made between three distinct works, the granting of the favor, the composition or writing of the rescript, and the expedition or sending of the rescript to the interested party.

Article I.—Before the Twelfth Century

If any Rescripts of Favor were granted before the fourth century, in all probability the group of seven *Notarii,* who at that time were in charge of the Pope's official correspondence, took care of them; and for any advice regarding the granting of special favors, the Pope probably conferred with the neighboring bishops who periodically gathered in synod at Rome.[1]

From the fourth to the twelfth century, the Popes sought advice in important matters from the Synods of Roman clergy, the Provincial Synods, the Synods of Primates and

[1] Hilling, *Procedure at the Roman Curia,* p. 8; Maroto, *Institutiones,* n. 826; Ayrinhac, *Constitution of the Church,* p. 51.

Patriarchs, and after Leo IX (1049-1054), from the General Western Synods. Toward the end of this period, the College of Cardinal Bishops, Priests, and Deacons assumed charge of the synodical assemblies.[2] The *schola* of seven "*Regionarii Notarii,*" with the "*Primicerius Notariorum*" at its head, continued for some time to compose and dispatch papal documents, including rescripts, but toward the end of the sixth century the palace officials, called the seven "*Judices Palatini,*" assumed charge of what was in substance the Papal Chancery. Among the "*Judices Palatini*" was the "*Nomenclator*" or Minister of Favors.[3] From the ninth century until the eleventh century, the "*Bibliothecarius*" presided over those who expedited papal documents:—he was succeeded by the Cardinal Chancellor. This marks the real beginning of the office of the Apostolic Chancery as now constituted, although in substance the Apostolic Chancery dates back to the time of the "*Judices Palatini.*" [4]

The organization established to take care of Papal Rescripts of Favor was, of necessity, still in its primitive stages, and the first sign of real progress dates from the time that the Popes selected Cardinals as their consultors and put them in charge of the work of dispatching papal grants of favor.

Article II.—Twelfth Century until the Reform of Sixtus V

As the volume of official business rapidly increased, the Popes abandoned synodical consultations and substituted frequent and even daily meetings or consistories of Cardinals. They also gradually formed official departments under the direction of the Cardinals, to take the place of the "*Pala-*

---

[2] Hilling, *Procedure at the Roman Curia,* pp. 10-14; Ayrinhac, *Constitution of the Church,* p. 52.

[3] Hilling, *Procedure at the Roman Curia,* p. 12; Maroto, *Institutiones,* n. 826; Ayrinhac, *Constitution of the Church,* p. 52.

[4] Hilling, *Procedure at the Roman Curia,* pp. 14, 116; Martin, *The Roman Curia,* p. 154; Ojetti, *De Romana Curia,* n. 157; Maroto, *Institutiones,* n. 826; Ayrinhac, *Constitution of the Church,* p. 78.

tine Judges," who disappeared by the end of the thirteenth century.[5]

Between the twelfth and sixteenth century, the Popes granted rescripts of favor principally through two offices, the *Apostolic Chancery* and the *Apostolic Penitentiary:*—the former was concerned with rescripts of the external forum, the latter, principally, but not exclusively, with those of the internal forum.

As the number of Papal reservations increased and greater leniency was shown in granting dispensations, the *Apostolic Chancery,* through which most of the rescripts of favor were dispatched, grew in importance:—in fact, in the thirteenth century it became necessary to establish a special office, the Communis Data, within the Chancery to care for favors, and in the following century another office, the Secretariate of Briefs, to dispatch documents of minor importance.[6]

The Apostolic Chancery was governed by the Rules of the Apostolic Chancery. Most of these rules were concerned with the petition for and granting of benefices, dispensations and other favors, and were so constituted as to safeguard the proper distribution of Papal favors.[7] Thus Rules 22, 32, 35, 55, 57 determine what must be stated in petitions for different favors; Rules 20, 21 state what qualifications are necessary to receive benefices and other favors; Rules 16, 25, 27, 40, 41, 47-53, 56, 58, 59, 61, 62 concern the form of different rescripts of favor; Rules 26, 39, 44-46, 60 contain regulations concerning the granting of benefices; Rules 30, 31, 36, 42, 43 decide what is necessary for the validity and what is necessary for the lawfulness of grants of benefices and other favors; Rule 18 safeguards acquired rights; Rules 17, 34 give the principles for precedence of rescripts; Rule 12 revalidates rescripts of favor, granted

---

[5] Wernz, *Jus Decretalium,* II, n. 637; Hilling, *Procedure at the Roman Curia,* p. 14; Maroto, *Institutiones,* n. 826; Ayrinhac, *Constitution of the Church,* p. 52.

[6] Hilling, *Procedure at the Roman Curia,* pp. 118, 119, 123, 15, 16; Maroto, *Institutiones,* n. 826; Ayrinhac, *Constitution of the Church,* p. 52.

[7] Baart, *The Roman Court,* n. 282; Hilling, *Procedure at the Roman Curia,* p. 16.

during the year previous to death of the preceding Pope but not presented for execution; Rule 52 concerns the use of favors granted by rescript; Rule 68 forbids exactions for rescripts; Rules 13-15, 63, 64, 69 revoke certain favors and faculties granted by the preceding Pope; and Rules 1-11, 68 determine which benefices are reserved to the Pope.[7a]

During the eleventh or twelfth century the *College of Apostolic Penitentiaries* was established by the Pope to care for the penitential office and dispensations of the internal forum. The cases brought before the Penitentiary became so numerous in the thirteenth century that a Cardinal was appointed to preside over it, and thus the present Tribunal of the Sacred Penitentiary came into existence.[8] The Sacred Penitentiary did not, however, confine itself to the internal forum, but as early as the thirteenth and fourteenth centuries, with the approval of the Roman Pontiffs, occupied itself in the external forum also.[9] Pius IV, in his constitution "*In sublimi*," issued on May 4, 1562,[10] greatly reduced its power for the external forum.

During this period, another office, the *Signature of Favor*, was established for the purpose of examining and giving advice regarding favors of an extraordinary character. At first the Signature of Favor was united to the Signature of Justice, but it was made a distinct and separate office by Innocent VIII (1484-1492).[11]

About the beginning of the sixteenth century, because of the ever increasing number of dispensations and grants of reserved benefices, the *Office of the Apostolic Datary* was separated from the Apostolic Chancery and given an iden-

---

[7a] Rigantius, *Commentarium in Regulas*.

[8] Baart, *The Roman Court*, n. 262; Hilling, *Procedure at the Roman Curia*, pp. 15, 127; Monin, *De Curia Romana*, p. 85; Eubel, Ak K R, t. 64, p. 3 ff.; Ferreres, *La Curia Romana*, n. 827 ff.; De Meester, *Compendium*, II, n. 598; Wernz, *Jus Decretalium*, II, n. 673; Kubelbeck, *The Sacred Penitentiaria*, pp. 14, 15.

[9] Martin, *The Roman Curia*, p. 120; Monin, *De Curia Romana*, pp. 87 ff.; De Meester, *Compendium*, II, n. 598; Ojetti, *De Romana Curia*, n. 124. Cf. Part III, Chapt. I, Art. III, §1 for details about the external and internal fora.

[10] *Bullarum . . . Taurinensis editio*, VII, 128, 129.

[11] Baart, *The Roman Court*, p. 253.

tity of its own.[12] Some authors[13] contend that the Apostolic Datary was established as a separate office at a much earlier date, sometime in the fourteenth century. As already mentioned, there was a *Communis Data* within the Apostolic Chancery as early as the thirteenth century, but not until the time of Martin V in 1420 was there any mention of a *Datarius*, and not until the end of the fifteenth century was the *Datarius* given an assistant with a permanent appointment. This hardly permits dating the beginning of the Apostolic Datary, as a separate office, before the beginning of the sixteenth century, although long before that time the office of the Datarius existed within the Apostolic Chancery.

Article III.—The Reform of Sixtus V

During the fifteenth and sixteenth centuries, the Roman Curia was the object of much criticism and ridicule. The reform and reorganization of the Roman Curia, so greatly needed, was accomplished by Sixtus V in his constitution "*Immensa,*" published on the 22 January 1588.[14] Sixtus V, in his constitution, retained the Sacred Chancery, the Datary, and the Sacred Penitentiary, and established fifteen Congregations including two that were already in existence, v.g., the Sacred Congregation of the Roman and Universal Inquisition, now more generally known as the Congregation of the Holy Office, established by Paul III,[15] and the Sacred Congregation of Cardinals Interpreters of the Council of Trent, now known as the Congregation of the Council, established by Pius IV.[16]

---

[12] Monin, *De Curia Romana*, p. 129; Ayrinhac, *Constitution of the Church*, p. 80; Celier, *Les Dataires du XVe Siècle; Revue Augustinienne*, XIII (1908), 569; *Canoniste*, XXXVIII (1915), pp. 19 ff.; De Meester, *Compendium*, II, n. 603.

[13] Wernz, *Jus Decretalium*, II, n. 677; Wernz-Vidal, *Jus Canonicum*, II, n. 505; Phillips, *Kirchenrecht*, VI, p. 385; Ojetti, *De Romana Curia*, n. 172; Hilling, *Procedure at the Roman Curia*, pp. 15, 123.

[14] *Bullarum . . . Taurinensis editio*, VIII, 117.

[15] Bull. "*Licet ab initio*," 21 July 1542, *Bullarum... Taurinensis editio*, VI, 43.

[16] Motu proprio "*Alias nos*," 2 Aug. 1564, *Bullarum . . . Taurinensis editio*, VII, 99.

The Congregations established by Sixtus V and his successors assumed much of the work done by the Consistories before the sixteenth century,[17] and, although it was not intended as their principal work, some of them began to share in the work of granting Rescripts of Favor. In the Constitution *"Immensa,"* at least the Congregation of the Sacred Inquisition, the Congregation of Sacred Rites and Ceremonies, and the Sacred Congregation of the Index were given power to grant papal favors. Thus, e.g., the Congregation of the Sacred Inquisition was given power to dispense from the impediments of Mixed Religion, Disparity of Cult, Solemn Profession, and Sacred Orders; from the laws prohibiting the reading of forbidden books, and holding conversation with heretics.

The entrance of Congregations into the affairs of Rescripts of Favor marks an important development in the history of Rescripts.

Article IV.—Sixtus V to Pius X

During this period, the Offices, Congregations and the Tribunal of the Sacred Penitentiary all took part in the granting, composition and expedition of Papal Rescripts of Favor.

Among the offices, the Apostolic Datary, the Apostolic Chancery and the Secretariate of Briefs were the most important.

The power of the *Apostolic Datary* rapidly increased so that by the middle of the seventeenth century it was one of the most important departments of the Roman Curia. It became the principal agent of the Pope in the distribution of favors, appointment to benefices, marriage dispensations, dispensations from irregularities, in fact, of all the ordinary concessions not reserved to other departments.[18] The Apostolic Datary ordinarily concerned itself only with the granting of the favors, the Apostolic Chancery and the

---

[17] Hilling, *Procedure at the Roman Curia,* p. 19; Martin, *The Roman Curia,* pp. 17, 18; Maroto, *Institutiones,* II, n. 826.

[18] Baart, *The Roman Court,* n. 255, 256; Wernz, *Jus Decretalium,* II, n. 677; Hilling, *Procedure at the Roman Curia,* p. 124; De Meester, *Compendium,* II, n. 603; Ayrinhac, *Constitution of the Church,* p. 81.

Secretariate of Briefs expediting the favors in the form of Bulls or Briefs. Only occasionally did the Apostolic Datary grant them by simple signature.[19] The Apostolic Datary was therefore not an office *"gratiae expeditae,"* but *"gratiae concessae,"* i.e., an office with power to grant papal favors, but dependent on other departments for the composition and expedition of the Rescripts.

During this period, the power of the *Apostolic Chancery* gradually diminished. When the Apostolic Datary was separated from it, it lost all power of *granting* favors and retained only the work, as far as Rescripts of Favor were concerned, of composing and expediting in the form of Bulls and Briefs certain favors granted by the Datary or the Congregations. In the seventeenth century, when the Secretariate of Briefs became a separate unit, the work of the Apostolic Chancery was confined to writing and sending, in the form of Bulls, the rescripts, which, by custom or law, were to be expedited in that form.[20] Thus it became an office *"gratiae expeditae."*[21]

The *Secretariate of Briefs* was both an office *"gratiae expeditae"* and *"gratiae concessae."* It was separated by Innocent XI in his bull *"Romanus Pontifex,"* 1 April 1678,[22] and given the task of composing and expediting favors of lesser moment in the form of Briefs. All favors not sent out directly by the Congregations or through Bulls of the Apostolic Chancery were composed and expedited through the Secretariate of Briefs.[23] Although principally an office for the composition and expedition of favors, it also had some power to grant favors. Benedict XIV, in his bull *"Gravissimum Ecclesiae,"* issued Nov. 26, 1745,[24] enumerates the favors granted by the Secretariate of Briefs independently of or with the Apostolic Datary, v.g., dispensations from the canonical age for Holy Orders, privileges

---

[19] Hilling, *Procedure at the Roman Curia,* p. 126; Ojetti, *De Romana Curia,* n. 176.

[20] Baart, *The Roman Court,* n. 274, 277; Hilling, *Procedure at the Roman Curia,* pp. 119, 121.

[21] Ojetti, *De Romana Curia,* n. 276.

[22] *Bullarum . . . Taurinensis editio,* XIX, 37.

[23] Baart, *The Roman Court,* n. 284.

[24] *Bullarii Romani Continuatio,* I, 145.

of a private altar, indults to reserve the Blessed Sacrament in a private chapel or a public non-parochial church, to bless and endow medals and rosaries with papal indulgences, to grant the privileged altar, to bestow papal honors, etc. Leo XIII, in his motu proprio, "*Christianae republicae*," issued Oct. 31, 1897,[25] gave it the exclusive power of granting indulgences.

Three other offices, the Secretariate of Memorials, the Secretariate of Briefs to Princes, and the Signature of Favor were of minor importance during this period. The Secretariate of Memorials had the power to grant indulgences for the moment of death, relics, small favors pertaining to the other departments, and favors which depended on the immediate intervention of the Pope. By the end of the nineteenth century it had lost most of its powers.[26] The Secretariate of Briefs to Princes composed and dispatched rescripts, in the form of Briefs, to Kings, Princes, Bishops and other dignitaries.[27] The Signature of Favor was consulted by the Popes in questions of extraordinary favors. By the middle of the nineteenth century it had practically disappeared.[28]

The *Congregations* participated both in the granting of favors, and in the writing and expedition of rescripts which neither by custom nor law had to be expediated through the Apostolic Chancery or the Secretariate of Briefs.[29] Nine Congregations were concerned with Rescripts of Favor, The Congregation of the Holy Office, The Sacred Congregation of the Index, The Sacred Congregation of the Council, The Sacred Consistorial Congregation, The Sacred Congregation for the Affairs of Bishops and Regulars, The Sacred Congregation of the Propagation of the Faith and Oriental Rites, The Sacred Congregation of Sacred Rites, The Sacred Congregation of Studies, and The Sacred Congregation for

---

[25] ASS, XXX (1897-8), 563 sq.

[26] Amort, *Elementa Juris Canonici*, III, p. 600; Baart, *The Roman Court*, n. 287.

[27] Hilling, *Procedure at the Roman Curia*, p. 115.

[28] Baart, *The Roman Court*, n. 253-255; Hilling, *Procedure at the Roman Curia*, p. 143.

[29] Baart, *The Roman Court*, n. 284.

Extraordinary Ecclesiastical Affairs.[30] Gradually many of the powers that had formerly been in the possession of the Apostolic Chancery and the Apostolic Datary were transferred to the Congregations. Unfortunately some of the powers pertaining to the same subject were divided between different Congregations, e.g., Religious, Bishops.[31]

The *Tribunal of the Sacred Penitentiary* continued to be the ordinary grantor, composer, and expeditor of Rescripts of Favor pertaining to the internal forum. Despite the attempts of Pius IV and Pius V to limit the Penitentiary to the internal forum, in the following centuries it received power, through papal grants, for the external forum also, e.g., for dispensations from public matrimonial impediments for the poor.[32]

Such was the condition in the Roman Curia regarding the granting and expedition of Papal Rescripts of Favor before the reform of Pius X:—its organization defective, inasmuch as the Tribunal of the Sacred Penitentiary was dealing with matters of the internal and external forum; inasmuch as the offices dealt extensively in the granting as well as the expedition of favors; and inasmuch as the system of division of power among the Congregations was faulty, some Congregations overcrowded with work and others with scarcely anything to do, and practically all dealing extensively in matters of the judicial forum, making the Tribunals of Justice tribunals in name only.[33]

Article V.—Pius X to the Present

The reform, for which many of the Cardinals and Bishops had written to Leo XIII and Pius X, was finally accomplished by Pius X in his constitutions, "*Sapienti Consilio*," 29 June 1908,[34] and "*Ordo Servandus*," 29 Sept.

---

[30] Hilling, *Procedure at the Roman Curia*, pp. 56, 59, 63, 64, 78, 74, 75, 83, 84, 88-92, 98; De Meester, *Compendium*, II, n. 598; Santi, *Praelectiones*, lib. I, tit. 31, n. 131.

[31] Hilling, *Procedure at the Roman Curia*, pp. 56, 75, 63, 74, 78.

[32] Martin, *The Roman Curia*, pp. 123-125; Ojetti, *De Romana Curia*, pp. 167, 168; De Meester, *Compendium*, II, n. 598.

[33] Martin, *The Roman Curia*, p. 14.

[34] AAS, I (1909), 7 sq.

1908.[35] Through this reorganization, the Roman Curia was so constituted that the primary and principal, though not entirely exclusive, function of the Tribunals was the exercise of the judiciary power; that of the Congregations, the exercise of the executive and administrative power; and that of the Offices, the exercise of the ministerial power.[36]

The *Sacred Penitentiary* was given full and exclusive power of granting all matrimonial dispensations, all dispensations, commutations, sanations, and condonations for the internal forum only, without territorial limitations or restrictions.[37] It was given not only power to grant but also to compose and expedite these favors in the form of Simple Rescripts or Briefs.[38]

To the *Congregations* was entrusted the power to grant practically all favors in the external forum; nearly all of their judicial power was taken from them and their field of labors was confined to administrative work; moreover, an orderly and systematic distribution of powers among the Congregations was effected.

The Congregation of the Holy Office was given power to grant indulgences, the Pauline Privilege, and dispensations from the matrimonial impediments of Disparity of Cult and Mixed Religion:—and in its sphere of activity there were to be no territorial limitations.[39]

The *Consistorial Congregation* was empowered to constitute new dioceses, cathedral and collegiate chapters, and to divide those already constituted; to propose Bishops, Administrators Apostolic, Adjutor and Auxiliary Bishops for appointment; to grant what was necessary for the ordinary government of dioceses and seminaries, e.g., dispensations from the law of residence, the faculty to delay the report of the diocese, etc., and to settle disputes about competency

---

35 AAS, I (1909), 36 sq.

36 Vermeersch-Creusen, *Epitome*, I, n. 317.

37 Pius X, const. "*Sapienti Consilio*," 29 June 1908, II-1°—AAS, I (1909), 15; Pius X, const. "*Ordo Servandus*," "*Normae Peculiares*," cap. 1, n. 1 g—AAS, I (1909), 60.

38 Wernz-Vidal, *Jus Canonicum*, II, n. 502.

39 "*Sapienti Consilio*," I—10°; "*Normae Peculiares*," cap. I, n. 1a—AAS, I (1909), 9, 59.

between the Congregations. It was to be limited in its powers by the limits of common law.[40]

The *Congregation of the Sacraments* was established by Pius X to bring together under one Congregation most of what pertained to the Sacraments. Its jurisdiction included the granting of matrimonial dispensations, sanations, dispensations *"super rato,"* separation of spouses and legitimation of children; the granting of dispensations for the other Sacraments, e.g., Holy Orders (except of religious), Holy Eucharist, Sacrifice of the Mass, reservation of the Blessed Sacrament and the like; the granting of faculties exempting the faithful, even of religious institutes, from the Eucharistic fast. For matrimony, not for the other Sacraments, its competence extended even to the territories of the Propagation of the Faith.[41]

The *Congregation of the Council* received power to dispense from the precepts of the Church; from what pertains to pastors, canons, pious unions and sodalities, pious legacies and works, Mass stipends, benefices, offices, ecclesiastical goods, collections, diocesan tributes and the like; from the necessary conditions to acquire benefices granted by Ordinaries. It was empowered, e.g., to exempt colleges of canons and chapters from the obligations of celebrating a ferial or vigil Mass, singing a conventual Mass, singing or reciting canonical hours; to permit anticipation of Matins by chapters and secular clergy. Its territorial limits were the limits of common law.[42]

The *Congregation for Religious Members* became a separate congregation. Its jurisdiction was to extend over all religious of both sexes, those, with or without vows, living a common life, and seculars of the Third Order. It was given power to dispense religious members from the common law, and to grant favors that concerned their state, discipline, studies and ordination, but not what concerned them as missionaries when they were in countries under

[40] *"Sapienti Consilio,"* I—2°; *"Normae Peculiares,"* cap. VII, art. II, n. 7; cap. I, n. 1b—AAS, I (1909), 9, 10, 83, 84, 59.

[41] *"Sapienti Consilio,"* I—3°; *"Normae Peculiares,"* cap. VII, art. III, n. 10; cap. I, n. 1c—AAS, I (1909), 10, 86, 87, 59.

[42] *"Sapienti Consilio,"* I—4°; *"Normae Peculiares,"* cap. VII, art. IV, n. 4; cap. I, n. 1d—AAS, I (1909), 11, 93, 69.

the jurisdiction of the Congregation of Propagation of the Faith; and to grant the "*Decretum Laudis*" and the "*Decretum Approbationis.*" [43]

The *Congregation of the Propagation of the Faith* was given power to grant favors for missionary countries and for the churches of the Oriental Rite, except in matters pertaining to Matrimony, rites, and religious as religious.[44]

The *Congregation of the Index* received power to grant permission to read forbidden books. It was to have no territorial limits.[45]

The *Congregation of Sacred Rites* obtained power to grant dispensations relating to the ceremonies and rites of the Mass, the Sacraments, etc.; to grant insignia and honorary privileges pertaining to the sacred rites and ceremonies. Its jurisdiction was limited to the Latin Rite.[46]

The *Congregation of Studies* was granted the power to approve new universities, to grant the faculty of conferring degrees, and, at times, to grant individual honors. Its jurisdiction was limited by the limits of common law.[47]

The *Congregation for Extraordinary Ecclesiastical Affairs* retained its right to grant extraordinary favors in any part of the Latin Church.[48]

Since the reform of the Roman Curia, the principal work of the Congregations, as far as Rescripts of Favor are concerned, has been the *granting* of papal favors by virtue either of general or special faculties or special papal concessions, but they have also *composed* and *expedited* some of the favors in the form of Simple Rescripts.

There are three forms in which favors granted by the Congregations are expedited:—either in the form of Bulls

---

[43] "*Sapienti Consilio,*" I—5°; "*Normae Peculiares,*" cap. I, n. 1e; cap. VIII, art. V, n. 6—AAS, I (1909), 11, 12, 60, 97.

[44] "*Sapienti Consilio,*" I—6°; "*Normae Peculiares,*" cap. I, n. 1f—AAS, I (1909), 12, 13, 60.

[45] "*Sapienti Consilio,*" I—7°; "*Normae Peculiares,*" cap. I, n. 1g—AAS, I (1909), 13, 60.

[46] "*Sapienti Consilio,*" I—8°; "*Normae Peculiares,*" cap. I, n. 1g—AAS, I (1909), 13, 14, 60.

[47] "*Sapienti Consilio,*" I—11°; "*Normae Peculiares,*" cap. I, n. 1d—AAS, I (1909), 14, 60.

[48] "*Sapienti Consilio,*" I—10°; *Normae Peculiares,*" cap. I, n. 1g—AAS, I (1909), 14, 60.

through the Apostolic Chancery, in the form of Briefs through the Secretariate of State, or by Simple Rescripts from the Congregations themselves. Law and custom determine the form that is to be used in specific instances. The "*Normae Peculiares*" contains examples of these three forms of Rescripts. Nominations of the Congregation of the Consistory, as well as the decrees of the constitution of dioceses, colleges of canons, or chapters, or the union of dioceses are sent in the form of Bulls.[49] Perpetual indulgences, temporary ones affecting a whole diocese, province, region or the whole church, perpetual faculties to apply indulgences to any pious articles, that are granted by the Holy Office; dispensations from matrimonial dispensation of major taxes, certain indults for private chapters, perpetual indults to reserve the Blessed Sacrament in a temple or chapel, that are granted by the Sacred Congregation for the Discipline of the Sacraments; and new constitutions of studies by the University or its faculty, or any great change in the status of the Faculty or University, that are granted by the Sacred Congregation of Studies:—all are sent in the form of Briefs through the Secretariate of State.[50] Matrimonial dispensations, except those of major taxes, and temporary indults to receive the Blessed Sacrament, that are granted by the Sacred Congregation for the discipline of the Sacraments, are sent out in the form of Simple Rescripts by the Congregation itself.[51]

Since 1908, the *Offices* are almost exclusively concerned with the *writing and expedition* of Rescripts, having very little to do with the *granting* of the favors.

The *Apostolic Chancery* was given the work of expediting Consistorial favors or any other favors that were to be granted in the form of Bulls.[52] The *Secretariate of State* assumed a part in the granting and expediting of Papal Rescripts of Favor through two of its Secretaries:—the Secretary of Briefs was commissioned to expedite, in

[49] "*Normae Peculiares,*" cap. VII, art. II, n. 10—AAS, I (1909), 84.

[50] "*Normae Peculiares,*" cap. VII, art. I, n. 14; cap. VII, art. III, n. 13, 15; cap. VII, art. XI, n. 4—AAS, I (1909), 78, 89, 90, 101.

[51] "*Normae Peculiares,*" cap. VII, art. III, n. 13-15—AAS, I (1909), 89, 90.

[52] "*Sapienti Consilio,*" III—1°—AAS, I (1909), 16.

the form of Briefs, the various favors committed to him by the different Congregations; and another Secretary was given the power to grant ecclesiastical insignia of honor.[53] The *Secretariate to Princes and of Latin Letters* retained its power to compose and expedite Briefs to Kings, Princes, Bishops and other dignitaries.[54] The *Apostolic Datary,* at one time the principal agent in the granting of Papal favors, was shorn of practically all its ancient powers. Its only remaining power was to grant and expedite non-consistorial benefices reserved to the Pope, and to grant exemption from the conditions necessary to obtain them. The favors emanating from the Datary were ordinarily to be expedited in the form of Bulls, but provision was made so that the custom of expediting some by a decree of simple signature could be retained.[55]

So satisfactory was the reorganization of the Roman Curia by Pius X that only a few changes have since been introduced. Benedict XV, in his motu proprio "*Seminaria,*" 4 Nov. 1915,[56] changed the name of the Congregation of Studies to that of the Congregation of Seminaries and Universities, adding to it the powers pertaining to Seminaries that had until then belonged to the Consistorial Congregation. In his *motu propio* "*Alloquentes,*" March 25, 1917,[57] he suppressed the Congregation of the Index, transferred the power to grant indulgences to the Sacred Penitentiary and the other powers to the Congregation of the Holy Office. The same Pope in his motu proprio "*Dei Providentis,*" May 1, 1917,[58] took away the affairs of the Oriental Church from the Congregation of the Propagation of the Faith and formed the new Congregation for the Oriental Church.

These changes have been retained in the Code,[59] nor have any changes occurred in the Congregation of the Council,

---

[53] "*Sapienti Consilio,*" III—4°—AAS, I (1909), 17.

[54] "*Sapienti Consilio,*" III—5°—AAS, I (1909), 17.

[55] "*Sapienti Consilio,*" III—2°; "*Normae Peculiares,*" cap. IX, art. II, n. 3—AAS, I (1909), 16, 104.

[56] AAS, VIII (1916), 493.

[57] AAS, X (1918), 167.

[58] AAS, X (1918), 529.

[59] Can. 248, 256, 253, 258, 247 §4, 257, 252.

the Congregation for Extraordinary Ecclesiastical Affairs, the Apostolic Chancery, the Apostolic Datary, the Secretariate of State, or the Secretariate of Briefs for Princes and of Latin Letters.[60] The exclusive power of the Congregation of the Holy Office to dispense priests from the Eucharistic fast connected with the celebration of Mass, as well as to grant favors that might also seem to fall within the jurisdiction of the Congregations of the Discipline of the Sacraments, for the Affairs of Religious Members, of the Propagation of the Faith, and of the Oriental Church, has been clearly maintained in the Code.[61] The exclusive power of the Congregation of the Discipline of the Sacraments for Matrimonial Dispensations of Subjects of the Congregation of the Propagation of the Faith has also been clearly stated.[62] Only two Congregations have had even slight modifications in their names. We now speak of the Congregation of the Discipline of the Sacraments, and the Congregation for the Affairs of Religious Members.[63] Finally provision was made so that all controversies about competency between the Congregation, Offices or Tribunals would be decided by a committee of Cardinals designated in each instance by the Roman Pontiff.[63a]

Since the Code, certain points relating to the competency of the different departments have been clarified. It is certain that the Congregation for the Affairs of Religious Members is competent to grant condonations and sanations regarding the past, and reductions for the future, for chaplaincies and legacies which although not concredited to an order or religious family as such, are, nevertheless, found erected or transferred in the churches of religious—but only as far as the administration and fulfillment of the legacies are accredited to the Religious; to grant dispensations from defect of age or an irregularity that prevents a Religious from receiving Sacred Orders; to grant

[60] Can. 250, 255, 260, 261, 263, 264.
[61] Can. 247, §5, 249, §1, 251, §3, 252, §4, 257, §2.
[62] Can. 252, §4.
[63] Can. 249, 251.
[63a] Can. 245.

permission to say Mass to those who are physically or morally unable to do so on account of a wound or any other cause;[64] and to grant to religious of both sexes dispensations from the law of the Eucharistic fast for the reception of Holy Communion. It has also been decided that matters pertaining to priests, either alumni or teachers of lay schools, and to clerical associations and federations come under the jurisdiction of the Congregation of the Council; and that the Congregation of Seminaries and Universities is competent to grant faculties that permit the alienation of goods pertaining to diocesan seminaries.[65] Finally, it was decided that non-Catholics, whether baptized or not, need permission from the Sacred Congregation of the Holy Office to appear as plaintiffs *(actores)* in ecclesiastical matrimonial trials,[66] and that petitions for dispensations "*super matrimonio rato et non consummato*" should be addressed to the same Congregation when one of the parties involved is a non-Catholic, baptized or not baptized.[67]

Otherwise, the Roman Curia has remained unchanged, as far as its work of granting, composing and expediting Rescripts of Favor is concerned. All the departments of the Curia, Tribunals, Congregations, and Offices, have some share in this work:—the Sacred Penitentiary, a tribunal, granting, composing and expediting favors for the internal

---

[64] Com. Card., 24 March 1919—AAS, XI (1919), 251.

[65] Com. Int., 13 and 27 Nov. 1922—AAS, XV (1923), 39.

[66] "I *Utrum in causis matrimonialibus acatholicus, sive baptizatus sive non baptizatus, actoris partes agere possit.*

"Ad I. *Negative seu standum Codici I. C., praesertim can. 87. Siquidem autem speciales occurant rationes ad admittendos acatholicos ut actores in huiusmodi causis, recurrendum ad Supremam Sacram Congregationem Sancti Officii in singulis casibus.*"—S. C. S. Off., 27 Jan. 1928, AAS, XX (1928), 75.

[67] "*Utrum in quibuslibet causis matrimonialibus inter partem catholicam et partem acatholicum, sive baptizatam sive non baptizatam, quocumque modo ad Sanctam Sedem delatis, Suprema Sacra Congregatio Sancti Officii exclusivam habeat competentiam.*

"*Ad II. Affirmative, habita praesertim ratione can. 247, §3, et salvo praescripto can. 1557, §1, n. 1.*"—S. C. S. Off., Jan. 27, 1928—AAS, XX (1928), 75; Kay, *Competence in Matrimonial Procedure*, pp. 76, 77; Roberti, "*Animadversiones*" Apollinaris, I (1928), 219. Cf. S. C. de Sacr., Instr., 7 Maii, 1923, reg. 9, §2; 98, §2—AAS, XV (1923), 393, 412, where such cases were included in the competency of the Sacred Congregation of the Sacraments.

forum; the Congregations granting, and frequently, composing and expediting favors for the external forum; while the Offices are concerned principally with the ministerial work of composing and expediting favors in the form of Bulls, Briefs and Simple Rescripts, with only a vestige left of their former power to grant favors, in the relatively few powers exercised by the Secretariate of State and the Apostolic Chancery. System and Order now prevail in the Roman Curia.

CHAPTER II

Form of Papal Rescripts of Favor

As has already been mentioned in the preceding chapter, the departments of the Roman Curia issue three kinds of Rescripts of Favor, namely, Bulls, Briefs, and Simple Rescripts.

The *Apostolic Bull,* the most solemn form of papal document, is reserved for Rescripts of greatest importance. The material for these documents, until the eleventh century, was papyrus, but since then, strong red parchment made of sheepskin has been used. Ordinarily only one side of the parchment is written on and the document has the shape of a horizontal rectangle. If the document, however, consists of many pages, both sides are written on, and the parchment assumes the shape of a vertical rectangle. The Bulls are written in Latin except when they are addressed to those of the Oriental rite, in which case, Greek is substituted. Since the time of Leo XIII (1878), the ordinary Latin character has been in vogue, but previous to that time, as far back as the time of the Papacy's sojourn in Avignon, it was customary to use the Gothic or Teutonic characters.[1]

There are many other characteristic features of Apostolic Bulls. Rescripts in this form commence with the name of the Pope, the place, and the date. The name of the Pope, without the number, is given first, followed by the phrase *Episcopus Servus Servorum Dei,* e.g., *Pius Episcopus Servus Servorum Dei.* They are concluded by the mention of the place from which they are sent, *Romae apud Sanctum Petrum,* followed by the date—year, day with the month, and the year of the pontificate. Since 1908, the

[1] Reiffenstuel, *Jus Canonicum,* lib. I, tit. II, n. 20; Hilling, *Procedure at the Roman Curia,* p. 120; Maroto, *Institutiones,* n. 338.

beginning of the year in the above date is reckoned from the Kalends of January instead of from the Feast of the Incarnation.[2] Although, as just observed, bearing the name of the Pope, the Rescripts, in this form, are signed by the Pope only in cases of Consistorial Bulls of great importance. In other cases, they are signed by the Cardinal Chancellor and another Official of the Apostolic Chancery, or by the Cardinal Chancellor and the Cardinal Prefect of the department in whose competency the matter belongs.[3]

The Seal is the really important distinguishing mark of the document. Before Leo XIII, all Bulls were marked with a special Seal of lead, attached to the document by a silken or hempen cord. On one side of the Seal was the representation of the heads of St. Peter and St. Paul, separated by a cross, with their initials *S.P.E.—S.P.A.* underneath; on the other side was the name and, oftentimes, the image of the reigning Pontiff. On December 29, 1878, Leo XIII, by a special act, reserved this Seal for Bulls of major importance, and ordered that a substitute Seal be used on all other Bulls, e.g., on those containing the grants of minor benefices and matrimonial dispensations. The substitute Seal is an impression, made in red ink on the lower left-hand part of the Rescript, representing the heads of St. Peter and St. Paul, separated by a cross, with the initials *S.P.—S.P.* underneath, and the name of the reigning Pope surrounding the heads of the Apostles.[4] At present, Bulls issued by the Apostolic Chancery bear the Seal of Lead, while those emanating from the Apostolic Datary bear the substitute seal.[5]

The *Apostolic Brief* is a form of Rescript used for matters of minor importance, e.g., some matrimonial dispensa-

---

[2] *"Sapienti Consilio,"* III—2°, n. 2, AAS, I (1909), 16.

[3] Monin, *De Curia Romana*, p. 361; Haring, *Grundzüge des Katholischen Kirchenrechts*, pp. 70, 71; Eichmann, *Lehrbuch des Katholischen Kirchenrechts*, pp. 30, 31; Maroto, *Institutiones*, n. 338; De Meester, *Compendium*, n. 23, 290.

[4] Rieffenstuel, *Jus Canonicum*, lib. I, tit. II, n. 17; De Justis, *De Dispensationibus*, lib. I, cap. VII, n. 299; Heiner, *Katholisches Kirchenrecht*, I, p. 34 ff.; NRT, XIV (1879), 117; De Meester, *Compendium*, I, n. 23.

[5] Maroto, *Institutiones*, n. 338.

tions since 1908.[6] The material used for the Brief is thin, white parchment made of animal skin, not very long, and oblong in shape. The Brief begins with the name of the Pope, with the number added, e.g., *Pius Papa XI*, or *Pius P.P. XI*. The date is given according to the ordinary calendar computation of time, in the order of day, month, year, and year of Pontificate. If the brief is of any importance, it is signed by the Secretary of State, otherwise by the Secretary of Briefs. The Seal used is the Fisherman's Seal, an image of St. Peter as a fisherman impressed in red wax on the parchment. Briefs have always been written in Latin characters.[7]

The *Simple Rescript* is the form most frequently used by the Roman Curia. It lacks the solemnities of the Bull or Brief, and is issued on ordinary paper in a rather simple style. Usually the Cardinal Prefect and the Secretary of the issuing department sign the document, but this is not a rigidly binding rule, since at times another Cardinal or Prelate of the department signs instead of the Cardinal Prelate, and a sub-secretary or some minor official instead of the Secretary, and in some instances, e.g., in most rescripts of this nature issued by the Congregation of the Holy Office, the simple signature of the Notary takes the place of the double signature. The Seal varies in nature according to the department that sends the Rescript or its presiding Cardinal. Although occasionally the Seal of the presiding Cardinal is used, ordinarily it is the seal of the department itself.[8]

Since the form of Simple Rescripts is so frequent it might be well to describe this form in detail. An examination of such Rescripts served as the basis for the following observations. Some Congregations have printed forms for different

---

[6] *"Normae Peculiares,"* cap. VII, art. III, n. 13, AAS, I (1909), 89.

[7] Reiffenstuel, *Jus Canonicum*, lib. I, tit. II, n. 16, 20; Monin, *De Curia Romana*, p. 368 sq.; De Meester, *Compendium*, I, n. 23; Maroto, *Institutiones*, n. 338.

[8] Maroto, *Institutiones*, n. 338, pp. 403, 404, nota (1).

kinds of favors, indicated by the titles on the back of the document, e.g., "*Facultas mutui contrahendi,*" "*Dispensatio in genere,*" "*Dispensatio a vetito can. 542, 1°.*" In these printed forms spaces are left so that different instructions may be added in writing. Other rescripts are typewritten or written by hand. The name of the department that grants the favor is always given, sometimes on the upper left-hand corner of the document, sometimes on the other side of the rescript. Usually it is given in two lines, e.g., *Suprema S. Congregatio,* and underneath, *Sancti Officii.* On the upper left-hand corner the number of the document and the year are indicated, e.g., N., Num., or Num. Prot. $\frac{720}{1924}$ or $\frac{692}{25}$; on the upper right-hand corner are the letter F and a number, e.g., F. 27[a], evidently referring to the number of the faculty. On the lower left-hand corner the place and date are indicated, e.g., *Datum Romae die... etc.;* underneath the date the Seal of the Congregation or Prefect is stamped. On the lower right-hand corner are the signatures of the Prefect and Secretary or the signature of the Notary alone:—the signature first and underneath the title.

Such are the main differences between Rescripts in the form of Bulls, Briefs, and Simple Rescripts. There are not the same differences in the body of the letter itself, aside from the style and language used. Just as it was customary, according to the tradition of the Roman Curia, for a petitioner for a favor to divide his petition into three parts, namely, the exposition of the facts, the reasons, and the object of the petition, so also was it customary, at one time, for the Rescript to have three corresponding parts, namely, the narrative part summing up the facts found in the first part of the petition, the motive part stating the reasons for the concession, and the dispositive part containing the concession of the favor together with the conditions to be observed.[9] At present, however, the departments concerned in the preparation of the Rescripts

---

[9] Reiffenstuel, *Jus Canonicum,* lib. I, tit. III, n. 9; Maroto, *Institutiones,* n. 281; Ayrinhac, *General Legislation,* p. 144.

are not bound so rigidly to this form, but quite frequently the narrative part is restricted to the name of the petitioner, the diocese or religious order, etc.; the motive is given in a very brief manner or omitted entirely; while the dispositive part, embodying the decision of the Pope, continues to be the main part of the document.[10]

Such details, although in themselves of minor importance, may at times be of value in determining the authenticity of Papal Rescripts.

[10] Wernz, *Jus Decretalium*, I, n. 152; Lombardi, *Institutiones*, I, p. 92.

CHAPTER III

Taxes, Componenda, Agents' Fees, and Carrier Expenses

On the occasion of grants of favors and dispensations, the Roman Curia imposes a *Tax* of a fixed determined amount of money on the recipients of the Rescripts. The tax is not meant to be a price placed on the favor, but is rather a legitimate method employed to maintain and defray the expenses of the departments of the Curia. Pius X in the reorganization of the Curia through his constitution, *"Ordo Servandus," "Normae Communes,"* 29 Sept. 1908, retained the ancient system of taxation and ordained exactly what the future taxes would be. He retained the taxes then in vogue for matrimonial dispensations, and placed a tax of ten lire on all other major rescripts and five lire on minor rescripts, with a provision added that in case a rescript contained more than one favor the tax would be increased in proportion to the number of favors.[1] This rule is not without its exceptions. The Congregation of the Holy Office does not exact a special tax for its dispensations of Mixed Religion and Disparity of Cult, but rather a chancery fee of fifteen lire, which includes the agent's fee. Moreover, petitioners from some countries, e.g., Germany and France, instead of paying the regular taxes, give certain offerings that are at times less than the corresponding taxes.[2]

Each department of the Roman Curia has special officials to care for the marking and collection of taxes. Ordinarily the tax is marked on the rescript, but in case of secret matters it is marked on another document. Each month the

[1] *"Normae Communes,"* cap. XI, n. 12, 13, AAS—I (1909), 57, 58.

[2] Wernz-Vidal, *Jus Canonicum,* p. 525, 526, nota (123); Chelodi, *Jus Matrimoniale,* n. 51.

Moderator of the department examines the tax report and gives an account of it to the Treasury of the Holy See.[3]

The *Componenda* is a certain sum of money, distinct from the tax, exacted from those who petition for favors that presuppose a fault on the part of the petitioner. The nature of the fault will appear in the petition either in the nature of the impediment or in the cause that is given in seeking the favor. The money obtained in this way is not used for the maintenance of the Curia, but is distributed by the Curia among works of charity. In this respect the Componenda differs from the almsgiving which, at times, is imposed upon the parties to be done personally by them: —in the first case the Roman Curia distributes the money, in the other, the parties are free to give the money to any charitable work that they select. The amount of the Componenda varies considerably according to the economic conditions of the petitioner and the gravity of the fault that was committed. At times it amounts to three thousand lire.[4]

A special fee is charged when an *Agent* is used by the petitioner of a favor in communicating with the Roman Curia. Before 1908, Bishops were obliged to transact their business with all the departments of the Holy See, except the Sacred Penitentiary, through Agents. Private individuals were allowed to petition for papal favors granted by the Sacred Penitentiary, with or without Agents. Although the Agents were not Officials of the Roman Curia, they were men thoroughly acquainted with the affairs and the manner of procedure of the Roman Curia and had a certain standing with the authorities there. Frequently they were domestic prelates or apostolic protonotaries *ad instar*. Their work consisted in composing the petitions of their patrons, correcting any mistakes or defects, submitting the petitions with the necessary explanations and paying the curial tax. Instead of the Agents,

[3] "*Normae Communes*," cap. XI, n. 4-7, AAS—I (1909), 56, 57.

[4] Kubelbeck, *The Sacred Penitentiaria*, pp. 113, 118; Wernz-Vidal, *Jus Canonicum*, V, p. 524, nota (123); De Smet, *De Sponsalibus et Matrimonio*, n. 857; Chelodi, *Jus Matrimoniale*, n. 51; Capello, *De Sacramentis*, III, n. 289.

the "*Procuratores Missionum*" transacted this business with the Congregation of the Propagation of the Faith.[5]

The Reform of the Curia by Pius X brought with it a great change in the status of Agents. Since then there are two kinds of Agents, Private Agents for Individuals, and Public Agents for Ordinaries.

The faithful were relieved of the obligation of recoursing to Rome through their Ordinaries and were permitted to deal with the Roman Curia either personally or through the medium of *Private Agents.* To act as a Private Agent one must be a Catholic, have a good reputation and not be personally concerned in the matter in question. A Private Agent has no official recognition, each particular Moderator being free to admit or to refuse to admit a particular Agent.[6]

Ordinaries were granted the option of treating with Rome with or without Agents, but were advised, in order to be sure of a speedy transaction of their business, to make use of *Public Agents.*[7] Public Agents have an official standing in Rome. To qualify they must be Catholics, of good reputation, and specially versed in Latin and Canon Law. If they are in sacred orders and belong to the secular clergy, they must have permission from the Office of the Vicar of Rome to remain in Rome; if religious, the permission of their Superior General. Pius X ordained that, excepting those who at the time were acting as Agents and had acquired rights, the Cardinal *a secretis* of the Consistorial Congregation, with the advice of his Congress, would determine whether or not a particular person would be admitted as a Public Agent. All public Agents must have their names inscribed in the tablet of the Procurators. The Ordinary, in selecting his Agent, can choose one who has or has not already been inscribed in the tablet of the Procurators, but before one who has not been inscribed can act as his Agent he must follow the ordinary procedure

---

[5] Hilling, *Procedure at the Roman Curia,* pp. 43, 44, 150, 152; Capello, *De Curia Romana,* I, p. 43; Kubelbeck, *The Sacred Penitentiary,* p. 86.

[6] "*Normae Communes,*" cap. IX, n. 1, 2; cap. X, n. 1, 2—AAS, I (1909), 49, 53.

[7] "*Normae Communes,*" cap. IX, n. 5, 6—AAS, I (1909), 54.

by being inscribed. Moreover, a mandate from the Ordinary must be presented by the Agent to the Office *a secretis* of the Consistorial Congregation.[8]

There are two ways in which the Public Agent may lose his Office, either by removal, or by the withdrawal of the mandate by the Ordinary. When guilty of acting in a manner unbecoming a Christian or of committing a serious fault in the exercise of his duties, the Public Agent may be suspended from office or even perpetually dismissed. The College of Consistorial Agents acts as the disciplinary court but in case of a publicly known fault, the Consistorial Congregation, or in case of a fault in which one of the other departments is concerned, the respective department can proceed from the sentence of the College to the admonition of the guilty party or to his temporary or perpetual dismissal.[9] The mandate of election may be rescinded by the Ordinary, not the Vicar Capitular, and there is no way for the Agent to recourse against the action of the Ordinary. The Vicar Capitular, as well as the Bishop, is always free to act directly with the Roman Curia, but in so doing, he must personally take care of the expenses, taxes, *componenda*, etc.[10]

The Public Agent can transact all business with the Holy See for the Ordinary, but must always send the sealed rescript to the Ordinary. He is bound, under pain of serious sin, to keep secret any information he obtains in the exercise of his office, except when the fact is public or notorious. As a compensation for his services, he receives a fixed fee of six lire for all major rescripts and three lire for minor rescripts, whether they contain one or more favors, and he cannot exact a larger amount. Any violation of this latter law makes the guilty party bound to restitution and liable to other penalties.[11]

Some Religious Institutes transact their business with the Holy See through a member of their own Institute, not

---

8 "*Normae Communes*," cap. IX, n. 3-8—AAS, I (1909), 49-51.

9 "*Normae Communes*," cap. IX, n. 13-16—AAS, I (1909), 52.

10 "*Normae Communes*," cap. X, n. 9, 10; cap. X, n. 4-6—AAS, I (1909), 55, 54.

11 "*Normae Communes*," cap. XI, n. 13; cap. IX, n. 9-13—AAS, I (1909), 58, 51.

through a regular Public Agent. At present, every Institute of Pontifical Right of men religious whether clerical or lay, must have a *Procurator General,* designated in accordance with the respective constitution of his order or congregation, through whom the business of the institute with the Holy See is transacted.[12] The position of procurator general is not an institution of the Code. Most of the older and more centralized religious orders had such officials for centuries, and in the early part of the nineteenth century all religious orders who were inadequately represented in the Papal states were obliged by Pius VII to have procurators general at Rome to transact the business of their orders with the Holy See.[13] Even when the separate Benedictine Congregations agreed to have an Abbot Primate they retained the right to have their individual procurators general at Rome.[14] The present law, as contained in the Code, does not impose upon the procurator general the obligation of residing in Rome, but the Sacred Congregation for the Affairs of Religious Members on June 4, 1920,[15] specified very definitely that the procurator general should not only be a member of the institute that he represented but should also habitally reside in Rome.

The procurator general not only takes care of the affairs of the Institute but he also ordinarily presents the petitions of the individual members to the respective departments of the Roman Curia.[16] This does not, of course, prevent the Major Superiors from occasionally recoursing directly to the Holy See as long as their respective constitutions do not forbid them to do so,[17] nor are the individual members strictly bound to recourse through the procurator general in every instance. Certainly when the matters of the internal forum are involved, especially when the sacramental seal is to be safeguarded, the religious can recourse either

12 Can. 517, §1.

13 S. C. Ep. et Reg., decr. "*Ubi primum,*" 22 Aug. 1814—Bizzari, *Collectanea,* pp. 42-45; Augustine, *A Commentary,* III, p. 151; Schäfer, *De Religiosis,* n. 517.

14 Leo XIII, litt. ap. "*Summum semper,*" 12 Julii 1893—Fontes, n. 402.

15 AAS, XII (1920), 301.

16 Schäfer, *De Religiosis,* n. 157; Coronata, *Institutiones,* I, n. 543.

17 Coronata, *Institutiones,* I, n. 543.

through the procurator general or directly to the Sacred Penitentiary. Usually, however, the Sacred Congregation for the Affairs of Religious Members or the other Congregations do not answer the petitions of members of religious institutes until they have received an oral or written opinion from the procurator general.[18]

Undoubtedly, it is of great advantage for an institute of men religious with a large membership that has considerable business to transact with the Holy See to have a procurator general at Rome, but the same cannot be said of small institutes, especially those that have no house in Rome. However, the Holy See is not unreasonable in this matter. She is always ready to dispense from the law of residence when circumstances are such that it would work an undue hardship upon the institute if the procurator was compelled to live in Rome.[19]

The Code has made provision[20] so that the religious superiors cannot lawfully[21] remove the procurator general before his term of office expires without first consulting with the Holy See. Upon the completion of his term of office, however, the religious superiors need not consult the Holy See about the appointment of another procurator general,[22] nor would it be necessary for them to consult with the Holy See about his removal when there is no time limit to the term of the procurator general and he is appointed and removed *ad nutum Superioris*, because the law imposes the obligation of consulting the Holy See only when the term of office is for a definite period of time.[23]

Only religious institutes of men have procurators general. Women religious, if they are exempt and aggregated to an Order of men, may recourse to Rome through the procurator general of the Order to which they are aggre-

---

18 Schäfer, *De Religiosis*, n. 157.

19 Vermeersch-Creusen, *Epitome*, I, n. 586; Fanfani, *De Jure Religiosarum*, n. 58.

20 Can. 517, §2.

21 Can. 11; Vermeersch-Creusen, *Epitome*, I, n. 586; Schäfer, *De Religiosis*, n. 157.

22 Fanfani, *De Jure Religiosorum*, n. 61.

23 Vermeersch-Creusen, *Epitome*, I, n. 586; Fanfani, *De Jure Religiosorum*, n. 61; Coronata, *Institutiones*, n. 543.

gated: other women religious may recourse only through the local Ordinary, through an Agent at Rome, or through their Cardinal Protector.[24]

The *Carrier Expense* is the sum of money expended in delivering or sending the rescript to the petitioner, e.g., postage, etc.

Whether or not the *tax,* the *componenda,* the *agent's fee* or the *carrier expenses* are to be paid in particular instances depends both on the nature of the department of the Curia and on the economic condition of the petitioner.

The Sacred Penitentiary requires no tax or componenda for its rescripts. If the petitioner makes use of an Agent, the Agent's fee and postal expenses must be paid, but if direct recourse is made to the tribunal, the petitioner does not have to pay even the postal expenses, unless he wishes to do so.[25] The Congregation of the Propagation of the Faith, since the time of Gregory XV, has granted rescripts without imposing any taxes.[26]

For the other departments of the Roman Curia distinction is made between the *"miserabiles,"* the *poor,* the *quasi poor,* and the *rest.* The Congregation of the Holy Office, in a decree 26 Sept. 1754,[27] determined what principles should be used in deciding the economic condition of petitioners. Persons who had no capital or fortune and lived off their labor and industry were to be considered as *"miserables;"* those living in Italy, having a capital of less than three hundred Roman *scutata* i.e., about sixteen hundred lire, and those outside Italy, having a capital of less than five hundred and twenty-five Roman *scutata* were to be considered as poor; while those in Italy, who had a fortune of more than three hundred Roman scutata and less than one thousand, and those outside Italy, who had a fortune varying between twice the above sums, were to be con-

---

[24] Schäfer, *De Religiosis,* n. 157; Fanfani, *De Jure Religiosorum,* n. 59.

[25] Gasparri, *De Matrimonio,* n. 324; Wernz-Vidal, *Jus Canonicum,* V, p. 526, nota (123) ; De Smet, *De Sponsalibus et Matrimonio,* n. 858.

[26] Gregory XV, const. *"Cum Inter,"* 14 Dec. 1622, *Bullarum . . . Taurinensis editio,* XII, 91; *"Normae Communes,"* cap. XI, n. 15, AAS, I (1909), 58.

[27] Fontes, n. 806.

sidered as quasi-poor. This norm was the general one followed ever since.[28] There have been some exceptions, e.g., for Spain and Portugal those with a fortune of less than fifteen hundred lire were considered poor, and those with a fortune of less than two thousand lire were considered quasi-poor, according to the formula of the Datary for 1901; e.g., some Ordinaries in specific instances have obtained special concessions in this matter.[29] But ordinarily the rule of the Holy Office is still in force. In estimating the capital of people, one should, however, take into account the stable returns from certain works and offices, e.g., as received by magistrates, physicians, lawyers, the value of money in different countries, and deductions for debts, taxes, and obligations.[30]

Those who are considered as "*miserables*" or "*poor*" need only pay for the postage expenses and half of the regular agent's fee, and not even all or any of that if they are unable to do so; those considered *quasi-poor*, must pay a tax and componenda of ten lire, the agent's fee and the postage expenses; while all other petitioners must pay the regular tax, a componenda proportionate to their means, the agent's fee and the postage expenses.[31]

---

[28] S. Poenit., 20 Jan. 1904—ASS, XXXVIII (1905-1906), 228.

[29] De Smet, *De Sponsalibus et Matrimonio*, n. 857; Chelodi, *Jus Matrimoniale*, n. 51.

[30] Wernz, *Jus Decretalium*, IV, n. 613, nota (38); Capello, *De Sacramentis*, III, n. 289.

[31] "*Normae Communes*," cap. XI n. 2-9—AAS, I (1909), 56, 57; Wernz-Vidal, *Jus Canonicum*, V, p. 525, nota (123); De Smet, *De Sponsalibus et Matrimonio*, n. 858.

PART III

Petitioning, Interpreting, and Executing Papal Rescripts of Favor

CHAPTER I

PETITIONING FAVORS FROM THE HOLY SEE

A Papal Rescript of Favor by its very nature presupposes that a previous petition was sent to the Roman Curia, so it is not surprising that a summary of the petition is found at the beginning of practically all rescripts. Because of the close connection existing between petition and rescript, this first chapter will be devoted to an explanation of the canonical principles that concern the petitioner and the petition.

Article I.—Persons who can Validly and Lawfully Petition for Papal Favors

From Decretal times until Pius X, there were very strict laws in force regarding those who could validly receive favors from the Holy See.[1] Heretics and schismatics,[2] false and revoked Procurators,[3] and all those who were excommunicated by major excommunication [4] were excluded from papal favors, whether their crime was public or occult, whether the excommunicated person was *vitandus* or

[1] Reiffenstuel, *Jus Canonicum,* lib. I, tit. III, n. 38-44; Schmalzgrueber, *Jus Ecclesiasticum,* pars. I, tit. III, n. 4; De Angelis, *Praelectiones,* lib. I, tit. III, n. 3; Wernz, *Jus Decretalium,* I, n. 151.

[2] C. 13, X, *de haereticis,* V, 7.

[3] C. 33, X, *de rescriptis,* I, 3.

[4] C. I, *de rescriptis,* I, 3, in VI°.

toleratus. The only exceptions admitted by law were petitions sent in the form of an appeal, and petitions seeking the remission of the penalty. The Sacred Penitentiary [5] on Sept. 9, 1898, made a further exception by declaring that although a person was punished by an occult excommunication he could still, as far as the internal forum was concerned, receive minor favors, e.g., the power to bless crosses, the faculty to read forbidden books.

The strict discipline of the Church regarding petitioners for her favors was modified somewhat, at least for excommunicated persons, by the custom that the Roman Curia had of inserting in rescripts granted *in forma gratiosa* or *in forma commissoria* an "*absolutio ad cautelam,*" temporarily suspending the censure so that the favor granted by the rescript could be received validly.[6] The customary formula inserted was "*Oratorem absolvimus et absolutum esse censemus ad effectum solummodo praesentium litterarum,*" [7] or "*Nos igitur eumdem N. N. a quibusve excommunicationibus suspensionibus et interdictis, aliisque ecclesiasticis sententiis et poenis a jure vel ab homine quam occasione vel causa latis, si quibus quomodolibet innodatus existit, ad effectum dumtaxat praesentium consequendum harum serie absolventes et absolutum fore censentes.*" [7a] This absolution, however, did not apply to all excommunicated persons. According to the 66th Rule of the Apostolic Chancery,[8] it was not intended to include those who, for four months remained excommunicated *a jure* or *ab homine* on account of the crimes of incendiarism, violation of churches, falsification of Apostolic letters, falsification of petitions, use or reception of falsified rescripts, giving protection to those guilty of falsification, giving forbidden things to heretics, violation of ecclesiastical liberty, non-

---

[5] ASS, XXXV (1902-1903), 754.

[6] Reiffenstuel, *Jus Canonicum,* lib. I, tit. III, n. 53; De Angelis, *Praelectiones,* lib. I, tit. III, n. 3; Wernz, *Jus Decretalium,* I, n. 151; Michiels, *Normae Generales,* II, p. 186.

[7] Santi, *Praelectiones,* lib. I, tit. III, n. 6.

[7a] Gennari-Boudinhon, *Consultations,* II, cons. 96, p. 222; Michiels, *Normae Generales,* II, p. 186, nota (6).

[8] Rigantius, *Commentarium in Regulas,* Reg. 66; Wernz, *Jus Decretalium,* I, n. 151, nota (31); Hyland, *Excommunication,* p. 161.

compliance with ecclesiastical mandates, and impeding Nuncios or Apostolic Executors and their officials in the execution of their commissions; nor for anyone, who for a year, remained under the penalty of any censure.

Any interference on the part of civil authority with petitions to Rome and all attempts on its part to nullify papal rescripts or to render persons "*inhabiles*" to receive papal favors were condemned by the Holy See.[9]

Pius X, in his constitution "*Ordo Servandus,*" introduced some very important changes regarding the status of the petitioner. The concession by which every "*christi fidelis* was allowed free access to the Holy See regarding their own affairs"[10] safeguarded petitioners to the Holy See from civil interference and permitted individual Catholics to send their petitions directly to the Roman Curia. Moreover, the number of censures, that rendered persons incapable of validly receiving papal favors, was greatly diminished by Pius X. Finally, it was decreed that favors and dispensations of all kinds granted by the Holy See were to be considered licit and valid even when granted to those laboring under censure, "*nisi de iis agatur qui nominatim excommunicati sint, aut a Sancta Sede nominatim pariter poena suspensionis a divinis mulctati.*"[11]

Disputes arose among canonists regarding the interpretation of this part of the constitution, "*nisi, etc.*" It was agreed that by "*nominatim excommunicati*" were meant those who were excommunicated by a public decree that designated the person in a very determinate manner either by publicly inflicting the penalty or by publicly declaring that the penalty had been incurred.[12] Discussion arose, however, as to whether only an excommunication inflicted

---

[9] Pius IX condemned the following propositions: "*Gratiae a Romano Pontifice concessae existimari debent tamquam irritae, nisi per Gubernium fuerint imploratae.*"—Pius IX, alloc. "*Numquam fore,*" 15 Dec. 1856, Fontes, n. 522; "*Civilus auctoritas potest impedire quominus sacrorum Antistites, et fideles populi, cum Romano Pontifice libere ac mutuo communicent.*"—Pius IX, alloc. "*Maxima quidem*" 9 Junii 1862, Fontes, n. 534.

[10] "*Normae Communes,*" cap. X, n. 1—AAS, I (1909), 53.

[11] "*Normae Peculiares,*" cap. III, n. 6—AAS, I (1909), 64.

[12] Martin, *The Roman Curia*, p. 269; Capello, *De Curia Romana*, I, p. 525.

or declared by the Holy See invalidated rescripts or whether an excommunication inflicted or declared by another Superior had the same effect. There was some room for divergence of opinion, since the phrase "*A Sancta Sede*" occurred only in the latter part of the sentence. Some, interpreting the law strictly, held that the qualifying phrase "*A Sancta Sede*" referred to both excommunication and suspension, while others [13] held that it modified only suspension. The phrase "*suspensionis a divinis*" was another source of dispute, some [14] maintaining that it referred to suspension from both jurisdiction and orders, while others [15] held that it referred to suspension from all powers arising from Sacred Orders. Can. 2279, §2, n. 2 now defines "*suspensio a divinis*" as suspension from all powers of Orders, whether arising from Sacred Orders or from a special privilege.

But whether the law of Pius X was strictly or broadly interpreted, it considerably decreased the number of persons who, on account of ecclesiastical censures, could neither licitly nor validly receive papal favors. This mitigation of the law ultimately led to the suppression of the "*absolutio ad cautelam*" clause in papal rescripts.[16]

The law of the "*Ordo Servandus*" is repeated in the Code, with some modifications, in the following terms:

Canon 36, §1.—Rescripta tum Sedis Apostolicae tum aliorum Ordinariorum impetrari libere possunt ab omnibus qui expresse non prohibentur.

§2.—Gratiae et dispensationes omne genus a Sede Apostolica concessae etiam censura irretitis validae sunt, salvo praescripto can. 2265, §2, 2275, n. 3, 2283.

The principle that Papal Rescripts can be asked by all those who are not expressly forbidden is an ancient principle of canon law,[17] resting on another legal axiom

---

[13] Martin, *The Roman Curia*, p. 269; Capello, *De Curia Romana*, I, p. 525.

[14] Eg. Martin, *The Roman Curia*, p. 269.

[15] Eg. Capello, *De Curia Romana*, I, p. 526.

[16] Ferreres, *La Curia Romana*, n. 235 ff.

[17] Reiffenstuel, *Jus Canonicum*, lib. I, tit. III, n. 33; Wernz, *Jus Decretalium*, I, n. 151.

"expresse intelligitur, quod non reperitur expresse prohibitum.[18] The word *"libere"* is used in the sense of the *"Ordo Servandus."*

At present, those who are excommunicated, personally interdicted, or suspended are forbidden to petition for certain kinds of favors, namely, dignities, offices, benefices, ecclesiastical pensions, any work in the church, or promotion to Orders.[19] This law applies to all excommunicated persons without exception; to all those who are under personal interdict, a penalty that directly forbids a person the use of sacred things, but not to those who are under penalty of local interdict, that affects the persons only indirectly through the place;[20] and finally to all those who are suspended from both office and benefice with all their effects, but not to those who are merely suspended from office, or from benefice, etc.[21]

When these penalties are *"latae sententiae,"* however, the guilty parties are excused from observing them before a declaratory sentence has been passed, if they cannot do so without losing their reputation, nor can the observance of the penalty be enforced before that time, unless the crime is nortorious,[22] i.e. publicly known, and committed in such circumstances that it can neither be concealed nor excused.[23] Chelodi,[24] commenting on this phase of the question, states that if the censure is juridically occult, it in no way affects the favors and dispensations asked of the Holy See, lest perhaps, while a guilty party is punished, an innocent party might also suffer. Without qualification, this statement is incorrect. If the censure is occult, the *validity* of a papal favor is not affected, but even then it would be unlawful to petition for the favors mentioned above, unless there was danger of loss of reputation involved. Cicognani[25] goes

[18] C. 2, X, *de translatione episcopi,* I, 7; c. 1, *de procuratoribus,* I, 19, in VI°.

[19] Can. 2265, §1, n. 2, 3, 2275, n. 3, 2283.

[20] Can. 2275, n. 3, 2268, §2.

[21] Can. 2283, 2278, §2; Chelodi, *Jus Poenale,* n. 45; Blat, *Commentarium,* V, n. 112.

[22] Can. 2232, §1.

[23] Can. 2197, n. 3.

[24] *Jus De Personis,* n. 76.

[25] *Commentarium,* p. 221.

even farther and says that "*ferendae sententiae*" penalties are of no value *(nihil)* before the sentence. This is not entirely correct, because "*ferendae sententiae*" penalties may be inflicted either by sentence or by precept,[26] and when inflicted by precept, although the guilty party cannot lawfully ask for certain papal favors, the validity of the favors is not usually affected: the validity is ordinarily affected only when the penalties are inflicted by judicial sentence.

The above-mentioned favors are not only unlawfully, but also invalidly received by an "*excommunicatus vitandus,*" or by an excommunicated, personally interdicted, or suspended person after a declaratory or condemnatory sentence has been passed; nor can *any* papal favor be validly received by any excommunicated, personally interdicted, or suspended person after a declaratory or condemnatory sentence, unless in the rescript itself explicit mention is made of the censure.[27] Santamaria [28] holds that the "*excommunicatus vitandus*" of can. 2343, §1, is capable of validly receiving papal favors. Ordinarily to become "*excommunicatus vitandus,*" one must be excommunicated by the Holy See by name, i.e., excommunicated by the Roman Pontiff or by one of the departments of the Roman Curia, with the name, family name, title, office, etc., explicitly stated; moreover, one must be publicly denounced in the "*Acta Apostolicae Sedis*" or in some other way judged by the proper officials as sufficient to bring the fact to the knowledge of the faithful; and finally one must be explicitly declared "*vitandus*" by decree or by sentence.[29] For only one crime, the laying of violent hands on the person of the Roman Pontiff, does one become *ipso facto vitandus,* i.e., *vitandus* without the necessity of a decree or a condemnatory or declaratory sentence.[30] There is no doubt that a person guilty of this crime is unable to validly receive ecclesiastical benefices, pensions, offices or dignities not only because of can. 2265, §2, but also because by can. 2343, §1,

---

[26] Can. 2217, §1, n. 2, 3, 2225.

[27] Can. 36, §2, 2265, §2, 2275, n. 3, 2283.

[28] *Comentarios al Codigo Canonico,* I, n. 78.

[29] Can. 2258, §2; De Meester, *Compendium,* n. 1755.

[30] Can. 2343, §1, n. 1.

n. 3, he becomes *ipso facto infamis* and therefore "*inhabilis*" to receive such favors.[31] However, it seems that he could validly receive other papal favors. In the latter part of can. 2265, §2, it is expressly stated that excommunication renders a person "*inhabilis*" to receive papal favors "*si haec sententia lata fuerit.*" Since in the case in question no sentence was passed, juridical principles governing penal legislation [32] require us to conclude that unless excommunicated by sentence the "*excommunicatus vitandus*" of can. 2343, §1, n. 1, can validly receive papal favors other than ecclesiastical benefices, pensions, offices, or dignities, despite the fact that Coronata [33] expressly declares that the *vitandus* of can. 2343, §1, n. 1, is *inhabilis*, and other authors,[33a] without discussing the case, or making any distinction, state that an "*excommunicatus vitandus*" is incapable of receiving Papal Rescripts of Favor.

For similar reasons it should be concluded that an "*excommunicatus vitandus*" who has been excommunicated by *decree* and not by sentence, can validly receive the same kind of favors.[34] Needless to say these cases are not of much practical importance.

Despite the fact that, according to can. 2232, §1, a declaratory sentence carries with it retroactivity of the penalty to the moment of the commission of the crime, the wording of can. 2265, §2, affords ample grounds for holding that a rescript granted after the crime had been committed, but before the declaratory sentence of excommunication, personal interdict, or suspension had been passed, would be valid.[35]

---

[31] Can. 2294, §1.

[32] Can. 2219, §1, "*In poenis benignior est interpretatio facienda*"; §3 "*Non licet poenam de persona ad personam vel de casu ad casum producere, quamvis par adsit ratio, imo gravior,*" . . . .

[33] *Institutiones*, I, p. 259, nota (7).

[33a] De Meester, *Compendium*, n. 292; Maroto, *Institutiones*, n. 280; Cicognani, *Commentarium*, p. 210; Chelodi, *Jus De Personis*, n. 76; Ojetti, *Commentarium*, I, p. 211; Vermeersch-Creusen, *Epitome*, I, n. 125.

[34] Can. 2258, §2, 2265, §2. Cf. Coronata, *Institutiones*, I, p. 259, nota (7), for opposite view.

[35] Chelodi, *Jus De Personis*, p. 134, nota (7); Coronata, *Institutiones*, I, n. 61.

Vindicative penalties, as well as medicinal penalties, prevent persons from validly receiving certain papal favors.[36] Thus can. 2291, §9, refers to a vindicative penalty rendering the faithful incapable of receiving any non-clerical favors or works in the Church or academic honors granted by ecclesiastical authority; can. 2298, §5, refers to a vindicative penalty rendering clerics incapable of receiving any dignities, offices, benefices or other clerical functions; while can. 2294, §1, states that the penalty of *"infamia juris"* renders one incapable of obtaining ecclesiastical benefices, pensions, offices or dignities.

Persons may become *"inhabiles"* to receive papal rescripts of favor in other ways than by penalties, medicinal or vindicative:—namely, by obstacles attached to their person, e.g., illegitimacy, bigamy, irregularities; by personal defects, e.g., defect of age, defect of the requisite order; and by possession of incompatible benefices or offices.[37]

Since Decretal times, heretics and schismatics have been excluded from Papal Rescripts of Favor, because, not being true members of the Church, and being guilty of contumacy, they were not considered worthy of the helps and favors of the Church.[38] Their present status in relation to papal favors is the cause of much dispute among canonists. It is clear that, as excommunicated persons, they are forbidden to ask for certain favors;[39] that if they give their name or publicly adhere to a non-Catholic sect, they become ipso factor *infames* and, therefore, incapable of validly receiving rescripts containing benefices, pensions, offices or dignities;[40] and that if they are excommunicated by sentence, they become incapable of validly receiving any papal favor, unless there is mention made in the rescript of the excommunication.[41] But difficulties and controversies arise when attempts are made to determine the status of heretics

[36] De Meester, *Compendium*, n. 292; De Smet, *De Sponsalibus et Matrimonio*, n. 862, 878; Ojetti, *Commentarium*, I, pp. 210, 233.

[37] Can. 1439, 156, 188, n. 3; Ojetti, *Commentarium*, I, pp. 210, 233; Augustine, *A Commentary*, I, p. 135.

[38] Wernz, *Jus Decretalium*, I, n. 151.

[39] Can. 2314, §1, n. 1, 2265, §1.

[40] Can. 2314, §1, n. 3, 2294, §1.

[41] Can. 2265, §2.

and schismatics, who are born and raised in heresy or schism, in relation to papal favors other than benefices, offices, dignities, and pensions.

Some canonists [42] hold that the status of heretics and schismatics has remained unchanged, that all, without distinction, are incapable of validly receiving Papal favors:—Augustine arguing from Decretal law; Ojetti, from the present law of the Code. Others [43] find strong indications that there has been no change from the old law in the status of those who are born and raised in heresy or schism in the fact that even though they are in good faith, they are considered guilty in the external forum, and moreover appear to be in the same condition as those who have been excommunicated by sentence, since can. 2232, §2 makes notoriety of the crime equivalent to a declaratory sentence, but still they do not consider the matter as certain, especially since it is a question of being "*in odiosis.*" Finally there are others [44] who maintain that as long as they are not "*vitandi*" or not sentenced, heretics and schismatics can validly receive papal favors, and still others [44a] who, although admitting that heretics and schismatics indirectly, on account of a sentence of excommunication, may be ineligible to receive any papal favors, or on account of the "*infamia juris*" contracted in virtue of can. 2294, §1, 2314, §1, n. 3, may be ineligible to receive certain papal favors, or on account of the style of the Curia, may be excluded from papal bounty, claim that there is no law by which heretics and schismatics as such become incapable of validly receiving papal favors.

Approaching the question from the viewpoint of penal legislation, one should conclude that the only time heretics and schismatics, born and raised in heresy or schism, are excluded from *all* papal favors is when a declaratory or

[42] Ojetti, *Commentarium,* I, p. 210; Augustine, *A Commentary,* I, p. 121; apparently also Blat, *Commentarium,* I, n. 100, since he confines §1 to "*fideles.*"

[43] Chelodi, *Jus De Personis,* I, n. 76; Cicognani, *Commentarium,* p. 211.

[44] Ayrinhac, *General Legislation,* p. 145; Coronata, *Institutiones,* I, p. 59, nota (2); Santamaria, *Comentarios al Codigo Canonico,* I, n. 78.

[44a] Michiels, *Normae Generales,* II, pp. 192-194.

condemnatory sentence has been passed by an ecclesiastical judge.[45] It is true that in can. 2232, §2, notoriety of the crime is made equivalent to a condemnatory sentence when there is a question of requiring observance of "*latae sententiae*" penalties in the external forum, but the laws of penal legislation do not permit a broad unfavorable interpretation, nor the extension of the law from person to person or from case to case, and in this particular instance they do not permit a declaratory sentence to be interpreted as including notoriety of crime, merely because, for practical purposes, they are equivalent in can. 2232, §2.[46]

The argument, however, offered by Ojetti,[47] namely, that can. 36 refers, not to all men, but only to all the faithful, i.e., to all those inside the Church, has real juridical foundation. It is significant that in the law of 1908, which forms the background for can. 36, it was clearly stated that every "*christi fidelis*" was allowed free access to the Holy See regarding their own affairs, and no mention was made of those who were not "*christi fidelis.*"[48] Moreover, the canonists of that time, notably Wernz,[49] maintained that only the faithful, not expressly forbidden, and "*capaces*" of ecclesiastical rights, not heretics and schismatics who were not considered to be true members of the Church, had the *right* to recourse to the Roman Pontiff. In the light of the preceding legislation, the word "*omnibus*" in can. 36, §1, may, therefore, be interpreted as signifying "*omnibus fidelibus*" as it does in other parts of the Code.[50] This interpretation is strengthened and confirmed by an answer given by the Congregation of the Holy Office, January 27, 1928, on a kindred question.[51] The question was asked: "*Utrum in causis matrimonialibus acatholicus, sive baptizatus sive non baptizatus, actoris partes agere possit,*" and the answer was given: "*Negative, seu standum Codici I.C., praesertim can. 87...*" The evident meaning of the answer

[45] Can. 2265, §2, 36, §2.
[46] Can. 2219, §1, n. 3.
[47] *Commentarium*, I, p. 210.
[48] "*Normae Communes,*" cap. XI, n. 1—AAS, I (1909), 53.
[49] *Jus Decretalium*, I, n. 151.
[50] Ojetti, *Commentarium*, I, p. 210.
[51] AAS, XX (1928), 75.

is that heretics and schismatics have received rights through Baptism, although not baptized as Catholics, but cannot use them because "*obstat obex ecclesiasticae communionis vinculum impediens;*"[52] that when the question arises as to their right to appear as plaintiffs *(actores)* in ecclesiastical trials, they are not to be considered as merely bound by the censure of excommunication, as merely bound by the penal legislation of the Church,[53] but as persons not in communion with the Church and therefore unable to exercise the rights ordinarily enjoyed by persons in the Church.[54] If this attitude is to be taken towards non-Catholics when there is question of their ability to become plaintiffs *(actores)* in ecclesiastical trials, a fortiori, it should be taken when there is question of non-Catholics, of heretics and schismatics, born and raised in heresy or schism, participating in the favors of the Church. In the latter case, just as well as in the former, the question of the effects of the censure of excommunication is not alone to be considered; in the latter case, as well as in the former, they should be considered as persons not in communion with the Church and therefore unable to exercise the rights ordinarily enjoyed by persons in the Church, among which should be numbered the right to recourse to the Holy See for favors. This would explain why the legislator in can. 36, § 1, used the word "*omnibus*" when really referring to "*omnibus fidelibus,*" i.e. "to all those who have received Baptism and have aggregated themselves into the family of Christ,"[55] "to all who have attached themselves to the Church, accepted her doctrines, and been initiated into her rites."[56]

There is a final reason why heretics and schismatics, born and raised in heresy and schism, cannot validly receive Papal Rescripts of Favor, namely, the Style of the Roman Curia. It has been and is an invariable rule of the Roman Curia, to grant favors to the Catholic party alone when they are to be enjoyed by the Catholic party in relation to the

[52] Can. 87.
[53] Cf. can. 1654.
[54] Roberti, "Animadversiones," Apollinaris, I, p. 216.
[55] Launoi, *Opera Omnia,* I, p. 560.
[56] Kilker, *Extreme Unction,* p. 123.

non-Catholic party, and to deny any favors that would be enjoyed by non-Catholics alone.[57] From this it would follow that, according to the Style of the Roman Curia, when petitioning for favors from Rome, they must mention the fact that they are not Catholics. If such a statement were made in the petition, the favor would, of course, be denied; and if it were not made, the grant of the *ordinary* rescript would be invalid.[58] If the case were viewed only from the standard of the Style of the Roman Curia, rescripts granted "*Motu Proprio*" or rescripts containing dispensations from the minor matrimonial impediments would still be valid, despite the fact that it was not mentioned in the petition that the petitioner was not a Catholic,[59] but, judged from the viewpoint of can. 36 and can. 87, even such rescripts should be considered invalid, because the petitioners are not able validly to receive papal favors.[60]

This problem really pertains to the theoretical rather than the practical canonical sphere, since no one can deny that it is always necessary to mention in petitions to the Roman Curia the fact that the petitioner is not a Catholic when he alone is to benefit by the favor. Obviously, the sacramental forum is in no way involved by the problem. For practical purposes the external forum is safeguarded by the style of the Curia which requires at least a letter of recommendation from the Ordinary in all petitions for papal favors pertaining to the external forum. But even if the fact, either purposely or through oversight, was not mentioned in a petition for a papal favor and the papal rescript was actually granted, one could not take advantage of the view favorable to heretics and schismatics by invoking the principle about doubtful laws contained in can. 15, because can. 6, n. 4, and not can. 15 applies to cases in which it remains doubtful whether the old law has been changed. Since in this particular instance it is at least doubtful whether the legislator modified in the Code the ancient law that prevented heretics and schismatics

[57] Ojetti, *Commentarium*, I, p. 210; Chelodi, *Jus De Personis*, I, n. 76; Cicognani, *Commentarium*, p. 211.

[58] Can. 42, §1.

[59] Can. 45, 1054.

[60] Can. 46.

from participating in the favors of the Holy See, there remains no other alternative than to consider the old law as still binding until the question is solved in a manner favorable to heretics and schismatics by an authoritative declaration of the Holy See.

While some controversy exists regarding the status of heretics and schismatics, it is certain that those who are not baptized are incapable of validly receiving Papal Rescripts of Favor,[61] because in no sense are they recognized as persons in the Church,[62] with the right to petition for papal favors.

Article II.—Petitioning Favors for Others

Canon 37.—Rescriptum impetrari potest pro alio etiam praeter eius assensum; et licet ipse possit gratia per rescriptum concessa non uti, rescriptum tamen valet ante eius acceptationem, nisi aliud ex appositis clausulis appareat.

The first principle contained in the present canon, namely, that Rescripts can be asked for another without his consent, without a mandate from him, has been recognized from Decretal times as a firmly established canonical axiom,[63] and rightly so, because if the Pope can grant a favor to a person who is neither present nor aware of the fact *motu proprio*, i.e., in the sense that no petition for the favor had been sent, he surely can grant it equally as well at the petition of another.[64] Naturally, one cannot validly obtain a favor for another person who is incapable of validly receiving the favor because such a procedure is forbidden by the general principle, *"Quum quid una via prohibetur alicui, ad id alia non debet admitti,"* [65] but there

[61] Coronata, *Institutiones*, I, n. 61; Haring, *Grundzüge des Katholischen Kirchenrechts*, I, p. 67.
[62] Can. 87.
[63] C. 17, *de Praebendis et dignitatibus*, III, 4, in VI°; Reiffenstuel, *Jus Canonicum*, lib. I, tit. III, n. 56; Schmalzgrueber, *Jus Ecclesiasticum*, pars I, tit. III, n. 4; Suarez, *De Legibus*, VI, cap. XIII, n. 6; De Angelis, *Praelectiones*, lib. I, tit. III, n. 3; Wernz, *Jus Decretalium*, I, n. 151.
[64] Schmalzgrueber, *Jus Ecclesiasticum*, pars I, tit. III, n. 4.
[65] R. J., 84 in VI°.

seems to be no regulation preventing a person who cannot validly obtain a favor for himself from petitioning the favor for another, since penal and inhabilitating laws must always be strictly interpreted.[65a] One can petition a favor for another person *without* his consent, but the same conclusion does not hold if a favor is asked *against* the will of the interested party. In the latter case the rescript would be invalid,[66] because although, strictly speaking, the Pope could grant favors even to those who are unwilling, it is to be presumed that he does not wish to force his favors on those who are unwilling to ask for them or receive them, according to the principle of Roman, law, "*Invito beneficium non dari et nihil acquiri posse nisi volenti.*" [67] The only exception that might be admitted would be when one party is willing and the other unwilling:—according to circumstances, the desire of the Pope to grant the favor, despite the objections of one of the parties, might be presumed.[68]

Before the Code, it was also generally admitted,[69] on account of the above-mentioned principle of Roman Law, that the acceptance of the favor was necessary for the validity of the rescript, e.g., a dispensation from a matrimonial impediment, except in those cases in which the necessity of acceptance was dispensed with by the grantor, e.g., by a "*sanatio in radice.*" In all cases some kind of acceptance was demanded, but the acceptance by the guilty party in case of a dispensation from an absolute matrimonial impediment, the acceptance by one of the parties in a relative impediment, and even the implicit acceptance

---

[65a] Can. 11, 19, 2219; Michiels, *Normae Generales*, II, p. 198, 199, contra Toso, *Commentaria Minora*, I, p. 122.

[66] Coronata, *Institutiones*, I, p. 59, nota (11); Santamaria, *Comentarios al Codigo Canonico*, I, pp. 78, 79.

[67] D. L. 17, 69.

[68] Vlaming, *Praelectiones Juris Matrimonii*, n. 472.

[69] Sanchez, *De Matrimonio*, lib. VIII, disp. XXVI, n. 7; Giovine, *De Dispensationibus*, I, §90; Caillaud, *Manuel des Dispenses*, III, 219, 381; St. Alphonsus, *Theologia Moralis*, VIII, n. 1145; Planchard, *Dispenses Matrimoniales*, n. 309; Gasparri, *De Matrimonio*, n. 398; Ojetti, *Synopsis*, n. 1824; D'Annibale, *Summula*, I, 223; Wernz, *Jus Decretalium*, IV, n. 641; Causa Baltimoren., 30 Junii 1910—AAS, II (1910), 596; Causa Divionen., 20 Jan. 1911—AAS, III (1911), 284.

contained in the fact that the party, knowing that the favor was asked for and granted, made no objections, were considered as sufficient.[70] Only a few authors[71] took the opposite view and claimed that the rescript was valid even before an implicit acceptance.

At present, it is commonly held[71a] that rescripts petitioned for others without their consent are not only valid but produce their effect without knowledge or acceptance on the part of the beneficiary, e.g., a matrimonial dispensation, applied for and granted without the parties in question being aware of the dispensation or the impediment, would be valid without the knowledge or acceptance of the parties and would produce its effect, i.e., remove the impediment upon its execution, if it is a rescript *in forma commissoria*, or upon its being granted, if it is a rescript *in forma gratiosa*.[71b] According to this interpretation of can. 37, the phrase "*et licet ipse possit gratia per rescriptum concessa non uti,*" refers to the *power of not using* a particular *favor that is in one's possession* as soon as the provisions of can. 38 are fulfilled, and to the fact that the recipient *is not bound* to use the favor, e.g., not bound to use a dispensation from a law forbidding the reading of certain books, but does not signify that the party has in all cases a choice of using or not using the favor, nor that the favor is granted in such a way that he always knows that he is actually taking advantage of the favor. A marriage between second cousins that had been performed after the dispensation from the impediment of consanguinity had, unknown to the parties, been granted and executed, would be considered by the defenders of this view as a validly contracted marriage.

Michiels,[71c] however, maintains that although such rescripts are valid they are not effective, do not produce their

[70] De Smet, *De Sponsalibus et Matrimonio*, n. 875.

[71] Engel, *Collegium Universi Juris Canonici*, I, III, n. 17.

[71a] De Smet, *De Sponsalibus et Matrimonio*, p. 733, 734, nota (2); Capello, *De Sacramentis*, III, p. 317, nota (9); Wernz-Vidal, *Jus Canonicum*, V, n. 447; Cicognani, *Commentarium*, p. 212; Ayrinhac, *General Legislation*, p. 146.

[71b] Can. 38.

[71c] *Normae Generales*, II, pp. 199, 200, 293.

effect, unless the recipients know about their existence and accept them. Otherwise, he says, the liberty of not using the favor granted by the phrase "*et licet...*" would be meaningless, if a person, upon refusing a favor obtained for him by another without his consent, did not have the same juridical state that he would have had if the favor had not been granted. As an example he cites the case of a religious, refusing to use a dispensation from his religious vows obtained by him by his superior, and thereby remaining bound by his vows. Vermeersch [71d] and Maroto [71e] seem to use the same interpretation of can. 37.

The more common view, however, seems to be more in harmony with the terms of the canon. In can. 37 there is no mention made of a freedom or a choice of using or not using the favor, nor of a distinction between the validity and efficacy of the rescript. Can. 38, not can. 37, speaks of the time when the rescript will produce its effects. In can. 37 only the power of not using the favor is granted to the person in question. The rescript is said to be valid, the favor is said to have been granted by the rescript: therefore, if the condition contained in can. 38 for the efficacy of the rescript is fulfilled, how can non-use be made synonymous with non-efficacy? Non-use should rather be considered in the present canon as denoting the same as it does in cans. 69, 76, and 86, where the non-use of the privilege or dispensation certainly refers to the non-use of a privilege or dispensation already in the possession of the person concerned. Moreover, it might be well to note that the canon states that the party is capable of not using the favor but does not say that knowledge and acceptance is necessary for the efficacy of the rescript. Finally, the example of the dispensation from religious vows is hardly representative, because such a rescript contains not a pure favor but a favor that at the same time deprives the party of the privileges of the religious, a favor that the Holy See is not accustomed to grant unless the party petitions for it and is willing to receive it.[72]

[71d] "Annotationes," Periodica, XI (1923), 150.
[71e] "Annotationes," CpR, IV (1923), 70, 71, 101.
[72] Voltas, "Annotationes," CpR, II (1921), 371, 372.

Some other authors seem forced to find exceptions to the law when no exceptions are permitted. Ojetti[73] says that knowledge and acceptance is necessary for the valid, as well as the licit, use of a favor *"ablativa oneris,"* because the law is in actual possession of its obligation, of which it cannot be deprived, unless it is clear that it has been derogated by the dispensation or favor of the Pope. Coronata[74] would like to limit the force of can. 37 when favors of the public good are involved.

The canon, however, is very clear:—acceptance or knowledge is not required for the validity except in one clearly specified case, namely, when the rescript states otherwise. Outside of this one case the Code permits of no exception. However, distinction between favors of a private or public nature is of importance in connection with the use or renunciation of favors granted by rescripts. Privileges or dispensations do not cease by non-use, if they are not burdensome to others; and even when burdensome to others, they cease only through legitimate prescription or tacit renunciation.[75] Private persons are free to renounce favors that concern themselves, not those which concern others or the common good; communities can renounce their favors if the renunciation is not prejudicial to the Church or to others:—but in both cases, to have juridical effect the renunciation must be intimated to the grantor and, at least, tacitly accepted by him.[76]

Article III.—Manner of Petitioning Favors from the Holy See

There are, as already explained, well defined regulations regarding the persons who are permitted to petition for papal favors, definite regulations about petitions made in the name of other persons:—but what is of more practical

[73] *Commentarium*, I, p. 213.

[74] *Institutiones*, I, n. 61.

[75] Can. 76, 86.

[76] Can. 72, 86; De Smet, *De Sponsalibus et Matrimonio*, n. 875; Wernz-Vidal, *Jus Canonicum*, V, n. 447.

use, there are certain guiding principles that are of assistance in formulating and directing petitions to the Roman Curia.

§1. *Department of Curia to which the Petition Must Be Sent*

A factor of prime importance in formulating and directing petitions to the Roman Curia is recognition of the two-fold forum in the Church, the external forum and the internal forum. The Church is an external society established by Christ to care for the spiritual welfare of individuals:—she must act as an external society when dealing with the social acts of the faithful, in those matters which concern the public or common good; she must act as a spiritual society when dealing with the private actions of the faithful, in those matters which concern the private good or conscience of the individual. The actions or omissions by which persons become guilty or just in the eyes of the Church as an external society, belong to the external forum; the actions, by which they become guilty or just in the eyes of God, belong to internal forum or the forum of conscience. In the internal forum, moreover, there is a further subdivision into the sacramental and non-sacramental, according as the power of the Church over the forum of conscience is exercised inside or outside the Sacrament of Penance.[77]

In granting favors, as well as in the exercise of her other powers, the Church takes cognizance of this two-fold forum. Since the reorganization of the Curia in 1908, the internal forum has been exclusively cared for by the Tribunal of the Sacred Penitentiary, while the external forum is under the direction of the Congregations and Offices. Petitions, of course, must be sent to the department that grants the favor, not to the one that composes and returns the rescript, if they happen to be different.

The general guiding principle for the petitioner is that when actions are public, recourse must be made to the external forum; when they are occult, recourse must be made to the internal forum.

[77] Vermeersch-Creusen, *Epitome,* I, n. 4, 276.

The definition of public and occult matrimonial impediments as given in can. 1037, namely, that an impediment is public when it can be proved in the external forum, and occult, when it cannot be proved, does not hold when there is question of obtaining dispensations from Rome. Rather the distinctions between impediments that are public or occult *by nature* and public or occult *in fact* must be taken into consideration. An impediment is said to be *public by nature* if it occurs in such circumstances that it ordinarily becomes known to others, if it arises from a fact that is *de se* or ordinarily public, i.e., from a fact that happens before the Church or in a gathering of the faithful, e.g., Orders, Public Vow, or from a fact that is kept in the public records, e.g., Age, Legitimate Consanguinity, etc., or from a fact that can *ordinarily* be proved by a qualified witness giving testimony "*ex officio,*" or by two private witnesses, e.g., ligamen; an impediment is said to be *occult by nature* if it proceeds from a fact that is not *de se* public, i.e., occurring in such circumstances that usually it will be known only to the parties concerned, e.g., Crime, Private Vow. An impediment is said to be *occult in fact* if it is known only to a few discreet persons, and no danger of divulgation is feared because of the character of the persons and the size of the place, etc.; otherwise the impediment is *public in fact.* The Sacred Penitentiary dispenses from impediments that are occult by nature and in fact, whether there is question of marriages invalidly contracted or marriages to be contracted, and also from some impediments public by nature but occult in fact, e.g., Affinity, Consanguinity, etc., for marriages invalidly contracted.[78] An impediment materially public but formally occult in fact on account of ignorance of the law is not considered occult by the Sacred Penitentiary, e.g., if it was generally known that the parties were guilty of crime

[78] Wernz-Vidal, *Jus Canonicum,* V, n. 147, 409; De Smet, *De Sponsalibus et Matrimonio,* n. 465, 830, 833; Chelodi, *Jus Matrimoniale,* n. 35, 40; Capello, *De Sacramentis,* III, n. 200, 227; Vermeersch-Creusen, *Epitome,* II, n. 297.

but it was not known that crime was an impediment.[79]

For penalties and for all other favors the criterion between public and occult acts is fairly simple. An act is considered public if it is already generally known or if it has been committed in such circumstances that it probably will become known:—otherwise it is considered occult, either materially occult, if the crime itself is hidden, or formally occult, if the imputability is hidden.[80] When only a few prudent, reliable persons know about an act, and there is not much danger that they will make it known to others, the act is considered occult; acts that were once public, but have been forgotten for a long time, are also considered occult;[81] and even when the guilty party has been unjustly absolved from the crime, the act is considered to be occult.[82]

Petitions for favors concerning public matters are to be sent to the respective Office or Congregation; petitions for occult favors, to the Sacred Penitentiary.[83]

The case may arise, however, when two dispensations, one public and the other occult, must be obtained from the Roman Curia for the same person. The proper procedure to follow is to send a petition for the external forum to the respective department of the Roman Curia making no mention of the occult impediment, and another petition to the Sacred Penitentiary, mentioning both impediments and also the fact that a petition had been sent in the external forum without mentioning the occult impediment. In this way the rescript granted by the Sacred Penitentiary will rectify any nullifying defect of subreption in the petition to the Congregation.

---

[79] Benedict XIV, *Institutiones Ecclesiasticae*, 87, n. 39 sq.; Feije, *De Impedimentis et Dispensationibus Matrimonialibus*, n. 94; Wernz-Vidal, *Jus Canonicum*, V, n. 409.

[80] Can. 2197, n. 1, 4.

[81] Chelodi, *Jus De Personis*, n. 173; Coronata, *Institutiones Juris Canonici*, I, n. 351.

[82] Sanchez, *De Matrimonio*, lib. II, disp. XXXVII, n. 12; lib. VIII, disp. XXXIV, n. 57.

[83] Cf. Part II, chapt. I, art. V, regarding the powers of the respective departments.

Before the Code, most canonists [84] held that it was immaterial which petition was sent first, so long as the petition to the Sacred Penitentiary mentioned both impediments, but there were some noteworthy canonists [85] who insisted that it was necessary to petition first in the external forum and then in the internal forum.

Since the Code, Vlaming [86] contends that *per se* it is immaterial which petition is sent first, since in either way the desired effect will be accomplished, namely, the removal of both impediments by one dispensation; but that *per accidens* it may be necessary for the confessor to send his petition to the Sacred Penitentiary first, if he fears that the rescript would otherwise not arrive in time for the celebration of the marriage; while De Smet [87] is of the opinion that when both impediments are diriment it is necessary, for the validity, to send the dispensation to the external forum first, but not when one is an impediment. Some other authors [88] even go so far as to say that in no case is it necessary, for the validity, to mention the public impediment in the petition to the Sacred Penitentiary, since the strictness of the law, contained in the Instruction of the Congregation of the Propagation of the Faith, May 9, 1877,[89] requiring that all impediments in a particular case be dispensed by one papal rescript, has been greatly mitigated by can. 1050.

Can. 1050, however, does not change entirely the preceding legislation but merely makes modifications for certain

---

[84] De Justis, *De Dispensationibus*, lib. I, cap. IV, n. 106; *Sanchez, De Matrimonio*, lib. VIII, disp. XXIII, n. 8; Pontius, *De Matrimonio*, lib. VIII, cap. XVII, n. 23; Corradus, *Praxis*, lib. VII, cap. VI, n. 79; Schmalzgrueber, *Jus Ecclesiasticum*, pars IV, tit. XVI, n. 178; Carriere, *De Matrimonio*, n. 1131; Van de Burgt, *De Dispensationibus*, p. 50; Pompen, *De Dispensationibus*, n. 75; Caillaud, *Manuel des Dispenses*, n. 226.

[85] Giovine, *De Dispensationibus*, II, §5, n. 12; Gasparri, *De Matrimonio*, n. 327; Feije, *De Impedimentis*, n. 689; D'Annibale, *Summula*, III, 348, nota (23); Konings, *Moralis Theologia*, n. 1628.

[86] *Praelectiones*, n. 448.

[87] *De Sponsalibus et Matrimonio*, n. 852, 853.

[88] Vermeersch, Gregorianum, VI (1926), p. 143; *Theologia Moralis*, III, n. 765; Vermeersch-Creusen, *Epitome*, II, n. 319; Capello, *De Sacramentis*, III, n. 227, 275.

[89] *Coll. de Prop. Fide*, n. 1470.

instances, namely, when the Ordinary has ordinary or delegated power to dispense from one impediment but must recourse to Rome for dispensation from the other impediment. In all other cases, according to the very clear words of the canon, recourse must be made to the Holy See for both impediments. The canon says nothing directly or indirectly about the further question, namely, whether or not it is necessary in these latter cases to mention both impediments in the petition to the Sacred Penitentiary. This should be decided, apparently, by the requirements of the Style of the Curia, and since there is no indication that the Style of the Curia has changed on this particular point, one should be guided by the old law.[90] In practice, the regular procedure to follow is to send the petition to the external forum first, and to mention both impediments in the other petition to the Sacred Penitentiary. However, because of divergence of opinion both before and since the Code, it cannot be maintained that reversing the mode of procedure would affect the validity of the grant, nor that, for the licitness of the act, special circumstances would not justify one to send the petition to the Sacred Penitentiary before the other.[91] The ordinary procedure in the execution of the two rescripts is to execute the rescript for the external forum first and then the one for the internal forum, but the validity of the execution of the rescript from the Sacred Penitentiary would not be affected by a change in the procedure.[92]

§2. *The Sender of the Petition.*

Since 1908, as explained in the preceding chapter, private persons have been permitted to deal directly with the Holy See in petitioning for favors, with the privilege of taking advantage of the services of a Private Agent. But right is one thing, and expediency another.

In practice, when favors of the external forum are concerned, it is more prudent to petition through the Ordinary

[90] Can. 6, n. 3, 4.
[91] Can. 6, n. 3, 15.
[92] Wernz-Vidal, *Jus Canonicum*, V, n. 445; Capello, *De Sacramentis*, III, n. 282.

of the place or, for some religious, through their Procurator General, or at least to accompany the petition with a letter of approval from the Ordinary, since it is the practice of the Roman Curia to consult with the Ordinary before granting such favors, if the petition is not accompanied by a commendatory letter. Consulting with the Ordinary before sending petitions will enable the person, at the same time, to take advantage of any special power that the Ordinary may possess, but of whose existence the person may be ignorant. In any event it is advisable to use the services of an Agent in Rome, who usually by virtue of long experience, is acquainted with the intricacies of Roman affairs.[93]

The pastor or delegated priest will generally bring the petition of the ordinary lay person to the attention of the Ordinary of the place, while the local Superior will usually take up the affairs of the members of the Institute with the Procurator General or the Ordinary of the place, according to the character of the favor that is to be petitioned and the nature of the Institute. In matrimonial matters, when there is question of an impediment in which only one party is directly concerned, e.g., vow, the pastor of that person will bring the matter to the attention of the Ordinary of the place; when each party is bound by the impediment, e.g., two vows, the respective pastor of each party; when the impediment is common to both, e.g., consanguinity, ordinarily the pastor of the bride; in case of Disparity of Cult or Mixed Religion, the pastor of the Catholic party.[94] The pastor, delegated priest or local Superior should prepare the data for the Ordinary, or for the Procurator General,[94a] when the latter are to send the petitions; otherwise, he should compose the petition itself, obtain the Ordinary's letter of approbation, and send them to the respective Congregation or Office, preferably through an Agent in Rome.

[93] Martin, *The Roman Curia*, p. 265; Capello, *De Curia Romana*, I, p. 43, *De Sacramentis*, III, n. 271; Maroto, *Institutiones*, n. 284, 835.

[94] Vlaming, *Praelectiones*, n. 442; De Smet, *De Sponsalibus et Matrimonio*, p. 698, nota (5).

[94a] Cf. can. 517, §1.

Petitions for the internal non-sacramental forum may be directed to the Sacred Penitentiary by the petitioner, Ordinary, pastor, Superior or any priest who may know about the matter outside the Tribunal of Penance.[95] Occasionally, when matters of the internal forum that later may become public are mentioned in confession, if it can prudently be done, it may be advisable to ask the penitent to mention the matter to some priest outside of Confession, so that the favor may be obtained in the non-sacramental internal forum. Then, in case the matter later becomes public, the favor granted in the internal non-sacramental forum, through the record of the case kept in the Secret Archives of the Diocese,[96] or in the Secret Archives of the Sacred Penitentiary, will become effective in the external forum, without need of a further dispensation. If, however, the case is of such a nature that the petitioner is unwilling to give information except in the Tribunal of Penance, the confessor should proceed in the sacramental forum. The confessor of each party, in case of an impediment proper to each party, or to the confessor who first detects the impediment if it is common to both, or the confessor of the guilty party if it is proper to one only,[97] will then take care of the petition for the penitent. The confessor must compose the petition and seal it, and send it either through the Ordinary, if there is no danger to the Seal of the Confession, or, preferably, directly to the Sacred Penitentiary.[98]

§3. *Form of the Petition.*

The petition should regularly be sent in writing through the mail:—only in extraordinary cases will a petition by telegraph or telephone be admitted by the Roman Curia,[99] and then only if the canonical cause, circumstances, etc., that are required in the written petition are given.[100]

---

[95] De Smet, *De Sponsalibus et Matrimonio*, n. 841; Maroto, *Institutiones*, n. 835.

[96] Can. 1047.

[97] Vlaming, *Praelectiones*, n. 444.

[98] Hilling, *Procedure at the Roman Curia*, p. 155; Kubelbeck, *The Sacred Penitentiary*, p. 86; Chelodi, *Jus Matrimoniale*, n. 47.

[99] Litt. Encycl. Secret. Stat., 10 Dec. 1891—*Coll. de Prop. Fide*, n. 1775.

[100] Capello, *De Sacramentis*, III, n. 272.

The practice of the Roman Curia regarding the language of the petitions has varied somewhat in the course of time. An encyclical letter of the Congregation of the Propagation of the Faith, Sept. 20, 1868,[101] protested against the practice of sending petitions in various languages, and strongly urged that they be sent only in Latin or Italian. Later, on May 18, 1898, the same Congregation [102] gave permission to write petitions in French. Since 1908, petitions to the Sacred Penitentiary may be written in any language, while petitions to the Congregations may be written in Latin, Italian, French, English, Spanish, German, or Portuguese, but always preferably in Latin.[103]

Petitions [104] to the Congregations should be addressed to the Pope, e.g., "*Beatissime Pater,*" whereas petitions to the Sacred Penitentiary should be addressed to the presiding official, e.g., "*Eminentissime Princeps*" or "*Eminentissime Domine.*" The favors should always be asked in the name of the petitioners, their real name, name and family name, being given in petitions for the external forum, fictitious names in petitions for the internal forum. In petitions for the external forum, besides the names, the diocese of domicile or quasi-domicile, or for "*vagi,*" the actual residence, should be mentioned.[105] After the indication of name and place, there follows the customary formula:—"*Ad pedes Sanctitatis Vestrae humillime provolutus,*" or the like.[106]

The body of the petition should be clear and concise. It ordinarily is divided into three parts:—the first, containing

---

[101] *Coll. de Prop. Fide,* n. 1335.

[102] *Coll. de Prop. Fide,* n. 1929.

[103] "*Normae Peculiares,*" cap. VI, n. 5—AAS, I (1909), 73; Capello, *De Curia Romana,* I, p. 44, 359.

[104] Cf. for forms of petitions: Capello, *De Curia Romana,* I, Index, p. 619, 620, v. Formulae; Martin, *The Roman Curia,* p. 271-279; Hilling, *Procedure at the Roman Curia,* p. 156-171; Tanquerey, *Synopsis Theologiae Moralis,* I, p. 674 sq.; Mothon, *Institutions Canoniques,* III, *Formulaire.*

[105] Wernz-Vidal, *Jus Canonicum,* V, n. 440; Capello, *De Curia Romana,* I, p. 44, De *Sacramentis,* III, p. 304, nota (16).

[106] Hilling, *Procedure at the Roman Curia,* p. 148.

a brief reference to the circumstances that occasions the presentation of the request; the second, setting forth the nature of the petition; and the third, indicating the reasons why the petition appears to be expedient or necessary. If, however, the favor is not of much importance the mere statement of the nature of the case will suffice.[107] The fact that the favor is or is not asked in "*forma pauperum*" should always be mentioned.[108] Moreover, special circumstances, like the extreme delicacy and gravity of the matter, may warrant application to have the names of petitioners for favors of the non-sacramental internal forum inscribed in the Secret Archives of the Sacred Penitentiary, instead of the Secret Archives of the Diocese.

The customary concluding formula is "*Et Deus...*" or "*Pro qua gratia...*," indicative of the prayer of gratitude that the petitioner addresses to God in anticipation of the expected favor.[109] Petitions to the Sacred Penitentiary should contain at the end, in the proper language of the country of the petitioner, the name and address of the sender or of the person to whom the rescript is to be sent, e.g., "*Dignetur Eminentia Vestra rescribere ad... (name, family name, address).*" [110]

The addresses of the various departments of the Roman Curia are as follows:—All' Eminentissimo Cardinale Penitenziere Maggiore (or Sacra Penitenzieria)—Palazzo del S. Officio, Via del S. Uffizio—Roma; All' Eminentissimo Cardinale Prefetto S. Congregazione (del Concilio, dei Riti, dei Religiosi, dei Sacramenti),—Palazzo della Cancelleria, Piazza della Cancelleria—Roma; All' Eminentissimo Car-

---

107 Hilling, *Procedure at the Roman Curia*, p. 149. Minute description of the circumstances to be mentioned for different favors is beyond the scope of this work. Authors on various subjects, matrimony, religious, indulgences, etc., may be consulted for the circumstances that must be mentioned for different favors, e. g., Ojetti, *Commentarium*, I, p. 234 for benefices.

108 "*Normae Communes,*" cap. XI, n. 3—AAS, I (1909), 55, 56.

109 Hilling, *Procedure at the Roman Curia*, p. 148.

110 Capello, *De Curia Romana*, I, p. 44, *De Sacramentis*, III, n. 273; Hilling, *Procedure at the Roman Curia*, p. 115.

dinale Prefetto S. Congregazione dei Seminari e delle Università degli Studi, Palazzo di S. Callisto, Piazza di S. Maria in Trastevere—Roma; All' Eminentissimo Cardinale Segretario della Concistoriale—Palazzo della Cancelleria, Piazza della Cancelleria—Roma; All' Eminentissimo Cardinale Segretario del S. Officio—Palazza del S. Officio, Via del S. Uffizio—Roma; All' Eminentissimo Cardinale Segretario di Stato di S. S. Pio XI—Citta del Vaticano—Italia.[111]

[111] Capello, *De Curia Romana*, I, p. 44, *De Sacramentis*, III, n. 273.

CHAPTER II

Interpretation of Papal Rescripts of Favor

The Code has enacted in can. 38 to can. 50 the main guiding principles for the interpretation of Rescripts. It has not confined itself to a mere statement to the effect that rescripts should be strictly or broadly interpreted, but has determined accurately and decisively the effect that falsehood, error, essential conditions, previous refusal, etc., have on the validity of rescripts. In this present chapter these various questions are treated; first, the general principles for interpretation of rescripts, and then, the more specific problems.

Article I.—General Principles of Interpretation

Two very important rules of interpretation are given in the following canon:

Canon 49.—Rescripta intelligenda sunt secundum propriam verborum significationem et communem loquendi usum, nec debent ad casus alios praeter expressos extendi.

Words, that are not ambiguous but clear, should be understood according to their proper signification [1] for the very simple reason that in rescripts, as well as in testaments, clear words do not admit of interpretation or conjecture of will,[2] except to avoid absurdity or to prevent the rescript from becoming useless.[3] Words, moreover, should be understood either according to their ordinary meaning, i.e., their ordinary legal meaning, which is not always the same

[1] D. XXXII. 1. 69; Reiffenstuel, *Jus Canonicum*, lib. I, tit. III, n. 19; Santi, *Praelectiones*, lib. I, tit. III, n. 13.

[2] D. XXXII. 1. 25; Pirhing, *Jus Canonicum*, lib. I, tit. III, n. 15 sq.

[3] Maroto, *Institutiones*, n. 287.

as the definition given in the ordinary dictionary, e.g., "benefice," or "cloister," as defined according to can. 1409, 597, or according to their accepted meaning at Rome, since papal rescripts emanate from the Roman Curia and are to be interpreted from the viewpoint of the grantor, e.g., the word "*collegium*" signifying schools for boys or girls.[4] Very frequently the text and context of the word as well as the style of the particular department of the Curia that sent the rescript will help to determine the precise meaning of a word.[4a]

Interpretation may be declarative, extensive, or restrictive:—*declarative,* if the meaning of a doubtful word or phrase is merely defined, or the meaning of a clear, but contested word or phrase, is asserted; *extensive,* if application is made to cases that are not included in the wording itself; *restrictive,* if cases, which would be included according to the literal meaning of the text, are excluded.[5] The law of the Decretals, which determined that rescripts could receive neither a restrictive[6] nor an extensive interpretation, but only a declarative one,[7] has been retained by the present law, and rightly so, since rescripts are granted to particular persons whose peculiar conditions and circumstances cannot be attributed to others.[8] From this it follows that interpretation by way of analogy cannot be applied to rescripts as it can to laws,[9] i.e., an interpretation which extends the meaning of the rescript to persons, cases, or things not contained or expressed in the rescript is forbidden, even when they are similar to those contained or expressed, or when there is an equal or greater reason for their inclusion in the terms and content of the rescript than

---

[4] Vermeersch-Creusen, *Epitome,* I, n. 137; Cicognani, *Commentarium,* p. 240.

[4a] Michiels, *Normae Generales,* II, p. 253.

[5] Ayrinhac, *General Legislation,* p. 123; Cicognani, *Commentarium,* p. 117.

[6] C. 27, *de praebendis et dignitatibus,* III, 4, in VI°

[7] C. 40, X, *de officio et potestate judicis delegati,* I, 29; R. J. 74, in VI°; De Justis, *De dispensationibus,* lib. I, cap. IV, n. 62, 63; Corradus, *Praxis,* lib. VII, cap. V, n. 57.

[8] Maroto, *Institutiones,* n. 287.

[9] Can. 20.

for those that are actually included or contained therein.[10] Although the present law makes no direct reference to it, undoubtedly, restrictive interpretation of rescripts is also forbidden. There is every reason to suppose, however, that the exceptions to the general rule forbidding restrictive interpretation that were admitted by representative pre-code canonists [11] are also allowed by the present law which adds nothing new to the old law.[12] Accordingly, a restrictive interpretation should be used when a declarative interpretation would presuppose an injustice on the part of the grantor of the favor, and rightly so, because one cannot presume that the Pope intends an injustice in a rescript of favor. This exception would be verified in case the favor that was granted would, on account of special circumstances of person, place, or time, be contrary to the divine natural or positive law, but not when it only appeared as though the Pope was too prodigal with his favors, since there might be special reasons, unknown to others, that could explain his extraordinary generosity. A further exception should be made to permit restrictive interpretation of rescripts when it can reasonably be presumed that the grantor did not intend what is understood according to the declarative interpretation. Thus, if the declarative interpretation would reveal a favor contrary to another favor granted by a former rescript, a restrictive interpretation must be used because the Holy See cannot be presumed to take a favor into consideration unless it makes specific mention of it. Moreover, general terms in the rescript should not be understood to include those things which the Pope would most likely specifically mention in granting favors,[13] because whenever things that are deserving of special mention are not specifically referred to, one should conclude that the grantor purposely omitted them.[14] Finally, general terms should not be interpreted as including those things which

---

[10] Michiels, *Normae Generales*, II, p. 254.

[11] Suarez. *De Legibus*, VIII, c. 28, n. 3-10.

[12] Can. 6, n. 2; Ojetti, *Commentarium*, I, p. 292; Michiels, *Normae Generales*, II, pp. 255-257.

[13] "*In generali concessione non veniunt ea, quae quis non esset verisimiliter in specie concessurus*"—R. J. 81, in VI°.

[14] C. 2, *de poenitentiis et remissionibus*, V, 10 in VI°.

legitimate custom or law excludes,[15] e.g., a general power to absolve from those censures that are reserved to the Apostolic See does not include the power to absolve from censures that are reserved in a special or most special way to the Apostolic See.[16] But, aside from these few exceptions, declarative and not restrictive or extensive interpretation of rescripts must be used.

The declarative interpretation which should ordinarily be applied to rescripts may, however, be either strict or broad: *strict,* if the words are taken in their rigorous and precise meaning, according to their species; *broad,* if they are taken in their full and entire significance, according to their genus. Thus sons, strictly interpreted, would include only those by birth, widely interpreted, also those by adoption; religious, strictly, only those who are professed, widely, even those who are novices; clerics, strictly, all who have received at least tonsure, seculars or religious, in the wide sense, all religious even those who are not tonsured; vacant benefices, strictly, benefices vacant in the ways specified by the rescript, widely, benefices, erected even after the date of the rescript, that become vacant in any way whatsoever.[17]

The following canon in very clear and precise terms decides which rescripts, in cases of doubt, should be interpreted strictly; which rescripts, broadly:

Canon 50.—In dubio, rescripta quae ad lites referuntur, vel jura aliis quaesita laedunt, vel adversantur legi in commodum privatorum, vel denique impetrata fuerunt ad beneficii ecclesiasa tici assecutionem, strictam interpretationem recipiunt; ceteromnia latam.

Whenever, at first sight, the meaning of a word or expression in a rescript appears doubtful, the ordinary means proposed in can. 18 for the interpretation of doubtful laws may be employed in determining the exact content of the rescript. Accordingly, the word or expression may be con-

---

[15] D'Annibale, *Summula,* I, n. 228.

[16] Can. 2253, n. 3.

[17] Maroto, *Institutiones,* n. 236; Cocchi, *Commentarium,* I, p. 157; Ojetti, *Commentarium,* I, p. 248; Michiels, *Normae Generales,* II, p. 258.

sidered in the light of the text or context, or in conjunction with various circumstances that help to clarify and determine with certitude the intention of the grantor,[18] e.g., by comparing the rescript with the petition, since the rescript is ordinarily supposed to be granted in accordance with what was contained in the petition, by examining the causes and circumstances that influenced the person to send the petition, or by a comparison with similar rescripts. In endeavoring to dispel the doubt by resorting to these means, one must, of course, be extremely careful not to be too easily influenced by mere presumptions or slight indications and to recognize the necessity of obtaining moral certitude before dismissing the doubt as non-existent. If moral certitude cannot be obtained, one must recourse to the principle contained in can. 50 that has been recognized since Decretal times, namely, that in case of doubt, rescripts of favor should ordinarily be broadly interpreted.[19] The only three exceptions to this general rule that were recognized by the Church in the past, as they are recognized by her at the present time, were rescripts that injured the acquired rights of others,[20] or were opposed to the law for the benefit of private persons,[21] or were granted in order that a person might obtain an ecclesiastical benefice: [22] these three kinds of rescripts of favor now, as in the past, must be strictly interpreted.

Acquired rights, referred to in the present canon, are rights that are obtained through juridical facts,[23] i.e., rights

---

[18] Suarez, *De Legibus*, VIII, c. 28, n. 14; Roelker, *Principles of Privilege*, p. 78; Michiels, *Normae Generales*, p. 258.

[19] "*Odia restringi, favores convenit ampliari*"—R. J., 15 in VI°; Wernz, *Jus Decretalium*, I, n. 155.

[20] C. 19, X, *de privilegiis*, V, 33; "*Locupletari non debet aliquis cum alterius injuria vel jactura*"—R. J. 48, in VI°; Reg. Cancell, XVIII, "*De quaesito non tollendo;*" Reiffenstuel, *Jus Canonicum*, lib. I, tit. III, n. 132; De Angelis, *Praelectiones*, lib. I, tit. III, n. 7.

[21] C. 1, *de filiis presbyterorum et aliis illegitime natis*, I, 11, in VI°; "*Quae a jure communi exhorbitant nequaquam ad consequentia sunt trahenda*"—R. J. 28, in VI°.

[22] C. 4, 5, *de rescriptis*, I, 3, in. VI°; c. 4, *de praebendis et dignitatibus*, III, 4, in VI°; Reiffenstuel, *Jus Canonicum*, lib. I, tit. III, n. 126-128; Schmalzgrueber, *Jus Ecclesiasticum*, pars I, tit. III, n. 28; Santi, *Praelectiones*, lib. I, tit. III, n. 17.

[23] Chelodi, *Jus De Personis*, n. 59; Cicognani, *Commentarium*, p. 26.

that have been obtained by the application of an existent law, or by the granting of privileges, indults, dispensations or other favors. Thus the rights that the pastor has to bring the Viaticum to the sick [24] is a right that is acquired by him when he becomes pastor; so also would the right to erect the Stations of the Cross, obtained by rescript, be an acquired right.[25] According to the present canon, doubtful rescripts that oppose the acquired rights of others must be strictly interpreted. The Code more than once shows her special concern for the acquired rights of persons. Acquired rights are considered to be sacred things worthy of the Church's protection:—hence her insistence that rescripts of favor opposed to them must be strictly interpreted. In can. 46, the law ordains that unless the rescript contains a derogatory clause to that effect, even "*motu proprio*" rescripts are not sustained against the acquired rights of others. By this the legislator evidently means, as shall be seen in the interpretation of can. 46, that although such rescripts are not invalidated by the mere fact that they are opposed to the acquired rights of others, they do become invalid when the interested party opposes them. In the present canon, the legislator rather refers to rescripts, opposed to the acquired rights of others, that contain the necessary derogatory clause. Such rescripts must be interpreted strictly, e.g., if the clause "*etiam fructus intercülares huiusque hospitalibus obvientes*" is contained in such a rescript that bestows upon the local Ordinary the right to use all the interculary beneficial fruits for the support of his diocesan seminary, the word "*hospitalibus*" would include only houses used for the care of the sick, not orphanages, etc.[26]

Dispensations that are granted for reasons of private nature, the good of society or religion, as well as privileges contrary to the law for the benefit of private persons, come under the category of favors that are opposed to the law

---

[24] Can. 850. Cf. can. 397, n. 3, 514 for special provisions for bishops and religious.

[25] Cicognani, *Commentarium*, p. 233; Vermeersch-Creusen, *Epitome*, I, n. 54.

[26] Michiels, *Normae Generales*, II, p. 260.

for the benefit of private persons,[27] and, accordingly, must be strictly interpreted, whereas dispensations that are granted for the public good, to promote the common good of society or religion, e.g., a dispensation that helps to promote public worship, or a dispensation from the conditions required to obtain a benefice granted to a cleric whose appointment will be particularly beneficial to society or religion, as well as the faculty to dispense non-designated persons must be broadly interpreted.[28] But even though privileges contrary to the law granted for the benefit of private persons must be strictly interpreted, the interpretation should be of such a nature that the recipient will receive some benefit from the rescript.[29]

The present law does not ordain that all rescripts of benefices, but only that those which are in answer to a petition asking for a benefice should be strictly interpreted. This distinction held true even before the Code. Since they were looked upon as favoring inordinate ambition, rescripts that were petitioned in order to obtain a benefice were strictly interpreted, while other beneficial rescripts, e.g., rescripts bestowing faculties to grant benefices, were broadly interpreted,[30] in all likelihood, just as in the case of rescripts granting powers to dispense, because they were exercised for the common good. It seems, however, that the limitation of strict interpretation laid down by common law for the interpretation of privileges contrary to the common law for the benefit of individuals, namely, that the interpretation should not be such that the favor becomes valueless to the individual, applies also to rescripts that are granted to persons who petition for benefices.[31]

Whenever, therefore, a doubtful word or expression appears in rescripts that are opposed to the acquired rights of others, or are opposed to the law for the benefit of

---

[27] Can. 85, 68; Reiffenstuel, *Jus Canonicum,* lib. I, tit. III, n. 138, 139; Chelodi, *Jus De Personis,* n. 79.

[28] Can. 85; Schmalzgrueber, *Jus Ecclesiasticum,* pars I, tit. III, n. 31; Michiels, *Normae Generales,* II, p. 261.

[29] Can. 68.

[30] C. 16, X, *de verborum significatione,* V, 40; c. 4, *de praebendis et dignitatibus,* III, 4, in VI°.

[31] Cf. can. 68; Ojetti, *Commentarium in Codicem,* I, p. 249.

private persons, or are granted so that a person may obtain an ecclesiastical benefice, a strict interpretation must be employed, but at the same time a strict interpretation that makes allowances for the limitations admitted by canonists under the old law.[32] Rescripts that injure the acquired rights of the *grantor* need not be strictly interpreted since the grantor, if he had desired, could have made specific mention of what concerned himself;[33] nor must rescripts that are granted with the clause *"motu proprio"* or the clause *"ex certa scientia"* be strictly interpreted, since it would be absurd to suppose that the special liberality of the Pope was intended to diminish rather than to increase the privilege.[34]

Article II.—Time when Rescripts become Effective

The element of time plays an important role in the interpretation of Rescripts. It is frequently a matter of considerable importance for the recipient of a rescript to know exactly when the rescript becomes effective, when the favors contained therein are actually granted to him, so that he may know when he can begin to take advantage of the papal favor and when he must stop using it, e.g., in using faculties that are granted for a certain length of time. The following canon makes the form in which the rescript is granted the deciding factor in the solution of this problem.

Canon 38.—Rescripta quibus gratia conceditur sine interiecto exsecutore, effectum habent a momento quo datae sunt litterae; cetera a tempore executionis.

The norm is very simple:—rescripts that are granted *in forma gratiosa*, i.e., without an executor, become effective at the very moment that they are dated; rescripts that are

---

[32] Can. 6, n. 2.

[33] Reiffenstuel, *Jus Canonicum*, lib. I, tit. III, n. 127; Roelker, *Principles of Privilege*, p. 81; Michiels, *Normae Generales*, II, p. 262.

[34] Suarez, *De Legibus*, VIII, c. 27, n. 8; Reiffenstuel, *Jus Canonicum*, lib. I, tit. III, n. 140; Roelker, *Principles of Privilege*, pp. 80, 83; Michiels, *Normae Generales*, II, p. 262.

granted *in forma commissoria,* i.e., with an executor, at the time they are executed.

There has been no change from the old law on this point regarding rescripts granted *in forma gratiosa,*[35] except that formerly the rescripts bore three different dates, and only at the time of the last date did the rescript become effective, whereas matters are simplified now by the fact that there is only one date in the rescript.[36] It must be remembered, however, that even though rescripts are generally sent from the Curia the day after they have been dated, a rescript granted *in forma gratiosa* is effective from the very moment the rescript itself is dated.[37]

A decided change from the old law has taken place regarding the time that rescripts granted *in forma commissoria* take effect. Before the Code, the time that the rescript was presented to the executor for execution was the deciding factor:[38] now, according to the clear words of the canon, these rescripts are effective only from the time of the execution, i.e., from the time that the favor is actually bestowed on the interested party by formal decree, and not from the time that the rescript is presented to the executor, as Chelodi,[39] in the desire to retain a classical term, claims. If no time intervened between the presentation of the rescript and its actual execution, it might not be necessary to give up the classical term, despite the fact that the Code has adopted a new one, but, as a matter of fact, rather frequently an appreciable lapse of time separates the two acts. There remains, therefore, no alternative:—since the legislator has changed the meaning as well as the wording of the law, the old law on this point cannot be retained.[40] The present law has its practical

---

[35] Reiffenstuel, *Jus Canonicum,* lib. I, tit. III, n. 77; De Angelis, *Praelectiones,* lib. I, tit. III, n. 6; Santi, *Praelectiones,* lib. I, tit. III, n. 19.

[36] Leurenius, *Forum Ecclesiasticum,* q. 272, 2; Ojetti, *Commentarium,* I, p. 214, nota (2).

[37] Cicognani, *Commentarium,* p. 214; Vermeersch-Creusen, *Epitome,* I, n. 130.

[38] Reiffenstuel, *Jus Canonicum,* lib. I, tit. III, n. 77; De Angelis, *Praelectiones,* lib. I, tit. III, n. 6; Wernz, *Jus Decretalium,* I, n. 155.

[39] *Jus De Personis,* p. 142, nota (3).

[40] Can. 6, n. 3.

advantages as far as proof is concerned, because if the prescriptions of the Code are carried out,[41] the time that rescripts for the external forum become effective can afterwards be determined by the date found in the written document of execution; whereas, if the time of presentation were the deciding factor, difficulties might arise in deciding the exact time that the rescripts produced their effects, since no law specifies that the act of presentation must be recorded in writing.

Michiels,[42] basing his claim upon an answer given by the Sacred Congregation for the Affairs of Religious Members on Aug. 1, 1922,[43] maintains that *any petitioner for papal favors* can effectively retract the virtual acceptance of the favor contained in his petition, can formally refuse the rescript, not only before the rescript has been executed, but even after it has been executed and notification of the execution has been made to him. This certainly seems to be concluding too much from the response of the Congregation. It should be noted immediately that the Congregation only stated that *a dispensation from vows or an indult of secularization* could be refused by the petitioner even after notification of the execution was made to him. The juridical foundation for this reply is to be sought not in the title on rescripts but in can. 640, §1, which treats of the indult of secularization and says "*Qui, impetrato saecularizationis indulto, religionem relinquit: A sua religione separatur...*" Practically, the answer of the Congregation amounts to saying that the dispensation from vows or the indult of secularization is not really effective, does not actually break the bond of the religious state, until the religious leaves

---

[41] Cf. can. 56.

[42] *Normae Generales*, II, pp. 293, 294.

[43] "*An religiosus qui saecularizationis indultum aut simplicium votorum dispensationem impetravit, possit primum aut alteram recusare cum a locali Superiore ejusdem notitiam accipit, quamvis Superior Generalis in scriptis jam executoriale decretum rescripti emiserit ad normam can. 56 Codicis juris canonici. Praerequisito igitur consultorum voto dubium propositum fuit Emis P. P. in plenario coetu diei 9 Junii 1922, qui re mature perpensa, respondendum censuerunt: Affirmative, dummodo Superiores graves rationes in contrarium non habeant, quo in casu ad Sacram Congregationem referant*"—AAS, XIV (1922), 501.

the religious institute *(relinquit religionem)* by accepting the favor after receiving notification that the rescript had been mandated to execution.[44] The special provision contained in the reply of the Congregation cannot, therefore, be extended to all rescripts because the special nature of the favor referred to and not the fact that it was granted by a rescript, explains the principle contained in the answer. Merely because the Holy See ordinarily desires, on account of the nature of religious vows, to leave the religious free, until the last moment, to accept or reject a favor that brings with it loss of privileges as well as freedom from obligations and burdens, one is not justified in concluding that the same principle applies to all rescripts of favor.

Article III.—Conditional Clauses in Rescripts of Favor

One of the main problems in interpretation concerns itself with the value that must be attached to conditional clauses in rescripts. The criterion to be used in distinguishing essential from accidental conditions is stated in the following terms of law:

Canon 39.—Conditiones in rescriptis tunc tantum essentiales pro eorundum validitate censentur, cum per particulas, si, dummodo, vel aliam ejusdem significationis exprimuntur.

Some conditional clauses in rescripts refer to the petitioner or the favor, others refer to the actions of the executor of the rescript, but for both kinds of clauses, as far as determining which conditions are essential, which conditions accidental, the same general principles apply, the main difference being that the clauses referring to the petitioner or the favor affect the validity or liceity of the rescript itself, whereas the other clauses affect only the execution of the rescript.[45]

Conditions in rescripts may be either essential or accidental:—essential, if the value of the rescript or of its execution depends upon the fulfilment or observance of the

[44] Maroto, "Annotationes," CpR, IV (1923), 105.

[45] Can. 39, 55.

conditions; accidental, if the rescript or the execution remains valid despite the fact that the conditions are not fulfilled or observed, but the execution of the rescript or the acts made in virtue of the rescript are rendered unlawful.[46] Accidental conditions are really more in the nature of monitions or precepts than conditions, and are inserted in the rescript to recall or urge an already existing obligation.

According to can. 39, conditions in rescripts are only to be considered as essential when they are expressed by the particles *si, dummodo,* or some other (particle) of the same meaning. If this canon were interpreted just as it reads, an essential condition would of necessity have to be introduced by a particle, either *si* or *dummodo,* or such particles as *non aliter, nisi, dumtaxat,* etc. However, it is generally admitted by canonists[47] that clauses restricting the use of the faculties, e.g., *"in ipso actu confessionis," "nec ullo modo uti potest extra fines dioecesis,"* are essential conditions despite the fact that they are not introduced by a particle. Moreover, practically all canonists, as shall be seen later, admit that the *"ablative absolute"* construction, at least in some instances, expresses an essential condition. Even under the old law, although certain grammatical constructions were, as a rule, looked upon as essential conditions, they were accepted as accidental when it was clear, on account of the style of the Curia, the nature of the thing, or the common opinion of authors, that the grantor of the rescript did not intend to have them taken as real conditions:—in other words, the grammatical construction was not the only thing considered in determining whether conditions were essential or accidental.[48] Taking into account not only the words of the canon but the clear meaning of

---

[46] Maroto, *Institutiones*, n. 284; De Meester, *Compendium*, n. 294; Cicognani, *Commentarium*, p. 215.

[47] Cicognani, *Commentarium*, p. 215; Chelodi, *Jus De Personis*, p. 136, nota (4); De Meester, *Compendium*, n. 294; Coronata, *Institutiones*, I, n. 62; Vermeersch-Creusen, *Epitome*, I, n. 131.

[48] Gasparri, *De Matrimonio*, n. 364; Zitelli, *De Dispensationibus*, p. 75.

the legislator,[49] the real meaning of can. 39 seems to be that conditions in rescripts are essential merely on account of the grammatical construction of the clause when they are introduced by the particles *si*, *dummodo*, or another particle of the same significance, but that other grammatical constructions can, in individual instances, be considered as essential conditions, if the style of the Curia, the nature of the thing itself, or the common opinion of authors requires that they be considered as essential.

The main source of controversy about conditions in rescripts seem to be the clauses that are expressed by the *ablative absolute*. Before the Code, while it was commonly held that the ablative absolute expressed an essential condition,[50] at the same time it was also generally admitted that some conditions expressed by the ablative absolute were not essential.[51] The common view maintained that ordinarily and *per se* the ablative absolute expressed an essential condition, but that *per accidens*, in particular instances it might be considered as expressing an accidental condition if the style of the Curia, the nature of the thing, or the common teaching of authors demanded that it be considered as such.[52] Since the Code, the common teaching of canonists regarding the force of the ablative absolute construction has been entirely changed. Now while the abla-

---

[49] *"Certum est, quod is committit in legem qui verba legis complectens contra legis nititur voluntatem"*—R. J. 88, in. VI°; Coronata, *Institutiones*, I, n. 62.

[50] Benedict XIV, *Institutiones Ecclesiasticae*, Inst. 87, n. 68, *"Certissimum est inter jurisperitos quod vera conditio ex ablativo absoluto consequitur."*; De Justis, *De Dispensationibus*, lib. I, cap. VII, n. 197; D'Annibale, *Summula*, I, 41, nota (33); Gasparri, *De Matrimonio*, n. 364, *"Communiter tradunt A A esse conditionem, si clausula exprimitur verbis postquam, si, dummodo, non aliter, sic nec alio modo, aut ablativo absoluto."*; Zitelli, *De Dispensationibus*, p. 75; Konings-Putzer, *Commentarium in Facultates Apostolicas*, p. 16.

[51] Sanchez, *De Matrimonio*, lib. VIII, disp. XXXIV, n. 29; De Justis, *De Dispensationibus*, lib. I, cap. VII, n. 209; Corradus, *Praxis*, lib. VII, cap. VII, n. 14; St. Alphonsus, *Theologia Moralis*, VII, n. 121; D'Annibale, *Summula*, I, 41, nota (33); I, 76.

[52] Gasparri, *De Matrimonio*, n. 364; Zitelli, *De Dispensationibus*, p. 75.

tive absolute is commonly considered[53] to be an essential condition only when the style of the Curia, the nature of the thing, or the agreement of authors requires that it be considered as essential, a few authors[54] still maintain that it expresses an essential condition unless it contains what by law or the nature of the thing is to be fulfilled for the lawfulness of the act.[55]

This is more than a mere theoretical question: it is one of great practical importance. Even though there may not be much disagreement about the character of particular ablative absolute clauses, it is precisely in such cases of dispute that one opinion or the other would play an important part in the solution of the doubts:—adherents to the first opinion would consider a doubtful clause as accidental, whereas the followers of the other opinion would presume the clause to be essential unless and until it was clearly proved to be accidental. The present common view seems to have a much stronger juridical basis for its interpretation of the existing law. The fact that the ablative clause is not a grammatical construction introduced by a particle, while not proving that it can never be considered an essential clause, shows that it should not be considered, merely on account of its grammatical construction, as ordinarily expressing an essential condition. The fact that the Code is silent about the ablative absolute construction, the fact that can. 39 does not explicitly or implicitly mention it as a grammatical construction that should be considered as essential, indicates that a change has taken place from the teaching of pre-Code canonists which placed it on an equal basis with the particles *si, dummodo,* and other constructions of essential conditions. Silence under such circum-

[53] Vermeersch-Creusen, *Epitome*, I, n. 131; De Smet, *De Sponsalibus et Matrimonio*, n. 870; Chelodi, *Jus De Personis*, p. 136, nota (4); Ojetti, *Commentarium*, I, p. 216; Wernz-Vidal, *Jus Canonicum*, V, n. 446; Capello, *De Sacramentis*, III, n. 284; Vlaming, *Praelectiones*, n. 476; Cicognani, *Commentarium*, pp. 215, 216; Blat, *Commentarium*, I, n. 104; Coronata, *Institutiones*, I, n. 62; Michiels, *Normae Generales*, II, p. 211.

[54] Maroto, *Institutiones*, n. 284; Ayrinhac, *General Legislation*, p. 147; Augustine, *A Commentary*, I, p. 129; Cocchi, *Commentarium*, I, p. 150.

[55] Maroto, *Institutiones*, n. 284.

stances indicates that it is no longer to be given the same value as *si, dummodo* and equivalent particles. Moreover, in view of the fact that the great majority of authors emphatically deny that it ordinarily expresses an essential condition, the very least that can be said is that the opinion of Maroto and the others is, both from the viewpoint of external and internal evidence, not very probable and, therefore, not binding.[56] This does not, of course, imply that an ablative absolute can never express an essential condition:—it only means that the mere fact that a clause appears in a rescript in such a construction no longer gives a presumption that it is an essential condition, that only when it is clear from the style of the Curia, the nature of the thing, or the opinion of authors can an ablative absolute be considered as essential.

Since the decree of the Holy Office issued on August 28, 1885,[57] the clauses used in rescripts by the various departments of the Roman Curia have become greatly reduced in number and more concise in form.[58] The following clauses comprise those which, at present, are more frequently used by the Roman Curia in Rescripts of Favor:—some concern the petitioners, others the executors. They are classified as essential or accidental according to the principle contained in can. 39, the present style of the Roman Curia, the nature of the things contained in the clauses, and the common teaching of canonists.[59]

---

[56] Can. 15.

[57] ASS, XXVIII (1895-1896), 512.

[58] Gasparri, *De Matrimonio*, n. 365 sq.; Wernz-Vidal, *Jus Canonicum*, V, n. 446.

[59] The following authors have been consulted: Barbosa, *Tractatus Varii, De clausulis usu frequentissimis;* Ferraris, *Bibliotheca*, v. Clausulae; Vermeersch-Creusen, *Epitome*, I, n. 131; II, n. 449, 465; De Meester, *Compendium*, n. 294; Chelodi, *Jus Matrimoniale*, n. 50, 59; Ojetti, *Commentarium*, I, pp. 219, 259; Wernz-Vidal, *Jus Canonicum*, V, n. 179, 272, 446, nota (154); De Smet, *De Sponsalibus et Matrimonio*, n. 871-887, p. 731, nota (1); Schaefer, *Compendium De Religiosis*, pp. 496, 566, 567, 573; Laaraona, CpR, II (1921), p. 218 sq.; Vermeersch, *De Religiosis*, p. 262; Kubelbeck, *The Sacred Penitentiary*, p. 100; Coronata, *Institutiones*, I, n. 77; I, p. 68, nota (6); Capello, *De Sacramentis*, III, n. 285-288; Cicognani, *Commentarium*, p. 216; Gasparri, *De Matrimonio*, n. 381, 391; Noldin, *De Sacramentis*, n. 323, 7; Instr. S. C. Indulg., 2 Jan. 1888, 14 Junii 1901—*Coll. de Prop. Fide*, n. 2115, nota.

Essential conditions affecting the validity of the rescript:—"*Si vera sunt exposita;*" "*Dummodo nullum scandalum intercedat,*" used in dispensations from the impediment of crime; "*Dummodo ignorantia hujusmodi impedimenti fuerit probabilis;*" "*Dummodo super publico impedimento dispensationis litterae obtentae fuerint, et nullitas eorum ex praemissis proveniens occulta remaneat,*" in rescripts of the Sacred Penitentiary for concurrence of public and occult impediments; "*Dummodo impedimentum occultum sit;*" "*Dummodo orator de novo titulo canonico sit provisus vel, ipsius Ordinarii judicio, ejus congruae sustentationi aliter cautum sit,*" in rescripts granting secularization to clerics in major orders; "*Dummodo servatum sit praescriptum can. 534, §2, et constito de vera necessitate,*" in *normam S. S. Canonum 554 et 564 Codicis Juris Canonici,*" "*Dummodo omnia habeantur quae de jure requiruntur ad normam S. S. Canonum 554 et 564 Codicis Juris Canonici,*" in rescripts granting permission to transfer Novitiate or Provincial houses; "*Dummodo libere petat,*" in dispensations from solemn vows.

Essential conditions affecting the validity of the execution:—"*Audita prius ejus confessione,*" "*in sacramentali confessione tantum,*" obliging, under pain of nullity of the execution, to execute the rescript after a sacramental confession, (the execution would be valid even after a sacrilegious confession), but not necessarily after the absolution; "*Dummodo per informationes etiam secretas . . . constet de enunciatae postulantis vitae honestate, religiosa conversatione et idoneitate morali,*" in rescripts granting permission to transfer from one religious institute to another; "*Dummodo per diligens examen eum repererit idoneum;*" "*Dummodo prius regulariter, ad praescriptum Cod. I. C. can. 1061, §2, cautum omnino sit conditionibus ab Ecclesia requisitis, et ipse R. P. D. Ordinarius moraliter certus sit easdem impletum iri, scilicet: ex parte nupturientis (conjugis), de amovendo a parte catholica perversionis periculo et ab utroque contrahente (nupturiente), de universa prole utriusque sexus (nata et forsan nascitura) in catholicae religionis sanctitate omnino baptizanda et educanda; declarata insuper parti catholicae obligatione, qua tenetur, pru-*

denter curandi conversionem conjugis ad fidem catholicam," in rescripts granting dispensations from the matrimonial impediments of Mixed Religion and Disparity of Cult, certainly essential as far as the obligations of obtaining the "*cautiones*" and being morally certain about their fulfillment are concerned.[60]

Accidental conditions affecting the petitioner or the executor of the rescript:—"*Vetito viro transitu ad alias nuptias,*

[60] Canonists are not agreed whether or not the parties must be in good faith in giving the promises in order validly to receive the dispensation. Woywood, *A Practical Commentary*, I, n. 1056; Harrington, "*The Importance of the Cautiones in Disparity of Worship*, AER, LXV (1921), 261, 262; Petrovits, *The New Church Law on Matrimony*, n. 257 affirm. O'Donnell, IER, XVIII (1921), 411-418; De Smet, *De Sponsalibus et Matrimonio*, p. 731, nota (1), where he refers to S. Romana Rota, 26 Nov. 1921—AAS (1922), 515 sq. in confirmation of his opinion; Schenk, *The Matrimonial Impediments of Mixed Religion and Disparity of Cult*, n. 356 ff. deny. The decision of the Rota, referred to by De Smet, is not, however, very conclusive. It merely states, incidentally, that the validity of *mixed marriages* is not effected by fictitious promises of the non-Catholic party unless it can be proved that the promises were considered and made a condition without which the marriage would not have been contracted, but does not state whether or not the *dispensation* would be validly granted despite a fictitious promise. The case under discussion was a marriage between two Catholics. The validity of the marriage was attacked on the ground that the promises, that had been made a *conditio sine qua non* of the marriage, had been made fictitiously by one of the parties. In the discussion of the case, it was stated that *mixed marriages* would not be invalidated by fictitious promises unless the promises were made a *conditio sine qua non* of consent. From the context, therefore, it appears that the question of the promises given in mixed marriages was viewed more in the light of consent than from the viewpoint of the dispensation or rescript. Moreover, the term *mixed marriages* may be taken in a general sense to include all marriages between Catholics and non-Catholics, whether the latter are baptized or not, but it may also be interpreted to mean marriages between Catholics and baptized non-Catholics, i. e., as opposed to "*disparate marriages*." In the decision of the Rota there does not seem to be anything that would exclude this latter interpretation, and, consequently, it is not clear that the decision even incidentally touches upon the point in question, because a *dispensation* from the impediment of Mixed Religion can be invalidated by a fictitious promise of the non-Catholic party without any effect on the validity of the *marriage*. Finally, viewing the case independently of the decision of the Rota, the *nature of a promise* seems to necessitate good faith, because, unless a person really intends to assume an obligation, there can hardly be any question of a *promise made* by a person, but only of a *promise* that is *simulated*. Hence a fictitious promise scarcely seems to fulfil the condition mentioned above.

inconsulta hac S. Congregatione," in dispensations "*super matrimonio rato et non consummato,"* granted on account of the probable impotency of the man; "*Cum licentia Ordinarii loci,"* or "*De consensu Ordinarii loci,"* in rescripts bestowing power to grant indulgences or to bless religious articles:—the consent should be express, if possible, but tacit, implicit, or, when necessary, even prudently presumed consent would suffice; "*Facta Superioribus gravi obligatione invigilandi ut religiosus quantum fieri potest Regulas suas observat,"* "*Firma tamen obligatione retinendi habitum Proprii Ordinis,"* in permissions to remain away from the religious house for more than six months; "*Sublata occasione peccandi;"* "*Quodque in pauperes faciant aliquam eleemosynam"* or "*Erogata ab eis aliqua eleemosyna juxta eorum vires judicio ipsius Ordinarii taxanda et definienda;"* "*Injuncta (imposita) oratoribus salutari poenitentia,"* a penance distinct from the sacramental penance and proportionate to the gravity of the crime, with due allowance made for the condition, age, health, office, sex, etc., of the respective person, imposed in dispensations from impediments of crime; "*Nullis super his testibus adhibitis aut litteris datis, sed praesentibus, post earum executionem, sub poena excommunicationis latae sententiae, per te laceratis (combustis),"* in rescripts from the Sacred Penitentiary:—destruction of the rescript to take place within three days; "*Discretioni tuae committimus, quatenus si ita sit,"* regarding investigation; "*Praevia expulsione oratoris ab ordine per modum poenae;"* "*Firma tamen obligatione transmittendi hoc anno relationem de statu dioecesis,"* in permissions granted by the Consistorial Congregation to defer the Visitation to the Holy See.

The clause "*Servatis canonicis praescriptionibus"* refers in a general way to the work of the executor, v.g., imposing juridical penance, juridical absolution, removal of scandal, giving alms, and the decree of execution. It is considered essential or accidental according as the specific prescriptions that it imposes are considered to be for the validity or the lawfulness of the execution.

Article IV.—Subreption and Obreption

Can 40.—In omnibus rescriptis subintelligenda est, etsi non expressa, conditio: *Si preces veritate nitantur*, salvo praescripto can. 45, 1054.

The most ancient as well as the most important essential condition requires that the petition be truthful. This condition is expressed by the clause *"si preces veritate nitantur,"* or by such substitute clauses as *"si ita est," "si vera sunt exposita,"* or *"veris existentibus narratis."* [61] Decretal Law, borrowing a principle from Roman Law,[62] ordained that the condition *"si preces veritate nitantur"* should be expressed in all rescripts,[63] or, if not expressed, at least understood.[64] This condition makes the valid granting of the favor depend not upon an *investigation* made by the executor about the truthfulness of the petition, but merely upon the *existence* of a truthful petition.[65] Before 1885, in rescripts of the Apostolic Datary or the Apostolic Chancery another clause, *"si preces veritate niti repereris,"* was usually inserted, a clause that not only conditioned the validity of the rescript on the truthfulness of the petition, but required for the validity of the execution that the executor investigate and judge whether or not the petition was truthful.[66] Since the Decree of the Holy Office August 28, 1885,[67] this latter clause has been suppressed and *"si preces veritate nitantur"* or one of the others has been substituted.

Can. 40 reiterates the Decretal Law principle, v.g., that the essential condition *"si preces veritate nitantur"* should be understood when not expressed, and at the same time refers to the special provisions that have been made for *"Motu Proprio"* Rescripts and for Rescripts that grant dispensa-

---

[61] Chelodi, *Jus De Personis*, p. 137, nota (1) ; Ojetti, *Commentarium*, I, p. 222.

[62] C. I. 23. 7.

[63] C. 16, C. XXV, q. 2.

[64] C. 2, X, *de rescriptis*, I, 3.

[65] Sanchez, *De Matrimonio*, *lib.* VIII, disp. XXXIV, n. 26, Ojetti, *Commentarium*, I, p. 222.

[66] D'Annibale, *Summula*, I, 241; Feije, *De Impedimentis*, n. 738.

[67] ASS, XXVIII (1895-1896), 512.

tions from minor matrimonial impediments. Before proceeding to the detailed explanation of can. 42, 45, 1054, the question of time will be treated. The following canon determines precisely when the petition must be truthful.

Canon 41.—In rescriptis quorum nullus est exsecutor, preces veritate nitantur oportet tempore quo rescriptum datum est; in ceteris tempore exsecutionis.

This principle might be put in a still more concise form by saying that the petition must be true at the time that the rescript becomes effective.[68] In the old law all canonists admitted[69] that, whether it was truthful before or afterwards, so long as the rescript was truthful at the time that the rescript was granted, the condition *"si preces veritate nitantur"* would be fulfilled in rescripts granted *in forma gratiosa;* but there was no such agreement regarding the time that the condition should be verified in rescripts granted *in forma commissoria.* Some few authors[70] maintained that in order to safeguard the validity of the rescript it was necessary and sufficient that the petition be true at the time the rescript was granted; others[71] claimed that the petition should be true at the time of the execution of the rescript; while still others[72] said that it was sufficient, for the validity of the rescript, if the petition was true at the time of the execution of the rescript, i.e., at the time that the favor was actually granted by the delegate or executor. The Code has accepted this last opinion as law for rescripts granted *in forma commissoria,* and at the same time has retained the accepted teaching regarding re-

---

[68] Cf. can. 38.

[69] Sanchez, *De Matrimonio,* lib. VIII, disp. XXX, n. 2, 4; D'Annibale, *Summula,* I, 239.

[70] Maschardus, *Conclusiones probationum omnium,* concl. 1123, 22.

[71] Pontius, *De Matrimonio,* lib. VIII, cap. XX, n. 3; Suarez, *De Legibus,* VI, c. 20, n. 13; De Justis, *De Dispensationibus,* lib. 1, cap. VI, n. 299; lib. I, cap. VIII, n. 138; Collet, *Traite des dispenses,* cap. VI, art. IV, resp. 2.

[72] Sanchez, *De Matrimonio,* lib. VIII, disp. XXX, n. 2; Garcia, *De Beneficiis,* lib. VI, cap. II, n. 283; Corradus, *Praxis,* lib. VII, cap. VI, n. 25; Schmalzgrueber, *Jus Ecclesiasticum,* pars I, tit. III, n. 23; D'Annibale, *Summula,* I, 239; Wernz, *Jus Decretalium,* I, n. 155.

scripts granted *in forma gratiosa.* Consequently, if in rescripts granted *in forma gratiosa* there is an invalidating lack of truth in the petition at the time that the rescript is granted, the rescript is invalid, even though the petition was true at the time the petition was sent to Rome, or immediately after the rescript was granted. In the same way the validity of a rescript granted *in forma commissoria* is affected if there is an invalidating lack of truth in the petition at the time the rescript is executed, nor will the fact that the petition was true before or afterwards remedy the defect.

Commenting on this canon, Coronata [73] remarks that a rescript granted *in forma commissoria* is valid if the reason given in the petition is true at the time of the execution of the rescript, even though the reason ceases afterwards. This statement is true but not sufficiently explained. As the case is given, the rescript itself would be valid, but if the rescript contained a dispensation that permitted of successive applications, e.g., permission to read forbidden books, dispensation from the law of fasting, the favor granted by the rescript would cease through a total and certain cessation of the motive cause.[74]

To be properly understood, the present canon should be taken in connection with can. 52, which states, in substance, that rescripts granted *in forma commissoria* that have no specified time within which presentation must be made to the executor, may be presented at any time, but that if by fraud or malice the rescript is kept from being presented until, e.g., the false cause becomes true, the executor may refuse execution or the rescript may be declared null by the grantor as a penalty for the fraud or deceit.[75]

As already stated, the essential conditional clause *"si preces veritate nitantur,"* expressed or understood in all rescripts, affects the validity of the rescript only when the petition is not true at the time that the rescript is effective. This does not mean, however, that the legislator looks upon false petitions as lawful or wishes to condone

[73] *Institutiones,* I, n. 62.
[74] Can. 86.
[75] Cf. Part III, Chapt. III, Art. II.

the lack of truthfulness in petitions:—it merely means that despite the fact that, through ignorance or oversight, the petition is not true when sent by the petitioner, despite the fact that the petitioner was morally responsible for an unlawful act by falsifying or omitting important facts, the legislator does not wish to nullify rescripts unless the petitions are lacking in truth at the time the rescripts actually become effective. Moreover, the essential condition "*si preces veritate nitantur*" should not be interpreted as meaning that any and every lack of truth in the petition at the time the rescript is effective renders the rescript invalid. Canons 42, 45, and 1054 explain the exact bearing of this condition on ordinary rescripts, on rescripts granted "*Motu Proprio,*" and on rescripts containing dispensations from the minor matrimonial impediments, respectively.

Canon 42, §1.—Reticentia veri, seu subreptio, in precibus non obstat quominus rescriptum vim habeat ratumque sit, dummodo expressa fuerint quae de stylo Curiae sunt ad validitatem exprimenda.

§2.—Nec obstat expositio falsi, seu obreptio, dummodo vel unica causa proposita vel ex pluribus propositis una saltem motiva vera sit.

§3.—Vitum obreptionis vel subreptionis in una tantum parte rescripti aliam non infirmat, si una simul plures gratiae per rescriptum concedantur.

Maroto[76] and Cicognani,[77] in summarizing the doctrine that existed before the Code about subreption and obreption, state that formerly rescripts were considered invalid when the subreption or obreption, caused by the malice of the petitioner, occurred in something substantial (in which impulsive causes were included), whether or not the Pope, knowing all the circumstances, would have granted the rescript; or when the subreption or obreption, caused by the ignorance or simplicity of the petitioners, occurred in the motive causes. Such an historical summary scarcely gives an adequate view of the teaching of old canonists about subreption and obreption.

---

[76] *Institutiones,* I, p. 319, nota (2).
[77] *Commentarium,* p. 224.

Ancient canonists distinguished between subreption and obreption, and defined them as they are defined in the present canon:—subreption, the concealment or suppression of the truth; obreption, the expression or narration of something false.[78] Subreption and obreption were judged according to the summary of the petition found in the rescript itself, not by the *libellus* sent by the petitioners to the Roman Curia.[79] Some canonists,[80] influenced by the fact that they had the same effect upon the validity of rescripts, refused to admit the existence of a real distinction between subreption and obreption.

The Corpus Juris Canonici contains the sources from which the complicated and controverted opinions of canonists evolved. Some Decretals declared that local Ordinaries should either remove from office those who had received office through subreption or obreption, or else refer their cases to Rome;[81] others positively declared that subreptious[82] and obreptious[83] rescripts were invalid; and one Decretal Letter[84] distinguished between subreption and obreption in good and bad faith. In this last Decretal, it was declared that if the petitioner had, in bad faith, committed subreption or obreption, the delegate could not proceed in the matter, but if the subreption or obreption had been done in good faith, the delegate could act according to the common form or procedure, not the special one specified in the rescript, provided that it could be presumed that the

---

[78] De Justis, *De Dispensationibus*, lib. I, cap. IV, n. 2, 3; Schmalzgrueber, *Jus Canonicum*, pars I, tit. III, n. 14.

[79] Sanchez, *De Matrimonio*, lib. VIII, disp. XXI, n. 57; D'Annibale, *Summula*, I, 236, nota (2).

[80] Sanchez, *De Matrimonio*, lib. VIII, disp. XXI, n. 2; Reiffenstuel, *Jus Canonicum*, lib. I, tit. III, n. 153.

[81] C. 2, X, *de filiis presbyterorum ordinandis, vel non*, I, 16; c. 6, X, *de corpore vitiatis ordinandis, vel non*, I, 20; c. 5, X, *de officio judicis ordinarii*, I, 31.

[82] C. 7, *de fide instrumentorum*, II, 22; c. 12, X, *de sententia et re judicata*, II, 27; c. 5, X, *de confirmatione utili vel inutili*, II, 30; c. 5, X, *de cohabitatione clericorum et mulierum*, III, 2; c. 6, X, *de concessione praebendae et ecclesiae non vacantis*, III, 8.

[83] C. 7, X, *de fide instrumentorum*, II, 22; c. 6, X, *de consanguinitate et affinitate*, IV, 14.

[84] C. 20, X, *de rescriptis*, I, 3.

Pope, had he been properly informed about the case, would have given permission to act according to the common form of procedure. It was upon these Decretals and particularly the last one that the conflicting opinions of canonists were founded.

Canonists distinguished first of all between rescripts that contained one favor and rescripts that contained more than one favor.

In rescripts containing a single favor, a further subdistinction was made between subreption and obreption that concerned matters other than the reasons or motives that were advanced by the petitioners to influence the grantor, and subreption and obreption that concerned the reasons or motives themselves. Some authors[85] taught that when the reasons or motives were not involved, the omission or false narration of something substantial would nullify the rescript, whether the subreption or obreption had been committed in good or bad faith, through malice, through ignorance or simplicity, whether the grantor would or would not have granted the favor, had he been cognizant of the real state of affairs. Others, on the contrary,[86] claimed that if the subreption or obreption was committed through ignorance or simplicity, the rescript would not be vitiated if it was clear that the Pope, acquainted with the true conditions of things, would have granted the favor in some form, even though not exactly in the form in which it was granted. When the question of subreption or obreption about the causes or motives was involved, a distinction was usually made between motive and impulsive causes. A few authors[87] maintained that, irrespective of the question of deceit, ignorance or simplicity, on account

[85] De Justis, *De Dispensationibus*, lib. I, cap. IV, n. 4, 9, 14, 19, 31, 51; Sanchez, *De Matrimonio*, lib. VIII, disp. XXI, n. 56; Pontius, *De Matrimonio*, lib. VIII, cap. XVII, n. 2; Layman, *Theologia Moralis*, lib. I, tract. IV, cap. 22, n. 18; D'Annibale, *Summula*, I, 240; De Becker, *De Sponsalibus et Matrimonio*, p. 334; Feije, *De Impedimentis*, n. 723; Wernz, *Jus Decretalium*, I, n. 153.

[86] Schmalzgrueber, *Jus Ecclesiasticum*, pars I, tit. III, n. 14-16; Reiffenstuel, *Jus Canonicum*, lib. I, tit. III, n. 161-163; De Angelis, *Praelectiones*, lib. I, tit. III, n. 4; Santi, *Praelectiones*, lib. I, tit. III, n. 11; Soglia, *Institutiones*, pars I, cap. I, par. 30.

[87] Garcia, *De Beneficiis*, pars VI, cap. II, n. 200.

of the clause "*si preces veritate nitantur,*" subreption or obreption even about the impulsive causes rendered the rescript invalid, but their opinion was not generally considered to have much juridical value.[88]

A *motive cause* was defined as a cause that moved the grantor to bestow the favor, a cause without which the favor would not be granted at all or at least not without the imposition of certain conditions; an *impulsive cause* was defined as a cause that was not necessary in order to obtain the grantor's consent, but helped to make the granting of the favor easier. When only one cause was given in the petition, it was accepted as a motive cause, and if it proved false, the rescript was considered to be invalid, because it was not to be presumed that the Pope would grant a favor without a cause.[89] However a rather important and practical exception to this general rule was admitted by a great number of authors:[90] it was said that if, in good faith, a cause was given in a petition for a matrimonial dispensation, and after the marriage had been contracted the causes were discovered to be false, the obreption in the rescript would not affect the validity of the marriage. When more than one cause was given in the petition it was commonly taught[91] that if one motive cause remained true, the rescript was valid, whether the obreption was committed

---

[88] De Justis, *De Dispensationibus*, lib. I, cap. IV, n. 29; Sanchez, *De Matrimonio*, lib. VIII, disp. XXI, n. 11; Reiffenstuel, *Jus Canonicum*, lib. I, tit. III, n. 184-187; Schmalzgrueber, *Jus Ecclesiasticum*, pars I, tit. III, n. 18.

[89] De Justis, *De Dispensationibus*, lib. III, cap. I, n. 46, 53, 56; Reiffenstuel, *Jus Canonicum*, lib. I, tit. III, n. 183, 194; Schmalzgrueber, *Jus Ecclesiasticum*, pars I, tit. III, n. 16, 18; D'Annibale, *Summula*, I, 238, nota (12); I, 238, where he says that the rescript would be invalid even if the cause was impulsive.

[90] Sanchez, *De Matrimonio*, lib. VIII, disp. XIX, n. 28; De Justis, *De Dispensationibus*, lib. III, cap. III, n. 68; Corradus, *Praxis*, lib. VII, cap. II, n. 27; Giovine, *De Dispensationibus*, I, §126; Caillaud, *Manuel des Dispenses*, n. 264; Carriere, *De Matrimonio*, n. 1116; Pompen, *De Dispensationibus*, n. 110, 5; Feije, *De Impedimentis*, n. 726; De Becker, *De Sponsalibus et Matrimonio*, p. 335; Van De Burgt, *De Dispensationibus*, n. 94, 126.

[91] Sanchez, *De Matrimonio*, lib. VIII, disp. XXI, n. 42; De Justis, *De Dispensationibus*, lib. III, cap. I, n. 59; Pontius, *De Matrimonio*, lib. VIII, cap. XVII, n. 41; Reiffenstuel, *Jus Canonicum*, lib. I, tit. III, n. 188; St. Alphonsus, *Theologia Moralis*, I, 185.

by deceit, or through malice or simplicity, but a few authors [92] maintained that the rescript was invalid if the obreption occurred through deceit. Finally it was taught that if all the proposed causes were impulsive, all had to be true; otherwise, the rescript would be invalid.[93]

In deciding the status of rescripts, containing more than one favor, in which the cause proposed for one of the favors was false, canonists applied the Roman Law principle "*Non solent quae abundant vitiare scripturas,*" [94] as well as the principle of the *Regulae Juris*, "*Utile non debet per inutile vitiari.*" [95] Some canonists claimed that in no case would obreption in one part of the rescript nullify the other favors,[96] but it was more commonly taught that if obreption were committed in one part of the rescript, not through ignorance or simplicity, but in bad faith, the whole rescript would be vitiated,[97] but since a penalty inflicted on the petitioner for his perversity was involved, it was claimed that invalidity would take place only after the sentence of the judge.[98]

If, after the rescript had been granted, the validity of the rescript was doubtful because it was not clear whether a circumstance that had not been mentioned or stated correctly was substantial or accidental, or whether the remaining cause was motive or impulsive, the rescript was con-

---

92 Aichner, *Compendium Juris Ecclesiastici*, p. 24,nota (8); De Becker, *De Sponsalibus et Matrimonio*, p. 335.

93 De Justis, *De Dispensationibus*, lib. III, cap. I, n. 64; Pontius, *De Matrimonio*, lib. VIII, cap. XVII, n. 41; D'Annibale, *Summula*, I, 238.

94 D. L. 17. 94.

95 R. J. 37, in VI°.

96 Schmalzgrueber, *Jus Ecclesiasticum*, pars I, tit. III, n. 17; Feije, *De Impedimentis*, n. 724.

97 Reiffenstuel, Jus Canonicum, lib. I, tit. III, n. 174-175; Santi, *Praelectiones*, lib. I, tit. III, n. 11.

98 Sanchez, *De Matrimonio*, lib. VIII, disp. XXI, n. 78; De Justis, *De Dispensationibus*, lib. I, cap. IV, n. 35-38; D'Annibale, *Summula*, I, 238.

sidered valid by virtue of the principle, *"in dubio standum est pro valore actus."* [99]

The present law has eliminated almost entirely, as far as the validity of rescripts is concerned, the distinction between subreption and obreption committed through malice, or through ignorance or simplicity, and, in doing so, has greatly lightened the task of interpreting rescripts. In only one instance, specifically mentioned by the Code, is the distinction any longer applicable to rescripts of favor, v.g., a general dispensation from irregularities applies to all irregularities that, *in good faith,* were omitted in the petition, excepting those which were incurred by homicide or by abortion, *"effectu secuto,"* or to those that were already brought to trial, but does not apply to those, which, *in bad faith,* were not mentioned [100] That the Church, however, still considers subreption and obreption, committed in bad faith, to be gravely sinful, can be concluded from the fact that she classifies them, even when they occur in rescripts granted *"Motu Proprio,"* or in rescripts containing dispensations from minor matrimonial impediments, as ecclesiastical crimes punishable by the Ordinary.[101]

Ordinary Rescripts of Favor are no longer invalidated by subreption unless something has been omitted which, according to the style of the Roman Curia, must be expressed for the validity of the rescript.[102] When such subreption occurs, the rescript becomes invalid *ipso jure.*[103] Canons 43 and 46 contain certain things which must be mentioned for the validity of the rescript:—the rest is determined by the style of the Curia, i.e., the rules of the

---

[99] Sanchez, *De Matrimonio,* lib. VIII, disp. XXI, n. 20, 25; De Justis, *De Dispensationibus,* lib. III, cap. I, n. 67; Pontius, *De Matrimonio,* lib. VIII, cap. XVII, n. 41; Reiffenstuel, *Jus Canonicum,* lib. I, tit. III, n. 196; Schmalzgrueber, *Jus Ecclesiasticum,* pars I, tit. III, n. 18; St. Alphonsus, *Theologia Moralis,* I, 185; Santi, *Praelectiones,* lib. I, tit. III, n. 11; D'Annibale, *Summula,* I, 240; Gasparri, *De Matrimonio,* n. 362; Lega, *S. R. Rota Decisiones,* Dec. IX, p. 134.

[100] Can. 991, §1.

[101] Can. 2361, 2195, §1.

[102] Can. 42, §1.

[103] Bartholinus, *De Subreptione Rescriptorum,* Quaest. XIV, n. 2; Wernz, *Jus Decretalium,* I, n. 153; Maroto, *Institutiones,* I, p. 320, nota (1).

various departments of the Curia which distribute papal favors, rules that have arisen from custom and statutes of Superiors, rules that vary with the department and with the specific favor involved.[104] When the petition omits something that, by common law or the style of the Curia, need not be mentioned for the validity of the rescript, the rescript remains valid even though the mentioning of the fact in the petition would have made the granting of the favor more difficult,[105] or even caused the Pope to refuse the favor.[106]

No attempt will be made to enumerate all the things that must be mentioned for the validity of different favors. The following are mentioned only by way of example. It is certain that in petitions for matrimonial dispensations it is necessary, for the validity of the rescript, to mention the species of the impediment and the degree of relationship. According to can. 1052, however, mentioning a closer degree of consanguinity or affinity would not invalidate the rescript. The petitioner is also bound to mention the nearer degree of relationship when the nearer degree in the mixed line is the first degree,[107] because before the Code both the style of the Sacred Penitentiary [108] and the style of the Apostolic Datary considered it as necessary for the validity of papal matrimonial dispensations, and there is no evidence that the style of the Sacred Congregation of the Sacraments has made any change in this regard.[110] There is no evidence, either, that the style of the Curia has changed

[104] Ayrinhac, *General Legislation,* p. 147-148; Cicognani, *Jus Canonicum,* II, p. 222.

[105] Sanchez, *De Matrimonio,* lib. VIII, disp. XXI, n. 11; Layman, *Theologia Moralis,* lib. I, tract. IV, cap. 22, n. 18.

[106] De Justis, *De dispensationibus,* lib. I, cap. IV, n. 31; Sanchez, *De Matrimonio,* lib. VIII, disp. XXI, n. 18; Pontius, *De Matrimonio,* lib. VIII, cap. XVII, n. 2; D'Annibale, *Summula,* I, 237.

[107] Chelodi, *Jus Matrimoniale,* n. 48; Ferreres, *Compendium Theologiae Moralis,* II, n. 960; Wernz-Vidal, *Jus Canonicum,* V, p. 529, nota (132); De Smet, *De Sponsalibus et Matrimonio,* p. 702, nota (4); Capello, *De Sacramentis,* III, n. 277; Vlaming, *Praelectiones,* n. 453 consider it as doubtful.

[108] Pius V, const. *"Sanctissimus,"* 20 Aug. 1566—Fontes, n. 114.

[109] Gasparri, *De Matrimonio,* n. 357, nota (1).

[110] Can. 6, n. 4. Cannot appeal to can. 96, §3, since the principle contained therein is already found in c. 9, X, *de consanguinitate,* IV, 14.

in regard to the necessity of mentioning, in petitions for dispensations to convalidate contracted marriages, the fact that the marriage had been contracted so that the dispensation could be obtained more easily. The obligation of mentioning this circumstance was contained in an instruction of the Propagation of the Faith issued on May 9, 1877,[111] and neither the decree of the Sacred Congregation of the Holy Office issued on June 25, 1885,[112] nor the decree of the same Congregation issued on March 18, 1891,[113] has altered the style of the Curia on the point in question, since in both cases reference was made to another circumstance, namely, the fact that the couple had committed an immoral act, *copula*, with or without the intention of being enabled to obtain a matrimonial dispensation. Since there is no evidence of change in the style of the Curia, it is necessary, in accordance with the old law, to conclude that the petitioners must mention the fact that they had invalidly contracted marriage in order to obtain the dispensation more easily.[114] Since it is not clear that the law of the instruction of the Sacred Penitentiary of May 9, 1877,[115] has been modified in their regard, it is also necessary to conclude that when more than one impediment of the same species in an equal or inferior degree must be dispensed from by Rome, all the impediments must be mentioned in the same petition,[116] and that when a public and occult impediment

---

[111] *Coll. de Prop. Fide*, n. 1470.

[112] "*. . . dispensationes matrimoniales posthac concedensas etiamsi copula incestuosa vel consilium vel intentio per eam facilius dispensationem impetrandi reticita fuerit, validas futuras.*"—*Coll. de Prop. Fide*, n. 1635.

[113] "*Dispensationes matrimoniales super quovis impedimentis, sive agatur de matrimoniis invalide contractis sive de contrahendis, esse validas etiamsi copula, vel consilium et intentio per eam facilius gratiam impetrandi reticita fuerint*"—*Coll. de Prop. Fide*, n. 1749.

[114] Can. 6, n. 4; De Smet, *De Sponsalibus et Matrimonio*, n. 848. Vlaming, *Praelectiones*, n. 432; Capello, *De Sacramentis*, III, n. 275; Kublebeck, *The Sacred Penitentiaria*, p. 91 deny that it is necessary. Wernz-Vidal, *Jus Canonicum*, V, p. 530, nota (134) considers both opinions as probable.

[115] *Coll. de Prop. Fide*, n. 1470.

[116] Can. 6, n. 4; De Smet, *De Sponsalibus et Matrimonio*, n. 847. Wernz-Vidal, *Jus Canonicum*, V, p. 530, nota (133); Capello, *De Sacramentis*, III, n. 275 consider it doubtful.

concur and both need the intervention of the Holy See, both must be mentioned in the petition to the Sacred Penitentiary.[117] In the law before the Code, it was doubtful whether the petitioner had to mention the fact of *"raptus non purgatus"*, [118] or the fact that the party whom the petitioner wished to marry was a heretic,[119] and since the present law has not clarified these points, they can still be considered as doubtful and therefore not binding.[120] In petitions made by religious persons to contract debts or obligations, under pain of invalidity of the rescript, mention must be made of the debts and obligations that already encumber the moral person, religion, province or house.[121] In petitions for dispensations from irregularities incurred by voluntary homicide the number of crimes must be mentioned.[122] Finally, in petitions for permission or consent to sell something that is divisible it is necessary, in order validly to receive the favor, to designate the parts that have already been sold.[123]

It is now definitely settled that obreption does not affect the validity of the rescript so long as there is one true motive cause mentioned in the petition, either the one proposed, or one of the many proposed.[124] Of course, if the obreption at the same time amounted to the omission of a circumstance that had to be mentioned for the validity,

---

[117] Can. 1050; De Smet, *De Sponsalibus et Matrimonio*, n. 853 bis; Genicot, *Theologia Moralis*, II, 527. Vermeersch, *Theologia Moralis*, III, n. 765; Vermeersch-Creusen, *Epitome*, II, n. 319; Capello, *De Sacramentis*, III, n. 275, 277 deny that it is necessary for validity.

[118] Zitelli, *De Dispensationibus*, pp. 73, 74; D'Annibale, *Summula*, III, n. 490 affirmed. Wernz, *Jus Decretalium*, n. 636, nota (179) denied.

[119] Feije, *De Impedimentis*, n. 701; Giovine, *De Dispensationibus*, II, §3; Wernz, *Jus Decretalium*, n. 636 affirmed. D'Annibale, *Summula*, III, n. 490, nota (19); Gasparri, *De Matrimonio*, n. 358, nota (1) denied.

[120] Can. 15. Chelodi, *Jus Matrimoniale*, n. 48 says both facts must still be mentioned for the validity. Capello; *De Sacramentis*, III, n. 277 says that it is more probable that it is not necessary to mention the *"raptus non purgatus,"* and probable, but not certain, that it is necessary to mention the heresy of the other party.

[121] Can. 534, §2.

[122] Can. 991, §2.

[123] Can. 1532, §4.

[124] Can. 42, §2.

e.g., if a non-Catholic in the petition claimed to be a Catholic, the case would be altered and the case would be judged according to the principles governing subreption. When only impulsive causes are proposed, they are considered as forming one motive cause, and obreption in any of them would nullify the rescript,[125] unless there are so many of them that the defect of one or the other would be considered as practically negligible.[126] In determining, in specific instances, which causes are motive and which causes are impulsive, one must be guided by the style and practice of the Curia, the law or the nature of the thing concerned,[127] not by conjectures about the intention of the grantor:—otherwise, continual perplexities and uncertainties would ensue.[128]

If, after the rescript has been granted, doubts arise about the character of the cause, v.g., whether the remaining cause is motive, or about the nature of certain circumstances that were omitted or incorrectly given, the old principle "*standum est pro valore actus*" still holds. Some authors,[129] while admitting this conclusion in theory, advise in practice, whenever there is available time, to seek a rescript "*Perinde Valere*," i.e., a letter that declares the rescript to be valid as if it were valid from the beginning. Seeking a rescript "*Perinde Valere*" in such circumstances seems entirely unnecessary, however, since the Code itself[130] states that a dispensation can be lawfully petitioned and validly and lawfully granted even if it is doubtful whether the cause is sufficient, and since the principle "*standum est pro valore actus*," offered by leading canonists and moralists, was intended not to solve theoretical questions but

[125] Ojetti, *Commentarium*, I, p. 226; Cicognani, *Commentarium*, p. 223.

[126] Coronata, *Institutiones Juris Canonici*, I, p. 63, nota (7); Capello, *Summa*, I, n. 152; Michiels, *Normae Generales*, II, p. 226.

[127] Sanchez, *De Matrimonio*, lib, VIII, disp. XXI, n. 19; Reiffenstuel, *Jus Canonicum*, lib. I, tit. III, n. 195; Cicognani, *Commentarium*, p. 223.

[128] D'Annibale, *Summula*, I, 238, nota (12); Coronata, *Institutiones*, I, n. 64.

[129] Chelodi, *Jus De Personis*, n. 78; De Smet, *De Sponsalibus et Matrimonio*, n. 921; Capellò, *Summa*, I, n. 152; Michiels, *Normae Generales*, II, p. 231.

[130] Can. 84, §2.

practical difficulties. Only in case it is *certain* that there is no true remaining motive cause or that something essential has been omitted or incorrectly stated is there any obligation to seek a rescript *"Perinde Valere."*[131]

When there is question, now, of obreption or subreption in rescripts containing more than one favor, the Old Roman Law and Decretal Law principles are to be applied strictly and absolutely;—the norm is very simple—only that part of the rescript, only that favor is invalidated, which is directly affected by the Subreption or Obreption.[132]

Michiels[133] claims that in the past, as well as at present, canonists more commonly maintained that subreption or obreption should be judged according to the petition that was sent to Rome, not by the summary of the petition contained in the rescript, and concludes that such a view is in accordance with right reason and substantiated by the words of the present law, since obviously the word *"preces"* refers to the petition sent by the petitioner, and only in the petition that he sent to Rome can the petitioner be said to *"reticere verum," "proponere causam," "exponere falsum"*, or to express the *"veritatem alioquin ad validitatem necessariam."* As a matter of fact, however, the external authority claimed by Michiels for his view really does not seem to be as imposing as he claims, since some of the authors quoted by him[134] did not *"ex professo"* discuss this question or state definitely and unmistakably that subreption or obreption was to be determined by the petition send to the Roman Curia and not by its summary in the rescript itself. At the same time, representative canon-

---

[131] De Meester, *Compendium,* I, n. 297; De Smet, *De Sponsalibus et Matrimonio,* n. 924.

[132] Can. 42, §3.

[133] *Normae Generales,* II, p. 214.

[134] Reiffenstuel, *Jus Canonicum,* lib. I, tit. III, n. 152; Chelodi, *Jus De Personis,* n. 78; Ojetti, *Commentarium,* p. 224. Reiffenstuel, *o. c.,* lib. I, tit. III, n. 194; Chelodi, *o. c.,* p. 139, nota (1), in particular instances, seem to view subreption and obreption in connection with the summary of the petition in the rescript.

ists of the old[135] and the new law[136] very definitely maintain that subreption and obreption must ultimately be judged by the summary of the petition contained in the rescript itself. The words of can. 42 can certainly be understood in this sense, because "*reticentia veri*" or "*expositio falsi in precibus*" in §1 and §2 can refer to the summary of the petition in the rescript, which generally contains the proposed causes and the necessary circumstances that were mentioned in the *libellus* sent to Rome, just as well as to the *libellus* itself, while the words of §3, "*Vitium obreptionis vel subreptionis in una tantum parte rescripti,*" favor the view that looks to the summary of the petition in the rescript for the substantiation and determination of subreption or obreption. Nor does such a view seem to be in opposition to right reason. After all, the presumption holds that the grantor of the favor was influenced by the circumstances and reasons as stated in the narrative and motive part of the rescript:—otherwise, their presence in the rescript would seem rather unnecessary. Finally, the circumstances and causes, as understood and acted upon by the grantor, are generally available for the executor or the beneficiary in the narrative and motive parts of the rescript[137] for comparison with the facts, whereas it might very easily happen that no copy of the petition sent to Rome would be retained by the sender. These reasons of authority and of fitness, as well as the juridical reason derived from the wording of the present law, undoubtedly justify adherence to the view formerly maintained by Sanchez and D'Annibale.

The special principles that determine the effects of subreption and obreption on Rescripts granted "*Motu Proprio*" and on Rescripts containing dispensations from minor

---

135 Sanchez, *De Matrimonio*, lib. VIII, disp. XXI, n. 57; D'Annibale, *Summula*, I, 236, nota (2).

136 Coronata, *Institutiones*, I, p. 60, nota (8); Haring, *Grundzüge*, p. 67, nota (7); Leitner, *Handbuck*, p. 49.

137 The circumstances are sometimes omitted when the circumstances or the favors are of minor importance.

matrimonial impediments are contained in the following canons:

Canon 45.—Cum rescriptis ad preces alicuius impetratis apponitur clausula: ***Motu proprio***, valent quidem ea, si in precibus reticeatur veritas alioquin necessario exprimenda, non tamen si falso causa finalis eaque unica proponatur, salvo praescripto can. 1054.

Canon 1054.—Dispensatio a minore impedimento concessa, nullo sive obreptionis sive subreptionis vitio irritatur, etsi unica causa finalis in precibus exposita falsa fuerit.

Two Decretals[138] declared that papal grants of favors were not invalidated by the concealment of certain circumstances when it was clear that the favor had been granted "*motu proprio*" by the Pope. Since the Decretals merely mentioned subreption as being affected by the "*motu proprio*" clause, canonists concluded that subreption of necessary circumstances, not obreption of a motive cause, lost its invalidating power when found in rescripts containing the "*motu proprio*" clause. They argued that subreption was not invalidating in such rescripts, because the Pope granted the favor as though he had not been petitioned for it, and, consequently, as though unconcerned whether or not certain circumstances had been mentioned in the petition; whereas obreption of the motive cause would remain invalidating, because there always remained the possibility that the grantor had been deceived by the motive cause, and, of course, even a "*motu proprio*" clause would not confirm a favor contrary to the intention of the grantor.[139] There has been no change introduced by the present law in this respect:—the only time that Subreption or Obreption affects the "*Motu Proprio*" Rescript is when the sole remaining motive cause is false. At present, obreption about the circumstances that otherwise must be

---

[138] C. 23, *de praebendis et dignitatibus*, III, 4, in VI°; c. 4, *de praebendis et dignitatibus*, III, 2, in Clem.

[139] Sanchez, *De Matrimonio*, lib. VIII, disp. XXI, n. 47, 52; De Justis, *De Dispensationibus*, lib. I, cap. IV, n. 40; Reiffenstuel, *Jus Canonicum*, lib. I, tit. III, n. 203-207; Schmalzgrueber, *Jus Ecclesiasticum*, pars I, tit. III, n. 11; D'Annibale, *Summula*, I, 240.

expressed for the validity of the ordinary rescript does not invalidate rescripts containing the *"motu proprio"* clause.[140] This was commonly taught by ancient canonists[141] and, although not explicitly stated in the present canon, is, nevertheless, therein implied. The canon states that the rescript containing the *"motu proprio"* clause remains valid despite the fact that circumstances that otherwise must be expressed for the validity of the rescript are omitted, but not if the sole final cause proposed is false. Evidently, the meaning of the legislator is that, despite any other defects arising from the omission of the truth or falsification, the *"Motu Proprio"* rescript remains valid as long as one motive cause remains true. Obreption about the necessary circumstances indirectly amount to subreption of them and, undoubtedly, as far as the validity of the rescript is concerned, the legislator in can. 45 combines obreption and subreption of the necessary circumstances under the single term of subreption of the necessary circumstances, as he does for all practical purposes in can. 42, §1, §2. Therefore, if circumstances that are required for the validity of the ordinary rescript are either omitted or falsely narrated in the petition for a rescript containing the clause *"motu proprio,"* the *"Motu Proprio"* Rescript will not thereby be invalidated. Therein lies the real and only difference between the ordinary and the *"Motu Proprio"* rescript, as far as the effect of subreption or obreption on them is concerned, since for both kinds of rescripts it is always necessary that one motive cause be true.

Since the law of 1908,[142] the validity of dispensations from the minor matrimonial impediments is in no way affected by subreption or obreption, even by obreption in the sole motive cause. The reason that has probably prompted the Church to grant this concession is the presumption that some reasonable cause prompts the parties to ask for such favors, even though the reason may not be

---

140 Michiels, *Normae Generales*, II, p. 227.

141 Sanchez, *l. c.;* De Justis, *l. c.;* Reiffenstuel, *l. c.;* D'Annibale, *l. c.*

142 *"Normae Peculiares,"* cap. VII, art. III, n. 21—AAS, I (1909), 92.

mentioned in the petition.[143] But even though no such reasonable cause existed, the dispensation would still be valid. The minor matrimonial impediments at present are consanguinity in the third degree of the collateral line, affinity in the second degree of the collateral line, public honesty in the second degree, spiritual relationship, and crime resulting from adultery combined with the promise or attempt to marry, even by a civil act.[144] Ordinarily, the only papal rescripts that will contain such dispensations will be rescripts from the Sacred Penitentiary, since local Ordinaries have in their Quinquennial Faculties the delegated power to dispense from minor impediments for the external forum.[145]

Article V.—The Effect of Error on the Validity of Rescripts

Canon 47.—Rescripta non fiunt irrita ob errorem in nomine personae cui vel a qua conceduntur, aut loci in quo ipsa moratur, aut rei de qua agitur, dummodo, iudicio Ordinarii, nulla sit de ipsa persona vel re dubitatio.

It has always been necessary to designate, clearly and specifically, by name, the persons to whom and by whom the favors were granted, their place of residence, and the favors that were granted. Before the Code it was somewhat uncertain exactly what effect an error in the name or family name of the petitioner or grantor would have upon the validity of the rescript. Some authors[146] contended that as long as the identity of the person for whom the petition was intended was certain, an error in the name of the person would not vitiate the rescript, because the Pope intended to grant the favor to the petitioner and not to Peter or Paul, and what influenced him to grant the

[143] Vermeersch-Creusen, *Epitome*, II, n. 318.

[144] Can. 1042, §2.

[145] Vermeersch-Creusen, *Epitome*, I, p. 537, nota (1).

[146] Sanchez, *De Matrimonio*, lib. VIII, disp. XXI, n. 37, 38; De Justis, *De Dispensationibus*, lib. I, cap. IV, n. 54, 55; Reiffenstuel, *Jus Canonicum*, lib. I, tit. III, n. 220; Layman, *Theologia Moralis*, lib. I, tract IV, cap. 22, n. 27.

favor was not the name, but the person and the intrinsic qualities of the petitioner. Others [147] made the following distinction:—if the error in the name merely concerned the quality of the person and it was clear which person was intended, the rescript would be valid, but if the error concerned the person itself, the rescript would be invalid, even though it was clear which person was intended. All agreed, however, that if the error was insignificant, e.g., the change or omission of a letter, the validity of the rescript would not be affected.[148] That invalidations from this source were not considered uncommon may be judged from the fact that power to sanate and convalidate papal matrimonial dispensations that had been vitiated by error in the names and family names of the parties, was formerly included in the faculties granted to the Ordinaries,[149] or Apostolic Delegates, Nuntios, etc., e.g., the faculties granted to the Nuntio of Spain to sanate and convalidate all marriages of the poor that had been invalidly contracted on account of the presence in papal dispensations of errors in the names of persons.[150] Even greater uncertainty existed about errors in the name of the place. Some [151] canonists said that as long as it was clear which place was meant, an error in the name of the place would not vitiate the rescript; others [152] said that even under such circumstances the rescript would more probably be invalid; while others [153] made the same distinction as they did about errors in the name of the person, namely, between errors about the quality of the place, and errors about the place itself. This latter opinion seems to have been the accepted teaching when errors about the thing, i.e., the favor, were concerned:—when it was

---

[147] Pirhing, *Jus Canonicum*, lib. I, tit. III, n. 63 sq; D'Annibale, *Summula*, III, 449, nota (4).

[148] C. 11, X, *de fide instrumentorum*, II, 22; Wernz, *Jus Decretalium*, I, n. 153.

[149] De Smet, *De Sponsalibus et Matrimonio*, p. 701, nota (4); Chelodi, *Jus De Personis*, p. 137, nota (3).

[150] Giovine, *De Dispensationibus*, II, §2, n. 4.

[151] Reiffenstuel, *Jus Canonicum*, lib. I, tit. III, n. 223.

[152] Sanchez, *De Matrimonio*, lib. VIII, disp. XXI, n. 39; De Justis, *De Dispensationibus*, lib. I, cap. IV, n. 67-69.

[153] Pirhing, *Jus Canonicum*, lib. I, tit. III, n. 63 sq.; D'Annibale, *Summula*, III, 449, nota (4).

clear what favor had been granted, errors about the thing itself would invalidate the rescript, whereas errors about the qualities of the thing would not nullify the rescript.

The present law clarifies somewhat the problem of errors in Rescripts. Now, no matter what errors in the names of the persons, place, or thing occur in the rescript, the rescript remains valid, unless, in the judgment of the Ordinary, there is a serious doubt about the identity of the person or thing. The fact that the particle "*dummodo*" [154] certainly modifies the clause "*nulla sit de ipsa persona vel re dubitatio,*" necessitates the conclusion that whenever a real doubt about the identity of the person or place continues, the rescript becomes invalid. The construction of the canon might also lead one to conclude that in cases of errors in the rescript, the rescript would not only be illicit but also invalid, unless the rescript is presented to the Ordinary for decision. It hardly seems possible, however, that the legislator intends to impose an obligation, under pain of nullity to the rescript, of presenting to the Ordinary all Rescripts of the Sacred Penitentiary that have been rendered doubtful by error; nor to some canonists is it entirely clear that he wishes to impose this obligation on others who are not usually required to present their rescripts to the Ordinary, e.g., recipients of rescripts granted in the external forum *in forma gratiosa,* in which the recipient alone is concerned.[155] Taking all things into account, one is justified in concluding that only the main clause "*dummodo nulla sit de ipsa persona vel re dubitatio*" is an essential condition in the present canon, and that the clause "*iudicio Ordinarii*" is only an accidental condition that imposes an obligation of presenting all doubtful rescripts to the Ordinary, excepting those which by their very nature forbid presentation. From such an interpretation, it follows that errors in the names of the person, place, or thing bring about invalidation of rescripts only when the identity of the persons or thing remains doubtful; that subjection of the doubt to the judgment of the Ordi-

[154] Can. 39.

[155] Can. 51; Ojetti, *Commentarium,* I, p. 239; Vermeersch-Creusen, *Epitome,* I, n. 135.

nary is never required for the validity of the rescript;[156] that submission of the doubt to the Ordinary for solution is required for the lawful use of the rescript, except when the nature of the rescript forbids it, e.g., rescripts of the sacramental internal forum.[157] To make any further exceptions to the duty of subjecting doubt to the judgment of the Ordinary would really deprive the clause "*iudicio Ordinarii*" of any real meaning in this canon, since there would be no necessity to repeat an obligation that would be already indirectly contained in can. 51 and 52. Moreover, it might be well to observe that the present canon does not speak of the local Ordinary, but of the Ordinary in general, and that it makes no distinction between the different rescripts, as far as submission of the doubt is concerned. There certainly is, however, sufficient justification to exempt rescripts of the internal sacramental forum from this obligation, but scarcely any positive reason to make any other exemption, especially since it is evidently the purpose of the legislator to provide so that all doubts arising from errors in the rescripts should be decided by someone in authority.

Undoubtedly, when the error in the rescript concerns the person or thing, the rescript becomes invalid whenever the identity of the person or the thing cannot be clearly and certainly ascertained. It seems that the same would hold true when the error concerns the place of residence,[158] and the identity of the person or the thing remains doubtful,[159] since the canon explicitly mentions error about the place of residence together with errors about person or thing and

---

156 Contra Michiels, *Normae Generales*, II, pp. 244, 245, who considers "*iudicio Ordinarii*" to be an essential element of the substantial condition. While maintaining that it is desirable that the judgment of the Ordinary be explicit, he admits that a tacit or implicit judgment suffices, and even a prudently presumed judgment, if there is question only of an accidental error of minor importance.

157 Contra Michiels, *Normae Generales*, II, pp. 244, 245, who claims that, in case of doubt, the confessor must have recourse to the Sacred Penitentiary.

158 Augustine, *A Commentary*, I, p. 135, nota (13), is not correct in stating that "diocese" is not included in "*loci in quo ipsa moratur.*"

159 Cf. Ojetti, *Commentarium*, I, p. 240, who holds the opposite opinion.

states that rescripts do not become invalid on account of the presence of these errors, provided no doubt remains about the person or the thing. As a matter of fact, it may very easily happen that an error in the name of the place may cause uncertainty about the person of the petitioner. We should conclude, therefore, that the same obligation rests upon those who receive rescripts that contain errors in the name of the place as upon those who receive rescripts containing errors in the name of the persons or thing.

Not only errors in the name of the persons, place, or thing, but also erasures, errors in latinity, and absence of the customary solemnities of rescripts were at one time considered important problems of interpretation. Decretal law stated that an important erasure in the dispositive part of the rescript,[160] not an erasure in another part, nor the mere change of a few letters without a change in sense,[161] would nullify a rescript. Some authors [162] modified somewhat the strict words of the Decretal by maintaining that an erasure in a suspected or substantial part, e.g., the dispositive part, merely rendered the rescript suspect, merely gave it a presumption of falsity, a presumption which would, however, give way if, from the document itself and various circumstances, it appeared certain that the erasure had been made by the notary; others,[163] however, insisted that an erasure in a substantial and suspected part would render the rescript invalid. The *"Normae Peculiares"* [164] instructed all officials of the Curia to make a particular note, with special signature, of any erasures in the papal documents, but even this precaution did not entirely remedy the situation.[165] Manifest errors of latinity were also considered by some

---

[160] C. 7, X, *de statu monachorum,* III, 36.

[161] C. 3, X, *de fide instrumentorum,* II, 22; Reiffenstuel, *Jus Canonicum,* lib. I, tit. III, n. 226; Wernz, *Jus Decretalium,* I, n. 153.

[162] Reiffenstuel, *Jus Canonicum,* lib. I, tit. III, n. 224-229; De Angelis, *Praelectiones,* lib. I, tit. III, n. 4; Santi, *Praelectiones,* lib. I, tit. III, n. 9.

[163] Soglia, *Institutiones,* pars I, cap. I, par. 31; Vecchiotti, *Institutiones,* pars I, cap. I, §53; Wernz, *Jus Decretalium,* I, n. 153; Smith, *Elements of Ecclesiastical Law,* p. 29. Cf. Santi, *Praelectiones,* lib. I, tit. III, n. 9, regarding matrimonial dispensations.

[164] Cap. VI, n. 6—AAS, I (1909), 73.

[165] Cicognani, *Commentarium,* p. 235.

as invalidating,[166] and by others as giving legitimate cause to suspect a rescript.[167] The canonists who upheld the latter view reasoned that, since the document passed through so many hands and received such careful attention from such competent officials, the presence of errors in the Latin would give a presumption that the rescript was falsified, a presumption which would, of course, yield to truth in particular instances if it could be shown that the document otherwise appeared authentic and that the errors of latinity could be ascribed to oversight on the part of the officials. Finally, canonists taught that defects in the customary solemnities of Rescripts, Bulls, Briefs, or Simple Rescripts, invalidated rescripts.[168]

In the present law, there is neither direct nor indirect reference made to erasures, errors in latinity, or absence of solemnities of Rescripts. The absence of solemnities, e.g., the omission of the year, month, day, place, name of Pope, or incorrect usage of forms of address, e.g., calling a Bishop "*dilectus filius*" instead of "*venerabilis frater,*" are considered now as merely giving basis for suspecting the authenticity of the rescript,[169] or as being of minor importance.[170] The vast majority of authors[171] also maintain that erasures and errors of latinity give sufficient cause to suspect the authenticity of the rescript, but do not *ipso facto* invalidate them. De Meester[172] claims that, on account of can. 47, in particular cases the Ordinary should be consulted in order to decide whether the rescripts are

---

[166] Wernz, *Jus Decretalium,* I, n. 153; Soglia, *Institutiones,* pars I, tit. III, §31; Smith, *Element of Ecclesiastical Law,* p. 29.

[167] Reiffenstuel, *Jus Canonicum,* lib. I, tit. III, n. 212-215; Schmalzgrueber, *Jus Ecclesiasticum,* pars I, tit. III, n. 13; Santi, *Praelectiones,* lib. I, tit. III, n. 9.

[168] Wernz, *Jus Decretalium,* I, n. 153.

[169] Maroto, *Institutiones Juris Canonici,* n. 284; Ojetti, *Commentarium in Codicem,* I, p. 235.

[170] Chelodi, *Jus De Personis,* n. 77.

[171] Maroto, *Institutiones,* n. 284; Augustine, *A Commentary,* I, p. 136; Cocchi, *Commentarium,* I, p. 153; Raus, *Institutiones,* n. 39; Toso, *Commentaria Minora,* I, p. 133; De Smet, *De Sponsalibus et Matrimonio,* n. 922; Coronata, *Institutiones,* I, p. 65, nota (1); Torrubiano Ripoll, *Novissimas Institutiones,* I, 178; Michiels, *Normae Generales,* II, p. 234.

[172] *Compendium,* n. 295.

valid or invalid. Ojetti, however,[173] retaining the strict view of some of the older canonists, insists that manifest and grave errors in Latin diction render the rescript invalid, and that erasures in a substantial and suspected place have the same effect, unless it is clear, from an annotation in the rescript itself, or from the fact that the rescript was given signed and sealed to the Ordinary, that the erasure was made by an official of the Curia.

It must be admitted that the importance of this question has been greatly diminished by the fact that the Holy See ordinarily acts in the external forum through the execution of the Ordinaries, who can usually ascertain whether the erasures or errors arise from mistakes of Roman officials.[174] Judging the case in the light of the past disputes of canonists, as well as the present view of authors, it seems difficult to claim more than that erasures and errors in Latin diction give reasonable grounds to suspect a falsified rescript.[175] The person to decide whether or not the suspicion is well founded will usually be the executor, for rescripts granted *in forma commissoria;* the Ordinary, for rescripts granted *in forma gratiosa* that must be presented to the Ordinary; and the recipient, for rescripts granted *in forma gratiosa* which need not be presented. There seems to be no evidence that a new obligation of presentation or subjection to others for judgment has been imposed by the legislator for such cases, and it seems entirely unnecessary to invoke can. 20, *"a legibus latis in similibus,"* since the doubts arising from such defects will not ordinarily require the intervention of one with authority.

Forgers or falsifiers of Papal Rescripts, as well as persons who knowingly use such forged or falsified documents, incur ecclesiastical penalties:—they incur *ipso facto* an excommunication reserved in a special way to the Holy See; if they are clerics, other penalties may be imposed upon them, even privation of benefice, office, dignity, and ecclesiastical pension; if they are religious, they may be deprived of offices held in the Order, active and passive vote, besides

---

173 *Commentarium,* I, pp. 235, 236.
174 Chelodi, *Jus De Personis,* n. 77.
175 Can. 6, n. 6, 11, 15.

the other penalties imposed by their respective constitutions.[176]

Article VI.—The Effect of Previous Refusal on the Favor

Innocent XII, in his decree *"Ut occuratur,"* issued on June 4, 1692,[177] ordained that once a person, of his own accord, had petitioned a favor from a Congregation and the Congregation accepted the petition, he could not, under any pretext, discontinue negotiations in order to send a petition about the same matter to another Congregation; and that if the second Congregation actually granted a rescript, it would be null and void. Although, in the reorganization of the Roman Curia, Pius X endeavored to eliminate the conflict of rights between the various departments of the Curia, in order to provide for particular cases in which doubt or error might still cause a conflict, he declared that once a petition for a favor had been sent to a department, transfer of the matter could validly be done only with the consent of the first department or by permission of the Congregation of the Sacred Consistory.[178] At present, only a few matters pertaining to the same forum are settled by different departments, e.g., reduction of obligations of masses by the Sacred Congregation of the Council and by the Sacred Congregation of the Fabric of St. Peter,[179] and, therefore, transferring from one department to another is very infrequent. Nevertheless, the legislator still finds it advisable to make the following special provisions for such cases.

Canon 43.—Gratia ab una Sacra Congregatione vel Officio Romanae Curiae denegata, invalide ab alia Sacra Congregatione vel Officio aut a loci Ordinario, etsi potestatem habente, conceditur, sine assensu Sacrae Congregationis vel Officii quocum ve quibuscum agi coeptum fuit, salvo iure S. Poenitentiariae pro foro interno.

---

[176] Can. 2360.

[177] Anal. Juris Pont., II (1857), p. 2279; Ojetti, *Commentarium*, pp. 227, 228.

[178] *"Normae Peculiares,"* cap. I, n. 1—AAS, I (1909), 53.

[179] Vermeersch-Creusen, *Epitome*, I, n. 127.

At present, the mere fact that a petition for a favor has been *sent* to one department of the Curia and has been *accepted* by it, does not prevent another department, with proper jurisdiction, from validly receiving and granting the favor to the person. The present canon specifies that only when the favor has been *denied* by one department, is the power of the other department suspended. The same holds true for local Ordinaries, because even though petitions for favors have been sent to the Roman Curia, their ordinary or delegated powers are not thereby suspended, nor do they act invalidly in granting the favor until the Holy See has refused the petition. If a petition has been sent to Rome they are merely *forbidden* to use their powers unless a grave or urgent reason requires it.[180] In the Roman Curia, in case one department denies a favor, the only time that another department can validly grant it without the consent of the first department is when the Sacred Penitentiary and the internal forum are involved, i.e., a favor denied by the Roman Curia in the external forum can validly be granted by the Sacred Penitentiary in the internal forum without receiving the consent of the other department.

Some authors,[181] while admitting that the case is not very practical, claim that a favor denied by the Sacred Penitentiary can be validly granted by the respective Congregation or Office in the external forum without obtaining permission from the Sacred Penitentiary to transfer the matter. They base their claim on the fact that the canon refers only to a denial by a Congregation or an Office, whereas the Sacred Penitentiary is a Tribunal. This claim is denied by most canonists who refer to the question,[182] and rightly so. The argument just mentioned is not very convincing when the full context of the canon is taken into account. The fact that the clause "*salvo iure S. Poenitentiariae pro foro interno*" is placed in the canon indicates

---

[180] Can. 204, §1, 1048.

[181] Ojetti, *Commentarium*, I, p. 230; Capello, *Summa*, I, n. 145; Michiels, *Normae Generales*, II, pp. 181, 182.

[182] Maroto, *Institutiones*, I, p. 322, nota (2); Ayrinhac, *General Legislation*, p. 150; Vermeersch-Creusen, *Epitome*, I, n. 127; Cicognani, *Commentarium*, p. 227; Chelodi, *Jus De Personis*, p. 138, nota (3); Coronata, *Institutiones*, I, n. 63.

that the terms *Congregation* and *Office* are not to be understood in this canon as excluding all Tribunals, but rather as embracing the Sacred Penitentiary which grants for the internal forum the favors that are granted by the Congregations and Offices for the external forum. Under any other interpretation of the terms, the insertion of the clause "*salvo iure...*" becomes useless and meaningless. There is no question here of invoking a strict interpretation,[183] because the context of the canon, the addition of the final clause, allows of only one interpretation. Moreover, the special reason for permitting the grant of a favor in the internal forum after it had been denied in the external forum does not apply to the case under consideration. When a favor is granted in the internal forum after being denied in the external forum, the favor is not effective in the forum in which it was denied, whereas a favor granted in the external forum after being denied in the internal forum, applies immediately for the forum in which it was denied, and applies despite the fact that the reasons that prompted the first denial were not mentioned in the application for the second rescript.[184] Evidently the intention of the legislator is to avoid anything of this nature. Consequently, there does not seem to be any strong juridical basis for the opinion that insists that a person, who is refused a favor by the Sacred Penitentiary, can obtain the same favor from a department of the Roman Curia that grants favors in the external forum without first obtaining permission of the Sacred Penitentiary.

Another disputed point concerns the status of Ordinaries other than local Ordinaries, v.g., Major Superiors in clerical exempt religious institutes.[185] There is no doubt that until the favor has been denied by the Roman Curia, they can validly grant a favor petitioned from Rome, and can even lawfully grant such a favor when a grave and urgent cause demands their intervention.[186] The controverted point

---

[183] Can. 19; Ojetti, *Commentarium*, I, p. 148.

[184] Cicognani, *Commentarium*, p. 227. Sometimes, of course, rescripts for the non-sacramental forum can be used for the external forum, but only *per accidens*.

[185] Can. 198.

[186] Can. 204.

concerns their power to validly grant a favor that has been denied by the Roman Curia. A few authors [187] claim that they are in the same status as local Ordinaries. Ojetti argues on the principle "*si a recta ratione alienum videatur mentiri voluntatem ex verbis, non oportet jus calumniari et verba captare, sed quae mens legislatoris fuerit, animadvertere,*" [188] and explains, by quotations from Barbosa,[189] that the principle "*inclusio unius est exclusio alterius*" is not true in all cases. Other authors [190] take the opposite view. While admitting that the exemption accorded Major Superiors of clerical exempt religious institutes seems strange, they accept the words of the canon as they are given, maintaining that it is impossible to presume that the legislator has used superfluous words, as the application of the words "*Ordinarii loci*" to Major Superiors would necessitate. Admitting also the strangeness of the exemption, it seems difficult to interpret the canon in any other way than according to the interpretation of this latter view. To interpret it otherwise would involve the application of not merely a broad but of an extensive interpretation to can. 47, since the Code itself states that "*Ordinarii loci*" is to be understood as excluding Major Superiors.[191] The context of the canon affords no reason for any other than a strict interpretation of the words "*Ordinarii loci.*" Therefore, since an invalidating law is concerned, a law which Ojetti [192] himself admits is included among the laws that restrict the free exercise of rights, it is difficult to see how, merely on the grounds of fitness, a broad declarative and much less an extensive interpretation can be applied in

---

[187] Ojetti, *Commentarium,* I, pp. 229, 230; Capello, *Summa,* I, n. 145.

[188] D. X. 4. 19; D'Annibale, *Summula,* I, 185.

[189] *Tractatus Varii, Axiomata juris usufrequentissima,* ax. 120.

[190] Chelodi, *Jus De Personis,* p. 138, nota (1); Coronata, *Institutiones,* I, p. 62, nota (1); Michiels, *Normae Generales,* II, pp. 179, 180, who considers that the presence of the word "*loci*" in the canon is most probably due to inadvertence or an error, but at the same time recognizes the necessity of accepting the word as it is found in the canon.

[191] Can. 198, §2.

[192] *Commentarium,* I, p. 148.

this case.[193] The least that can be said is that the law, as far as Major Superiors are concerned, is doubtful and, therefore, not binding.[194]

The present law forbids, under penalty of nullity of the rescript, the unauthorized transferring of a petition for a favor to another department of the Roman Curia or to the local Ordinary after the favor had been denied by a department of the Roman Curia, but it does not forbid a person to go to the same department of the Roman Curia without mentioning a previous denial,[195] or to recourse to the Roman Curia without mentioning that the favor had been denied by the Ordinary. In the latter case, however, if no letter of recommendation from the Ordinary accompanies the petition, or if it is known that the Ordinary possesses the power to grant the favor, the petition or the petitioner will be referred to the Ordinary. In the same way it is possible, theoretically, to recourse to the person of the Pope without mentioning a previous denial by the Roman Curia, but in practice the attempt would be unavailing because invariably the response would be "*Accede ad S. Congregationem,*" or the like.[196] Some authors [197] claim that if the Pope orally denies a favor it cannot be validly granted by the Roman Curia or by the Ordinary, but other canonists,[198] with strong juridical arguments, deny that the oral refusal of a favor by the Pope invalidates a later rescript. There is nothing in the present law on Rescripts that directly or indirectly

---

[193] Can. 19. N. B. The words *Congregation* and *Office,* in this canon, were given a broad interpretation not merely on account of reasons of fitness but especially because the context of the canon clearly indicates the sense in which the words are to be taken.

[194] Can. 15.

[195] Vermeersch-Creusen, *Epitome,* I, n. 127; Coronata, *Institutiones,* I, n. 63.

[196] Maroto, *Institutiones,* n. 284; Cicognani, *Commentarium,* p. 226.

[197] Maroto, *Institutiones,* n. 284; Ayrinhac, *General Legislation,* p. 150; Cicognani, *Commentarium,* p. 226; De Meester, *Compendium,* I, p. 194, nota (4).

[198] Vermeersch-Creusen, *Epitome,* I, n. 127; Michiels, *Normae Generales,* II, pp. 178, 179; Capello, *Summa,* I, n. 145; Coronata, *Institutiones,* I, n. 62.

settles this question. Consequently, although it may seem somewhat strange, one should conclude from canons 11 and 19 that oral refusal of a favor by the Pope would not invalidate a later rescript of the Holy See or of another Ordinary granting the same favor.

Article VII.—Certain Limitations of "Motu Proprio" Rescripts

In Article IV of this Chapter, mention has been made of the limitation that common law has placed upon *"Motu Proprio" Rescripts* as far as Subreption and Obreption are concerned:—other limitations of these rescripts are treated in the present Article.

The Church has always insisted that there are certain circumstances of persons, places, and things, namely the fact that certain persons are incapacitated by law from receiving favors,[199] legitimate customs and statutes of particular localities,[200] and the acquired rights of others,[201] that cannot be presumed to be known or taken into account by the Pope when he grants Rescripts, even *"Motu Proprio"* Rescripts, unless reference is made to them by a special clause in the rescript. It was definitely stated, before the Code, that a *"Motu Proprio"* Rescript, without a special clause, did not change the status of a person who was unable to receive papal favors, nor grant a favor against the custom or particular statute of a church or place, nor become prejudicial to the acquired rights of others,[202] but it was admitted that if the parties, whose rights were interfered with, knew of the prejudicial rescript and did not

---

[199] Reiffenstuel, *Jus Canonicum,* lib. I, tit. III, n. 208.

[200] C. 10, *de rescriptis,* I, 3, in VI°; Menochius, *De Praesumptionibus,* lib. VI, praes. XXXIX, n. 3 sq.; Leurenius, *Forum Ecclesiasticum,* q. 300, n. 5; Reiffenstuel, *Jus Canonicum,* lib. I, tit. III, n. 200.

[201] C. 6, X, *de rescriptis,* I, 3; Reg. Cancell., Reg. XVIII, *"De non tollendo jus quaesitum"*; Barbosa, *Tractatus Varii, De Clausulis usufrequentissimis,* claus. 79, n. 19; Reiffenstuel, *Jus Canonicum,* lib. I, tit. III, n. 210.

[202] Reiffenstuel, *Jus Canonicum,* lib. I, tit. III, n. 200, 208, 210.

oppose it, the rescript would not be invalid.[203] This ancient law has been retained by the Code in the following canon:

Canon 46.—Rescripta etiam *Motu Proprio* concessa personae de iure communi inhabili ad consequendam gratiam de qua agitur, itemque edita contra alicuius loci legitimam consuetudinem vel statutum peculiare, vel contra ius alteri iam quaesitum, non sustinentur, nisi expressa derogatoria clausula rescripto apponatur.

Disqualification, as far as papal favors are concerned, may be *absolute,* i.e., extending to all favors, e.g., disqualification incurred by censures after a declaratory or condemnatory sentence,[204] or *relative,* i.e., extending only to certain favors, v.g., disqualification arising either from personal defects, e.g., illegitimacy, bigamy, irregularity, lack of age or orders, from possession of an incompatable office or benefice,[205] or from vindicative penalties.[206] *Custom,* referred to in the canon, is a legitimate custom of a nation, diocese, province or religious order, in existence for forty continuous and complete years; *particular statute,* is a law of a Bishop or of a particular Synod or Council. *Acquired rights* are to be understood here as rights in the broad sense of the term and, therefore, including rights that have been acquired by law, privileges, indults, dispensations, or favors.[207]

There is a wide divergence of opinion regarding the effect that these various circumstances have upon "*Motu Proprio*" Rescripts. Some canonists [208] claim that they render the rescripts invalid; Michiels [209] maintains that although the rescripts are not invalidated, i.e., although they still have the intrinsic requisites necessary for a re-

---

[203] D'Annibale, *Summula,* I, 237, nota (7).

[204] Can. 36, §2, 2265, §2, 2275, n. 3, 2283; cf. Part III, Chap. I, Article I.

[205] Can. 156, 1439.

[206] Can. 2291, n. 4, 2294, 2291, n. 9, 2298, n. 5.

[207] Cicognani, *Commentarium,* p. 233.

[208] Ayrinhac, *General Legislation,* pp. 152, 153; Augustine, *A Commentary,* I, pp. 134, 135.

[209] *Normae Generales,* II, p. 232.

script to be valid, they do not have any effect, do not *de facto* grant the favor because of extrinsic circumstances which, irrespective of the opposition of Superiors or the injured parties, render the rescripts inefficacious; Coronata,[210] basing his claim on the general modifying words "*non sustinentur,*" insists that, even without a derogatory clause, "*Motu Proprio*" Rescripts, whether granted to persons who are "*inhabiles*", or opposed to particular customs, statues, or the acquired rights of others, are not "*de se*" invalid, but become invalid only when contested; finally, the more common view [211] maintains that now, just as before the Code, "*Motu Proprio*" Rescripts granted to persons incapable of receiving the favors contained therein, or opposed to legitimate customs or statutes, are invalid because the "*motu proprio*" clause does not make an incapable person capable of receiving favors, nor cause a favor granted against legitimate custom to become valid; but that even when no mention is made in the "*Motu Proprio*" Rescripts of the acquired rights of others, the rescripts do not become invalid unless they are contested by the interested parties. This latter view that looks upon the present law as a repetition of the old law seems to give the proper interpretation of this canon. The phrase "*non sustinentur,*" qualifying all three classes of circumstances, does not state that the clause "*motu proprio*" changes the power of disqualified persons, or validates rescripts that are contrary to particular customs or statutes, nor, on the other hand, does it declare that rescripts opposing the acquired rights of others become invalid *ipso facto,* without any chance of being indirectly validated by the consent of the other party to the execution of the rescript. And, after all, from the viewpoint of reasons of fitness, the fact that "*Motu Proprio*" Rescripts, granted to ineligible persons, or against particular statutes, are not contested, does not presuppose or imply the consent

---

[210] *Institutiones,* I, p. 64, nota (6). Cf. I, n. 61, where he seems to contradict or at least to qualify his opinion, by stating that inhabilities arising from can. 36 affect even "*Motu Proprio*" Rescripts.

[211] Maroto, *Institutiones,* n. 285; Vermeersch-Creusen, *Epitome,* I, n. 134; Chelodi, *Jus De Personis,* p. 140, nota (2); Cicognani, *Commentarium,* p. 233.

necessary for an indirect validation, as it does in the case of non-contested rescripts that are opposed to the acquired rights of others. Since, therefore, it is far from clear that the old law has been modified, the old law must be followed.[212]

The present law retains the value of the derogatory clauses that declare that the favor is granted either despite the personal disqualification of the petition, or despite the fact that the favor is contrary to particular statutes, customs, or the acquired rights of others. The insertion of clauses counteracting the effects of personal disqualification or opposing a particular custom or statute is not uncommon in papal rescripts, but only on very rare occasions is the clause derogating the acquired rights of others found in papal rescripts.[213] When the clause definitely and precisely mentions that one or the other of these circumstances has been taken into consideration by the grantor of the rescript, the rescript is and remains valid despite the circumstance referred to, despite any opposition of others. There is another clause, "*supplentes omnes et singulos tam juris quam facti defectus,*" sometimes contained in papal rescripts, that must not be confused with the derogatory clause referred to in can. 46. This clause offsets any lack of solemnities in the rescript required by positive law, not the defects of the divine or natural law, nor the personal defects of the petitioner.[214]

Article VIII.—Conflicting Rescripts

Conflicting rescripts may occur in beneficial as well as judicial matters. During the centuries in which the Holy See was actively engaged in granting Rescripts of Benefices, definite principles were needed to decide which rescript would prevail when the same benefices were granted to different parties. Since the Council of Trent,[215] when

---

212 Can. 6, n. 4.

213 Michiels, *Normae Generales,* II, p. 233; Toso, *Commentaria Minora,* I, p. 132.

214 Ferraris, *Bibliotheca,* v. Clausulae, art. II, n. 2; Ojetti, *Commentarium,* I, p. 234.

215 Sess. XXIV, *de Ref.,* c. 19.

the granting of expectative favors was forbidden, these principles have not been of much practical importance, as far as rescripts of favor are concerned,[216] but they have been retained in the Code to be used when occasions arise. The following rules decide which rescript prevails when a conflict arises between a general and a special rescript, or between general rescripts or special rescripts granted either at different times or at the same time.

Canon 48, §1.—Si contingat ut de una eademque re dua rescripta inter se contraria impetrentur, peculiare, in iis quae peculiariter exprimuntur, praevalet generali.

§2.—Si sint aeque peculiaria aut generalia, prius tempore praevalet posteriori, nisi in altero fiat expressa mentio de priore, aut nisi prior impetrator dolo vel notabili negligentia suo rescripto usus non fuerit.

§3.—Quod si eodem die fuerint concessa nec liqueat uter prior impetraverit, utrumque irritum est, et, si res ferat, rursus ad eum qui rescripta dedit, est recurrendum.

To solve one of the problems of conflicting rescripts, a principle of Roman Law, *"In toto iure generi per speciem derogatur et illud potissimum habetur quod ad speciem directum est,"* [217] was adopted by Decretal Law.[218] Canonists consequently taught that a special rescript of favor prevailed over a general one, whether the general rescript was [219] or was not granted first.[220] The present law accepts this principle without change, specifying very definitely that a special rescript prevails over a general one, but only in those things that are expressed as special, i.e., in those

[216] De Angelis, *Praelectiones*, lib. I, tit. III, n. 8.

[217] D. L. 17. 80.

[218] C. I, X, *de rescriptis*, 1, 3, *"Speciale mandatum derogat generali"*; c. 38, *de praebendis et dignitatibus*, III, 4, in VI°, *"Species derogat generi"*; *"Generi per speciem derogatur"*—R. J. 34, in VI°.

[219] Reiffenstuel, *Jus Canonicum*, lib. I, tit. III, n. 115; Schmalzgrueber, *Jus Ecclesiasticum*, pars I, tit. III, n. 35; Wernz, *Jus Decretalium*, I, n. 154.

[220] Santi, *Praelectiones*, lib. I, tit. III, n. 23.

things that are given by way of exception to the general rescript.[221]

Decretal Law [222] also recognized the principle that, ordinarily, priority of time would decide the prevalence between rescripts that are equally general or special. Priority of time was reckoned by the time that the rescripts were granted, not by the time that they were presented or executed, whether the rescripts were granted *in forma gratiosa* or *in forma commissoria.*[223] That this principle is also retained by the Code is evidenced by the fact that in can. 48, §2, §3, there is question not of the time that the rescript is effective but of the time that the rescript is granted.[224] And, after all, it is fitting that this standard should apply even to rescripts granted *in forma commissoria,* since at the time that the rescript is granted the favored party receives a *"jus ad rem"* and some kind of priority claim.

In the old law, the priority of time principle was limited by two exceptions, that are also incorporated in the present canon, namely, when special mention is made of the former rescript in the later one, and when the recipient of the first rescript failed, through malice or notable negligence, to make use of his rescript.

When the grantor makes specific and express mention of the former rescript, he clearly manifests his intention to revoke his first decision, and, therefore, it is no longer possible to presume that he is acting through ignorance in granting the second rescript.[225] Formerly, the clause *"anteferri"* also gave priority to the second rescript even when there was no specific mention made of the first

---

[221] Michiels, *Normae Generales,* II, p. 247.

[222] C. 12, X, *de officio et potestate judicis delegati,* I, 29; *"Qui prior est tempore, potior in jure"*—R. J. 54, in VI°.

[223] Reiffenstuel, *Jus Canonicum,* lib. I, tit. III, n. 96; D'Annibale, *Summula,* I, 222.

[224] Cf. in can. 48, §2, par. 3 the words *"impetrator," "impetraverit," "impetrentur,"* which refer to the time of granting; Maroto, *Institutiones,* n. 286; Chelodi, *Jus De Personis,* n. 79.

[225] Reiffenstuel, *Jus Canonicum,* lib. I, tit. III, n. 113; Schmalzgrueber, *Jus Ecclesiasticum,* pars I, tit. III, n. 35.

rescript.[226] Ojetti [227] claims that since there is no longer any mention of this clause in the present law, it has lost its former value. It seems, however, that since in the old law the same general exceptions existed as at present, and still the *"anteferri"* clause was considered by pre-Code canonists to have the same practical meaning as an express mention of the first rescript, the clause would still retain its force, i.e., would still give priority rights to the possessor of the rescript in which the clause appears.[228] Whether or not the clause is used at the present time depends, of course, on the practice or style of the Curia.

Priority of time is not taken into account, however, in deciding prevalence between rescripts that grant identically the same favor when the one that ordinarily would be preferred was not used on account of the malice or notable negligence of its possessor. In one case the possessor of the prior rescript is punished on account of a deliberate and intentional fault; in the other case, on account of an inexcusable delay in using the rescript.

The penalty attached to the non-use of the rescript on account of *dolus*, i.e., *"omnis calliditas, fallacia, machinatio ad circumveniendum, fallendum, decipiendum alterum adhibita,"* [229] is merely an application of the principle *"fraus et dolus nemini debeant patrocinari."* Accompanying circumstances may help to prove that the recipient maliciously deferred using his rescript so that he could put a later petitioner to considerable inconvenience, but it is extremely difficult to decide just when one is guilty of *notable negligence* in not using a rescript of favor. The mere fact that it was not used for a year would suffice to prove notable negligence in the non-use of a rescript of justice,[230] but not

---

[226] Reiffenstuel, *Jus Canonicum*, lib. I, tit. III, n. 101; Santi, *Praelectiones*, lib. I, tit. III, n. 24; De Angelis, *Praelectiones*, lib. I, tit. III, n. 8.

[227] *Commentarium*, I, p. 244, nota (7).

[228] Can. 6, n. 2.

[229] D. IV. 3. 1. 2.

for a rescript of favor.[231] The solution of this problem must be left, in particular instances, to the judgment of a good man, especially a Judge or ecclesiastical Prelate, who in reaching a decision must take into account the character of the person, the nature of the case, the distance, etc.[232]

Some canonists [233] maintain that the general principle of priority of time admits of another exception, mentioned by some authors before the Code,[234] namely, that when the second rescript had not only been executed but had fully produced its effects, some kind of possession was acquired by the recipient, and, consequently, it was to be preferred to the first rescript. It seems perfectly in accord with the principles of the Code to admit this further exception, since the present law of can. 48, §2, which merely repeats the law that existed before the Code, should be understood according to the interpretation of approved authors of the old law.[235]

Outside of these few exceptions, the rescript of favor that was granted first will prevail over all contrary rescripts that are equally particular or general. Ordinarily the day, not the moment, that the rescript was granted, will determine priority of time, since the hour and moment are not generally recorded in the rescript,[236] but if in a particular case it is possible to determine the exact time of the day that the rescript was granted, e.g., by the testimony of witnesses, or by the confession of the other party, the moment of granting must be taken into consideration

---

230 C. 23, X, *de rescriptis*, I, 3.

231 Contra. Augustine, *A Commentary*, I, p. 137; and apparently Coronata, *Institutiones*, I, n. 70. Cf. c. 11, *de praebendis et dignitatibus*, III, 4, in VI°, where no mention is made of year for rescripts of favor; Reiffenstuel, *Jus Canonicum*, lib. I, tit. III, n. 66, 67; Schmalzgrueber, *Jus Ecclesiasticum*, pars I, tit. III, n. 35.

232 Reiffenstuel, *Jus Canonicum*, lib. I, tit. III, n. 66; Maroto, *Institutiones*, n. 286.

233 Maroto, *Institutiones*, n. 286; Vermeersch-Creusen, *Epitome*, I, n. 136; Coronata, *Institutiones*, I, n. 70; Michiels, *Normae Generales*, II, p. 250.

234 Reiffenstuel, *Jus Canonicum*, lib. I, tit. III, n. 99.

235 Can. 6, n. 2.

236 Vermeersch-Creusen, *Epitome*, I, n. 136.

in arriving at a decision.[237] Michiels,[238] distinguishing between the time *"impetrationis,"* and the time *"concessionis,"* of the rescript, claims that priority of time for prevalence of rescripts is determined by the *day "concessionis,"* when the rescripts are issued on different days, and by the *moment "impetrationis,"* when the conflicting rescripts are issued on the same day. This view does not, however, seem to take into consideration the whole context of can. 48. In the first two paragraphs of can. 48, especially in the second paragraph, *"impetratio"* and *"concessio"* are evidently considered as synonymous words. It certainly does not seem proper to adopt an interpretation that supposes that the legislator uses the word *"impetratio"* in two different meanings in the same canon, especially since the canon can be understood when the same meaning is attached to the word throughout the canon. Consequently, there does not seem to be any convincing motive for departing from the ordinary interpretation of the present canon which determines priority of time, whether the rescripts were granted on different days or on the same day, by the time that the rescript was granted.

In what has preceded, there has always been question of prevalence between rescripts, between a rescript that is general and one that is particular, or between rescripts that are equally general or particular. The law contained in paragraphs 1 and 2, states that one rescript *prevails* over another, not as in paragraph 3, that one or both are *invalid.* From this it follows that the general or the second rescript is not null *ipso facto,* but becomes null and void if a dispute arises and the recipient of the special or the first rescript claims his right. When no dispute arises, the general or the later rescript retains its force and produce its effect.[239] Before the Code, when it was impossible to determine which one of equally general or special rescripts had been granted first, other criteria were used to determine which rescript would prevail, e.g., the time of presentation, the fact of

---

[237] Reiffenstuel, *Jus Canonicum,* lib. I, tit. III, n. 106; Maroto, *Institutiones,* n. 286; Cicognani, *Commentarium,* p. 238; Coronata, *Institutiones,* I, n. 70.

[238] *Normae Generales,* II, p. 248.

[239] Maroto, *Institutiones,* I, p. 328, nota (1).

actually receiving the favor first, the vote of the canons, etc.[240] Now the law definitely states that when it is impossible to determine which rescript was granted first, both rescripts are invalid, and recourse must be made to the grantor to settle the question.[241] Since it is explicitly stated that both rescripts are invalid, one party cannot relinquish his rights to permit the other to enjoy the favor:—the grantor alone can revalidate one of the rescripts.

It is generally admitted [242] that the rule of can. 48, §3, does not apply to rescripts that are issued by different grantors, that when two rescripts are granted on the same day, one by the Holy See, and the other by another Ordinary, and there is no way of determining which was granted first, the Papal rescript will prevail over the rescript of the inferior Ordinary,[243] provided, of course, that acquired rights are safeguarded.[244]

---

[240] Reiffenstuel, *Jus Canonicum*, lib. I, tit. III, n. 108; De Angelis, *Praelectiones*, lib. I, tit. III, n. 8.

[241] Can. 48, §3.

[242] Maroto, *Institutiones*, n. 286; Ayrinhac, *General Legislation*, p. 155; Ojetti, *Commentarium*, I, p. 245; Cicognani, *Commentarium*, p. 239; Vermeersch-Creusen, *Epitome*, I, n. 136; Coronata, *Institutiones*, I, n. 70. Contra Michiels, *Normae Generales*, II, pp. 251, 252, who thinks that no distinction should be made since no distinction is found in the Code.

[243] C. 31, *de praebendis et dignitatibus*, III, 4, in VI°.

[244] Cf. can. 46; Reiffenstuel, *Jus Canonicum*, lib. I, tit. III, n. 103; Vermeersch-Creusen, *Epitome*, I, n. 136.

CHAPTER III

Execution of Papal Rescripts of Favor

Article I.—Presentation of Rescripts

Rescripts of Favor are granted either *in forma gratiosa* or *in forma commissoria:* in the former, the favor is granted by the Pope directly to the interested party with no one employed as an intermediary or executor; in the latter, the favor is granted through an executor. The obligation of presenting the rescript to someone in authority for examination is common to both kinds of rescripts:—rescripts granted *in forma gratiosa,* if presented, are presented to the Ordinary; rescripts granted *in forma commissoria,* when sent to the interested parties, must be presented to the executor. The element of time enters into the question of presentation of some rescripts granted *in forma commissoria,* since it is expressly stated in some of them and not in others that presentation of the rescript to the executor must be made within a definite period of time. These various phases of the problem of presentation will be treated in their respective places in the following paragraphs.

§1. *Presentation of Rescripts granted in Forma Gratiosa*

The Council of Trent[1] ordained that unless rescripts granted *in forma gratiosa* were presented to the Ordinary so that he might, as a papal legate, determine whether or not the petitions contained subreption or obreption, they would be invalid. In 1908, Pius X[2] greatly modified this ruling by declaring that thereafter only two kinds of rescripts *in forma gratiosa* would have to be presented to the

[1] Sess. XXII, de Ref., c. 5.
[2] *"Normae Peculiares,"* cap. III, art. I, n. 4—AAS, I (1909), 63, 64.

Ordinary, namely, rescripts that contained favors intended for public use, e.g., certain indulgences, permission to expose relics for public veneration, or permission to wear a special dress, and rescripts that necessitated the verification of certain conditions, e.g., a fitting place for a private chapel. The Code, in the following canon, has added a third exception to the two made by Pius X.

Canon 51.—Rescriptum Sedis Apostolicae in quo nullus datur exsecutor, tunc tantum debet Ordinario impetrantis praesentari, cum id in eisdem litteris praecipitur, aut de rebus agitur publicis, aut comprobare conditiones quasdam oportet.

The exception added by the Code, namely, when presentation is demanded by the rescript itself, is self-evident and needs no explanation. At present presentation is prescribed in all rescripts *in forma gratiosa* that grant dispensations *"super matrimonio rato et non consummato."* [2a] By a *public thing* is meant something that pertains to the general good of the people, of the Christian people, of the University, etc., e.g., churches, benefices, pious foundations accepted by the Church, seminaries, cemeteries, indulgences, titles of honor, sacred rites, etc.[3] Public is not to be taken here as opposed to occult, but rather as opposed to private. One cannot use as a criterion for the public character of the favor the fact that the favor was granted by one of the departments of the Roman Curia in charge of the external forum, namely, the Congregations and Offices, because, while as a general rule, private favors are also occult and are usually granted by the Sacred Penitentiary, in some cases they are distributed by the Congregations or Offices. Presentation is required for rescripts that are concerned with public favors because, on account of their importance for the community, the Church desires them to be recognized by some public authority before they are used. Rescripts that *contain certain conditions* that must be fulfilled should also be presented to the Ordinary. Since the Code does not speak of rescripts with essential conditions

[2a] S. C. de disc. Sac., 7 Maii 1923—AAS, XV (1923), 413.
[3] Cicognani, *Commentarium*, p. 244.

but merely states "*quasdam conditiones,*" even rescripts containing accidental conditions are included in this category.[4] The use of the taxative words "*tunc tantum*" in the canon show that only these three kinds of rescripts *in forma gratiosa* must be presented to the Ordinary. When the Ordinary receives this kind of rescript, he does not execute it but merely puts his "*Visum*" on the document. Such cases of presentation to the Ordinary do not occur very frequently, however, for the simple reason that rescripts are very rarely granted by the Holy See *in forma gratiosa.*[5]

Badii[6] claims that presentation is required for the validity of the rescript. This claim seems to be too exacting. Whenever the words of the rescript itself clearly require presentation under penalty of nullity of the rescript, the case is clear:—but since there is no invalidating formula in the canon, presentation of rescripts *in forma gratiosa* cannot be considered as ordinarily necessary for the validity of the rescript.[7] A confirmation of this conclusion may be found in the fact that in similar matters, e.g., the clause "*de consensu Ordinarii loci,*" the consent of the Ordinary is not required for the validity of the rescript.[8]

§2. *Presentation of Rescripts granted in Forma Commissoria*

Rescripts granted *in forma commissoria,* as a general rule, must be presented to the executor of the rescript, not to the Ordinary:—only *per accidens* must they be presented to the Ordinary, namely, when the rescript specifically enjoins the obligation, e.g., in some rescripts for the internal non-sacramental forum, or when the Ordinary happens to be the executor, e.g., in most rescripts for the external forum.[9] Even the obligation of presenting rescripts *in forma commissoria* to the executor is not as strict and

---

[4] Cicognani, *Commentarium,* p. 244, Michiels, *Normae Generales,* II, p. 266.

[5] De Meester, *Compendium,* I, p. 201, nota (1); De Smet, *De Sponsalibus et Matrimonio,* n. 740, 861.

[6] *Institutiones,* I, n. 69.

[7] Can. 11; Cicognani, *Commentarium,* p. 244; Ojetti, *Commentarium,* I, p. 251; Coronata, *Institutiones,* I, n. 72; Toso, *Commentaria Minora,* I, pp. 138, 139; Michiels, *Normae Generales,* II, p. 266.

[8] Cf. Part III, Chapt. II, Art. III.

[9] Coronata, *Institutiones,* I, n. 72.

absolute in practice, as it is in theory, for the very simple reason that the Holy See usually sends the rescripts directly to the executors and not to the interested parties, as was her custom in former times.

Since rescripts *in forma commissoria,* if not sent, must be presented to the executor for execution, it may be appropriate to mention here the persons whom the Holy See generally selects as executor of her rescripts.

In ancient times, the Roman Curia generally selected clerics with ecclesiastical dignity and jurisdiction in the external forum, e.g., Bishops, Vicars General, Vicars Capitular, Regular Prelates, even local Superiors, etc., to execute papal rescripts for the external forum.[10] Bishops and *Ordinarii Nullius* executed rescripts for religious in matters pertaining to the enclosure, alienation of property, secularization, and erection of new convents or monasteries, as well as all rescripts for nuns, whereas the Regular Superiors, General or Provincial, and Abbots of Monasteries generally executed rescripts pertaining to the religious discipline and rule.[11] Whenever the Roman Curia desired to depart from the ordinary custom and appoint as executor a cleric without ecclesiastical dignity, the clause *"ex certa scientia"* was inserted in the rescript.[12] The Council of Trent [13] ordained that all matrimonial dispensations for the external forum should be executed by the Ordinaries of the petitioners. Thereafter, when the *"Ordnarius loci"* was designated as the executor of the rescript, either the Bishop or the Vicar General could execute the rescript, but when the Bishop or the Vicar General was designated, only that individual could execute the rescript, because the executor was then considered to be appointed executor on account of his personal qualifications for the work, not on account of the office he was holding.[14] The Holy Office on

[10] Schmalzgrueber, *Jus Ecclesiasticum,* pars I, tit. III, n. 32; Soglia, *Institutiones,* lib. I, tit. III, par. 32; Bizzari, *Collectanea,* p. 613; Wernz, *Jus Decretalium,* I, n. 155.

[11] Bizzari, *Collectanea,* p. 613.

[12] Schmalzgrueber, *Jus Ecclesiasticum,* pars I, tit. III, n. 32.

[13] Sess. XXII, *de Ref.,* c. 5.

[14] Santi, *Praelectiones,* lib. I, tit. III, n. 29.

February 20, 1888,[15] declared that matrimonial dispensations, granted to the local Ordinary for execution, could be executed by Bishops, Administrators and Prefects Apostolic, Prelates or Prefects with jurisdiction over separate territories, and their Vicars General, and during the vacancy of the See, by the Vicars Capitular or legitimate Administrators; and on September 5, 1900,[16] the Holy Office decided that the same rulings would apply to matrimonial dispensations that were committed for execution to Bishops.

In ancient times, the Holy See appointed Doctors in Theology or Canon Law, privileged religious confessors, e.g., Jesuits,[17] or other capable ecclesiastical personages [18] to execute rescripts for the internal forum. Later they committed these rescripts for execution to any confessor among those approved by the Ordinary to hear confessions, v.g., "*Discreto viro Confessario ex approbatis ab Ordinario,*" or to a designated confessor, v.g., "*Discreto viro N. Confessario.*" [19]

At present, there are no general qualifications required by the Code for executors of papal rescripts for the external forum, but the law ordains that matrimonial dispensations must be executed by the Ordinary who sent the petition or added his testimonial letter to the petition.[20] Ordinarily, according to the style of the Roman Curia, other rescripts for the external forum are also given to the local Ordinary or the Ordinary of the petitioners for execution.[21] The Superior General of Clerical Religious Institutes, whether exempt or not exempt, executes the rescripts for the religious members of his Institute, whereas the local Ordinary usually executes rescripts for lay Religious Institutes.

---

[15] ASS, XX (1887), 543.

[16] ASS, XXXIII (1900-1901), 225.

[17] Gregory XIII, const. "*Exponi,*" 3 Aprilis 1582, *Bullarii Romani Continuatio*, VIII, 137.

[18] Sanchez, *De Matrimonio*, lib. VIII, disp. XXXIV, n. 3; Schmalzgrueber, *Jus Ecclesiasticum*, pars I, tit. III, n. 32; Maschat, *Institutiones Canonicae*, lib. I, tit. III, n. 13, 14; Wernz, *Jus Decretalium*, I, n. 155.

[19] Konings-Putzer, *Commentarium in Facultates Apostolicas*, p. 90.

[20] Can. 1055.

[21] De Meester, *Compendium*, n. 301; Cicognani, *Commentarium*, p. 247.

Occasionally, rescripts of religious of lay Institutes are executed by their Cardinal Protector.[22] When no one is designated as the executor, the choice is left to the judgment of the party to whom the rescript is addressed.[23]

Rescripts for the internal non-sacramental forum are now sent for execution to the Bishop, pastor, or priest who sent the petition to the Roman Curia, whereas rescripts for the internal sacramental forum are at times committed to a designated confessor, but more commonly to any confessor among those approved by the Ordinary.[24] When the rescript is to be executed by "*Confessario ex approbatis ab Ordinario,*" only a confessor who is approved by the Ordinary can validly execute the rescript,[25] a confessor, moreover, who can hear the confession of the party in question, e.g., one who is approved to hear confessions of women, if the party concerned is a woman.[26] When the confessor must be one approved by the local Ordinary, the confessor can execute the rescript only in the diocese in which he is approved to hear confessions, which, however, need not be the diocese of the penitent.[26a] The person who receives such a rescript may change confessors if the first confessor refuses to execute the rescript, e.g., on the grounds that the rescript is vitiated by subreption or obreption.[27] When the same rescript of favor is intended for more than one person, e.g., a matrimonial dispensation, and the confessor is not designated, each person is free to select his own confessor. The procedure is as follows:—the first penitent, after the rescript has been executed for him, obtains

---

[22] Vermeersch-Creusen, *Epitome*, I, n. 123; Cocchi, *Commentarium*, I, p. 158; Michiels, *Normae Generales*, II, p. 274, nota (3).

[23] Maroto, *Institutiones*, n. 288.

[24] De Smet, *De Sponsalibus et Matrimonio*, n. 865; Maroto, *Institutiones*, n. 288; Chelodi, *Jus De Personis*, n. 80.

[25] Capello, *De Sacramentis*, III, n. 283.

[26] D'Annibale, *Summula*, I, 242, nota (45).

[26a] De Justis, *De Dispensationibus*, lib. I, cap. VIII, n. 99; Ferraris, *Bibliotheca*, v. Executor, n. 45; De Smet, *De Sponsalibus et Matrimonio*, n. 882.

[27] Sanchez, *De Matrimonio*, lib. VIII, disp. XXVII, n. 40; Corradus, *Praxis*, lib. VII, cap. IV, n. 72; D'Annibale, Summula, I, 242; De Smet, *De Sponsalibus et Matrimonio*, n. 865; Capello, *De Sacramentis*, III, n. 288.

the rescript from the confessor and gives it to the other party, who, in turn, presents it to her confessor.[28]

Rescripts granted *in forma commissoria* must, therefore, be presented to the executor, not for the "*Visum,*" but for execution. The rescripts sometimes specify that within a certain time the rescript must be presented to the executor; at other times, no mention is made of time. Prior to the Code, it was taught [29] that when the limits of time for presentation were stated in the rescript, the rescript could not be validly presented or executed after the prescribed time had elapsed, because the presumed will of the grantor was that the rescript would have value only if it was presented within the specified time allotted for presentation. Some authors since the Code [30] still retain this opinion, but Michiels [31] more accurately points out that the time limit placed on the presentation does not affect the validity of the rescript or its execution unless the time for presentation is inserted in the form of an essential conditional clause,[31a] is given in express or equivalent words as invalidating, or is connected with the time limit for execution. In the latter case, the validity of the execution would be affected if the executor proceeded after the time limit was up, because, after the time granted for the execution elapsed, his mandate would cease and, with it, the efficacy of the rescript.[31b]

When no time for presentation is mentioned in the rescript, the following rule must be observed.

Canon 52.—Rescripta, quorum praesentationi nullum est definitum tempus, possunt exsecutori exhiberi quovis tempore modo absit fraus et dolus.

---

[28] S. Poenit., 15 Nov. 1748—Collet, *Traite Des Dispenses,* III, n. 41; Gasparri, *De Matrimonio,* n. 402; Vlaming, *Praelectiones,* n. 502; Noldin, *De Sacramentis,* n. 624; Coronata, *Institutiones,* I, n. 78; Capello, *De Sacramentis,* III, n. 288; cf. Ferreres, *Compendium Theologiae Moralis,* II, n. 976, who says, for the lawfulness of the act, it is necessary for both parties to go to the same confessor.

[29] Reiffenstuel, *Jus Canonicum,* lib. I, tit. III, n. 67; Schmalzgrueber, *Jus Ecclesiasticum,* pars I, tit. III, n. 20.

[30] Cocchi, *Commentarium,* I, p. 159; Ojetti, *Commentarium,* I, p. 252.

[31] *Normae Generales,* II, p. 267.

[31a] Can. 39.

[31b] Can. 55.

Adhering strictly to the principles of Decretal Law,[32] ancient canonists[33] maintained that when no definite time was prescribed for presentation, the rescript could be presented at any time, as long as the delay in presentation was not caused by malice, nor constituted a notable negligence.

The present law has merely changed the exception of notable negligence to that of fraud. *Fraus* and *dolus* should not be considered as synonymous terms, not so much because *fraus* consists in words, *dolus,* in facts, because in *fraus* the action is done openly, in *dolus,* secretly, or because *fraus* designates a culpable act with a certain amount of cleverness attached to it, but not necessarily combined with the intention of deceiving, whereas *dolus* has both cleverness and the intention of deceiving,[34] but principally because *fraus* is *"omnis actus directus ad eludendam legem,"*[35] whereas *dolus* is *"omnis calliditas, fallacia, machinatio ad circumveniendum, fallendum, decipiendum alterum adhibita,"*[36] i.e., because *fraus* is an act seemingly in accordance with the law but actually evading the law, e.g., when presentation is deferred so that certain circumstances will arise to render the person capable of receiving the favor, or the petition true, whereas *dolus* is an act intended to deceive men, e.g., when a person defers the presentation so that when another party obtains a similar rescript, he can present his rescript and, thereby, nullify the later rescript.[37] Most canonists[38] take this view of the present law and say that *"et"* in the clause *"fraus et dolus"* is to be taken disjunctively and not conjunctively. Michiels,[39]

---

[32] C. 12, *de rescriptis,* I, 3, in VI°; *"Decet concessum a Principe beneficium mansurum"*—R. J. 16, in VI°.

[33] Reiffenstuel, *Jus Canonicum,* lib. I, tit. III, n. 66, 67; Schmalzgrueber, *Jus Ecclesiasticum,* pars I, tit. III, n. 20; De Angelis, *Praelectiones,* lib. I, tit. III, n. 6.

[34] Calvinus, *Lexicon Juridicum,* v. Fraus, Dolus; Ojetti, *Commentarium,* I, p. 253.

[35] D. I. 3. 29.

[36] D. IV. 3. 1. 2.

[37] Cicognani, *Commentarium,* p. 246; Ojetti, *Commentarium,* I, pp. 253, 254.

[38] Vermeersch-Creusen, *Epitome,* I, n. 140; Cicognani, *Commentarium,* p. 245; Ojetti, *Commentarium,* I, pp. 253, 254; Coronata, *Institutiones,* I, n. 75.

[39] *Normae Generales,* II, p. 268.

while admitting, as most probable, the view that distinguishes between *fraus* and *dolus* and considers the one to have for purpose the deception of men, and the other to have for purpose the evasion of the law, thinks, however, that there is sufficient reason to interpret *"fraus et dolus"* as including *"per modum unius"* any case in which the presentation was deceitfully postponed in order to avoid the harmful or less pleasant effects that would have arisen from a quicker execution of the rescript. Such an interpretation scarcely gives full value to the words *"fraus"* and *"dolus,"* since one can be guilty of *"dolus"* and still have nothing to fear for himself from a quicker execution of the rescript, as far as harmful or unpleasant effects are concerned. From the point of view of fitness there surely is as much, if not more, reason to punish a person who defers presentation in order to deceive and harm others, as there is to punish one who defers presentation for his own benefit without harming or intending to harm others. Consequently, to give the words their true value as well as to make proper allowances for the intention of the legislator, this canon should be interpreted to mean that if presentation is deferred by the recipient of a rescript, either through deceit or fraud, he may no longer present his rescript to the executor.

A further question arises:—does the rescript become null and void by the mere fact that its presentation is fraudulently or maliciously deferred? Toso [40] claims that under such circumstances the rescript would become invalid, but most authors, who refer to the question,[41] correctly maintain that, while the executor can refuse to execute the rescript and the grantor can declare the rescript null or recall the favor, the rescript is not rendered *ipso facto* null and void by fraudulent or malicious deferring of the presentation, since it is far from clear that the canon expressly or equivocally contains an invalidating clause.[42]

---

[40] *Commentaria Minora,* I, p. 140.

[41] Vermeersch-Creusen, *Epitome,* I, n. 140; Cicognani, *Commentarium,* p. 220; Coronata, *Institutiones,* I, n. 75; Michiels, *Normae Generales,* II, p. 269.

[42] Can. 11, 15.

Article II.—Reception and Recognition of the Rescript by the Executor

Decretal Law[43] definitely stated that the time assigned for the judgment of a case commenced only when the rescript was presented to the judge. Canonists, applying this same principle to rescripts of favor, declared that an executor, even though he had previously received a copy of the rescript, could not validly execute the rescript until he had received the authentic letters.[44] D'Annibale,[45] however, taught that when an executor living in a country far distant from Rome proceeded to execute a rescript for an urgent case after he had received telegraphic notification that the rescript had been granted, the parties who took advantage of the favor should not be disturbed. The Holy Office, on August 24, 1892,[46] decided that matrimonial dispensations could not be validly executed before the reception of the authentic document of the rescript unless telegraphic notification was sent by the authority of the Holy See. This teaching about matrimonial dispensations has been extended by the following canon to all rescripts:—

Canon 53.—Rescripti exsecutor invalide munere suo fungitur, antequam litteras receperit earumque authenticitatem et integritatem recognoverit, nisi praevia earumden notitia ad eum fuerit auctoritate rescribentis transmissa.

The present law is very clear and definite:—the execution of any rescript is invalid unless the executor has received and recognized the authenticity and integrity of the letters or has been officially notified that the rescript has been granted. By receiving the letters is meant having actually in one's hands the mandate of execution and the rescript, which usually constitute one document.[47] The

[43] C. 12, X, *de appelationibus*, II, 28.

[44] Sanchez, *De Matrimonio*, lib. VIII, disp. XXIX, n. 10; De Justis, *De Dispensationibus*, lib. I, cap. VI, n. 2, 3; Schmalzgrueber, *Jus Ecclesiasticum*, pars IV, tit. XVI, n. 222; Wernz, *Jus Decretalium*, I, n. 155; Gasparri, *De Matrimonio*, n. 393.

[45] *Summula*, I, 241, nota (36).

[46] ASS, XXIX (1896), 642.

[47] Chelodi, *Jus De Personis*, n. 80; Cicognani, *Commentarium*, p. 248.

executor, at some time before execution, must have in his possession the original document, or, in case the original document was lost on the way, an authentic copy,[48] which can be obtained by asking for the rescript in forma *"Vidimus."*[49] The authenticity of the letters is recognized by inspecting the seal, signature, form of address, etc.; their integrity, by determining whether or not the rescript contains all that is essential. The executor should devote as much time and attention to this work as to any other serious matter.[50] Even though the letters are destroyed after they have been received and recognized, the rescript can be validly executed without obtaining even an authentic copy, provided, of course, that the executor remembers distinctly the essential parts of the letters.[51] Notification of the granting of the rescript, transmitted by telegraph or by telephone, by the grantor or by an official instructed by the grantor to send the message, serves as a substitute for the actual reception of the letters. Private telegraphic notification is not sufficient for the valid execution of a rescript,[52] but telegraphic notification by a Roman Agent may be acted upon in urgent cases, since the Holy See, especially the Congregation for the Discipline of the Sacraments, sometimes commits to the Agent the task of transmitting the official notification.[53] Notification by the Agent can certainly be considered official whenever the general tenor of the rescript is contained in the message together with some indication that the Holy See authorized the Agent to notify the executor to proceed.

The canon states that failure to receive and recognize the authenticity and integrity of the letters invalidates the

---

[48] Wernz-Vidal, *Jus Canonicum*, V, n. 445; Ayrinhac, *General Legislation*, p. 159.

[49] D'Annibale, *Summula*, I, 241, nota (36); Gasparri, *De Matrimonio*, n. 393; Ojetti, *Commentarium*, I, p. 255.

[50] Cicognani, *Commentarium*, p. 249.

[51] S. Poenit, 29. Febr. 1904—LQS, 195, p. 382.

[52] Opinion of D'Annibale, *Summula*, I, 241, nota (36) is no longer tenable.

[53] Durieux, *Les Dispenses Matrimoniales*, p. 130, nota; Cicognani, *Commentarium*, 250; Michiels, *Normae Generales*, II, pp. 272, 273. De Smet, *De Sponsalibus et Matrimonio*, p. 737, nota (4), thinks that this style of the Roman Curia needs official confirmation before the above-mentioned practice can be safely followed.

execution of the rescript, not the rescript itself. To rectify this kind of invalid execution, the executor merely awaits the arrival of the official notification or letters and then begins a new execution.[54]

Coronata [55] states that in order validly and licitly to use a rescript granted *in forma gratiosa,* it is sufficient to receive any kind of notification of the granting of the rescript, even notification by telegraph or telephone. It might be inferred from this statement that if no notification is received, the rescript cannot be validly or licitly used. It certainly would be unlawful to proceed without receiving notification, but there hardly seems to be any grounds for saying that the use of the rescript would be invalid if the rescript had actually been granted at the time it was used, since acceptance is not necessary for the validity of rescripts,[56] since rescripts *in forma gratiosa are effective* from the moment the rescripts are granted,[57] and nowhere in the Code is it expressly or equivalently stated that notification of their issuance is necessary for their valid use.[58]

Article III.—Power of the Executor

The respective powers granted to different kinds of executors are defined in the following canon:

Canon 54, §1.—Si in rescripto committatur merum exsecutionis ministerium, exsecutio rescripti denegari non potest, nisi aut manifeste pateat rescriptum vitio subreptionis aut obreptionis nullum esse, aut in rescripto apponantur conditiones quas exsecutori constet non esse impletas, aut qui rescriptum impetravit adeo, iudicio exsecutoris, videatur indignus ut aliorum offensioni futura sit gratiae concessio; quod ultimum si accidat, exsecutor, intermissa exsecutione, statim ea de re certiorem faciat rescribentem.

§2.—Quod si in rescripto concessio gratiae exsecutori committatur, ipsius est pro suo prudenti arbitrio et conscientia gratiam concedere vel denegare.

---

[54] S. Poenit., 5 Jan. 1894, ad II—*Coll. de Prop. Fide,* n. 1858; can. 59, §1.

[55] *Institutiones,* I, n. 72.

[56] Can. 37.

[57] Can. 38.

[58] Can. 11.

In the old law, Rescripts *in forma commissoria* were generally subdivided into three classes, the mere, the necessary or mixed, and the voluntary or free, corresponding to the three different kinds of commissions granted to executors. The *mere* executor was an executor who received a mere ministry of execution without jurisdiction or without knowledge of the case:—the matter had already been fully investigated and discussed by the grantor and the only thing that remained for the executor to do was to apply the rescript to the designated party. The *necessary* or *mixed* executor was ordered to apply the rescript if, after a diligent investigation, he was sure that the petition was true:—once he found that the petition was verified, he was obliged to execute. Finally the *voluntary* or *free* executor, instead of being ordered to grant the favor or execute the rescript, was granted the necessary faculties and left to judge for himself whether or not to grant the favor.[59] The customary formulae for the commissions of these three kinds of execution of rescripts were as follows:—for the mere executor, "*S. C. diligenter perpensa benigne annuit ac propterea mandavit committi Episcopo, ut petitam gratiam oratori concedat;*" for the necessary or mixed executor, "*S. C. benigne annuit et propterea mandavit committi Episcopo, ut veris existentibus narratis oratori petitam gratiam pro suo arbitrio et conscientia concedat;*" for the voluntary or free executor, "*S. C. oratoris preces remisit arbitrio et conscientiae Episcopi cum facultatibus necessariis et opportunis,*"[60] or "*dispenses, absolvas, si expedire judicaveris.*[61] The clause "*pro tuo arbitrio et conscientia,*" inserted in rescripts with a necessary or mixed

---

[59] De Justis, *De Dispensationibus,* lib. I, cap. VI, n. 286, 505, 506; Reiffenstuel, *Jus Canonicum,* lib. I, tit. III, n. 257, 258; lib. I, tit. XXIX, n. 157; Sanchez, *De Matrimonio,* lib. VIII, disp. XXVII, n. 14; lib. VIII, disp. XXVIII, n. 87; Santi, *Praelectiones,* lib. I, tit. III, n. 31, 36; lib. I, tit. XXIX, n. 9; Bizzari, *Collectanea,* pp. 612, 613; D'Annibale, *Summula,* I, 222, nota (5); I, 72, nota (20). Cf. Corradus, *Praxis,* lib. IX, cap. V, n. 5; De Rosa, *De Executoribus,* pars I, cap. VI, n. 1, 2, where they refer to the mere executors.

[60] Bizzari, *Collectanea,* pp. 612, 613.

[61] D'Annibale, *Summula,* I, 222, nota (5).

executor, was considered to be placed in the rescript merely out of politeness or as mark of reverence.[62]

Both the mere executor and the necessary executor received the *ministry of execution,* i.e., both were *ordered to execute the rescript,* but whereas the mere executor had no power to investigate the petition, the necessary or mixed executor was obliged to investigate before executing the rescript. The voluntary or free executor differed from the two other kinds of executors, inasmuch as he was not ordered to execute the rescript but was *left free to grant or deny the favor* as he saw fit.

Practically all authors of the present day[63] distinguish only between mixed or necessary, and free or voluntary executors, and in interpreting can. 54, refer §1 to the necessary executors and §2 to the free executors, explaining that the necessary executor is bound to execute the rescript except in three specified cases, whereas the free executor is free to grant or deny the favor according to his own prudent judgment. A few authors[64] still retain the three-fold distinction, and Coronata,[65] using the term absolute for the free executor, and naming the other two executors mixed and mere, refers can. 54, §1, to the mere executor, and can. 54, §2, to the mixed executor. He maintains that the *absolute (free)* executor has not only real power to grant the favor but also freedom to judge about the opportuneness of granting it, and being a true delegate is required only by equity to grant the favor to a worthy person; that the *mixed* executor can grant the favor only

---

[62] Trombetta, *Praxeos,* cap. VI, par. 3; D'Annibale, *Summula,* I, 222, nota (5).

[63] Maroto, *Institutiones,* n. 288; Chelodi, *Jus De Personis,* n. 80; Vermeersch-Creusen, *Epitome,* I, n. 142; Ojetti, *Commentarium,* I, pp. 249, 250, 256; Cicognani, *Commentarium,* pp. 205, 251, 252; Ayrinhac, *General Legislation,* pp. 158, 159; Kearney, *The Principles of Delegation,* p. 88; Badii, *Institutiones,* I, n. 70; Augustine, *A Commentary,* pp. 125, 142; Cocchi, *Commentarium,* I, pp. 158, 160; De Smet, *De Sponsalibus et Matrimonio,* n. 740, 864 *bis.*; Capello, *De Sacramentis,* III, n. 280; Vlaming, *Praelectiones,* II, p. 113, nota (3); Ferreres, *Compendium,* II, n. 979; Michiels, *Normae Generales,* II, pp. 275-277.

[64] Coronata, *Institutiones,* I, n. 58, 73, 77; Eichmann, *Lehrbuch des Katholischen Kirchenrechts,* p. 55.

[65] *Institutiones,* I, n. 58, 73, 77.

after he has investigated the truth of the petition, and, therefore, is not free to grant or deny the favor at will but only when, in his prudent judgment, he decides that it should or should not be granted; and that the *mere* executor cannot investigate the truth of the petition, and cannot deny execution of the rescript unless it is clear, without any investigation, that the rescript is vitiated by subreption or obreption, the conditions inserted in the rescript are not fulfilled, or the person to whom the rescript is addressed is so unworthy of the favor that to grant the favor to him would prove offensive to others in the future. He bases his claim for this interpretation on the teaching of the "*Normae Peculiares*" as well as the words of the present law.

Judging the present law not only from its present wording but also in the light of the law that preceded the Code, the correct interpretation of can. 54 refers §2 to the voluntary or free executors, and §1 to the mixed or necessary executors, as well as to the mere executors, if it is still the practice of the Holy See to issue rescripts in this latter form. According to this interpretation, the voluntary executor is left free by the Holy See to grant or deny the favor according to his own prudent judgment in the matter; whereas the mixed and mere executors are obliged to execute the rescript in all cases except the three that are mentioned in can. 54, §1, with this difference, however, that the mixed executor is obliged to investigate and determine, by investigation, whether the rescript is clearly invalidated by subreption or obreption, etc.; and the mere executor can deny execution only when the exceptions are clear without any investigation, since he has neither the duty nor the right to investigate. This interpretation, despite the contention of Coronata, is perfectly in harmony not only with the teaching of canonists before Pius X, but also with the law of the "*Normae Peculiares.*"

The "*Normae Peculiares*" [66] distinguished between papal favors granted through the persons and offices recognized by law, i.e., granted by the Holy See, "*interposito nemine,*" and papal favors granted by sending the petition through the legally recognized persons and offices to the Ordinary

[66] Cap. III, n. 3, 4—AAS, I (1909), 63.

or some other ecclesiastical person, together with the faculties to grant the favor, with or without limitations. A further subdistinction was made in the first class between favors granted *in forma gratiosa* and those granted *in forma commissoria.* It was definitely stated by the "*Normae Peculiares*" that when favors were granted *in forma commissoria,* the executor, the Ordinary, could not refuse execution and refer the case to the Holy See unless the petition was manifestly vitiated by subreption or obreption, or the petitioner was so unworthy that the granting of the favor would prove offensive to others in the future; but that when the petition and faculties were sent to the Ordinary, the granting of the favor was left to his "*aequo judicio rectaeque conscientiae, habita ratione formae rescripti, rerum Sanctae Sedi expositarum et opportunitatis gratiae concedendae.*" Evidently, when the "*Normae*" refer to the favors granted by sending the petitions and faculties to the Ordinary or some other ecclesiastical person, it refers to the free or voluntary executors, not to the necessary or mixed executors, since there is question of *receiving power to grant or deny the favor,* not of being *ordered to execute* after an investigation has been made; and when it speaks of the favors granted *in forma commissoria, "interposito nemine,"* it refers to the necessary and, probably also, the mere executors, since according to the previous teaching of canonists both the necessary and the mere executors were bound to execute the rescript, unless it was clear that the rescript was not invalidated by subreption or obreption, clear to the necessary executor from an investigation, clear to the mere executor, without investigation:—the "*Normae*" merely added another instance when execution should be refused, namely, the unworthiness of the petitioners. This conclusion is confirmed by the fact that evidently the main distinction made in the "*Normae Pecularies*" was between *gratiae faciendae,* i.e., when the power was given by the Pope to someone else with freedom to grant or deny the favor according to his own prudent judgment, and the *gratiae factae,* i.e., papal favors granted by the Holy See, *"interposito nemine,"* either without an executor, in *forma gratiosa,* or with an executor, in *forma commissoria;* and by the further fact that the necessary executor had always been considered as belonging to the class of *gratiae factae,* not *gratiae faciendae.*[67]

When the present law, contained in can. 54, is viewed in the light of the ancient teaching of canonists and the law of 1908, there can be no doubt that §1 refers to necessary and, if still extant, mere executors, while §2 refers to the free or voluntary executors, since the distinction in can. 54 between rescripts in which the *mere ministry of education* is committed to the executor and rescripts in which *the granting of the favor* is committed to the executor is exactly the same distinction that the *"Normae Peculiares"* referred to. Coronata argues that since §1 speaks of an executor with a mere ministry of execution, the mere executor is referred to. He forgets, however, that ancient canonists[68] held that the *"nudum"* or *"merum ministerium executionis"* was committed not only to the mere but also to the necessary executors and that the only difference between them was the power of investigation. Can. 54, §1, does not speak of executors who have *only* the ministry of execution without the power of investigation, but of executors who have the *mere* ministry of execution, which, in the light of the preceding law, includes necessary as well as mere executors:—in fact, the distinction of the canon does not refer at all to the power of investigation, but to the mere ministry of execution and the power of freely granting or denying the favor. There seems to be no real juridical basis, therefore, for the interpretation of Coronata, which would entirely change the ancient teaching regarding the power entrusted to the necessary or mixed executor.

---

[67] Sanchez, *De Matrimonio,* lib. VIII, disp. XXVIII, n. 87; De Justis, *De Dispensationibus,* lib. I, cap. VI, n. 505, 506; Garcia, *De Beneficiis,* VI, II, 309, 310; Layman, *Theologia Moralis,* lib. I, tract. IV, cap. 23, n. 18; De Angelis, *Praelectiones,* lib. I, tit. III, n. 10; D'Annibale, *Summula,* I, 222, nota (5); Gasparri, *De Matrimonio,* n. 363, 392.

[68] Sanchez, *De Matrimonio,* lib. VIII, disp. XXVII, n. 43; De Rosa, De Executoribus, pars I, cap. X, n. 37; De Justis, *De Dispensationibus,* lib. I, cap. VI, n. 313.

In the old law,[69] it was never claimed, as is claimed by the interpretation of Coronata, that the necessary executor should *investigate to judge whether to deny or grant the favor,* but it was always stated that he was *obliged to execute the rescript unless* it was found by investigation that the rescript was vitiated by subreption or obreption, or, after 1908, unless the interested party was found to be unworthy of the favor. It must be concluded, therefore, on account of the practically unanimous teaching of canonists and the strong juridical reasons that indicate that the present law has not changed from the ancient teaching,[70] that can. 54, §1, refers to the power of the necessary or mixed executor and, if still extant, the mere executor, while can. 54, §2, refers to the power of the voluntary or free executor.

To determine in a particular instance, from the form of the rescript, whether a mere or a necessary execution is committed, it is sufficient to see whether or not a clause like "*S. C. diligenter perpensa*" is included in the commission of execution:—if such a clause is present, it will indicate that no obligation of investigation is imposed on the executor and, consequently, that the executor is a mere executor. Aside from the matter of investigation, the limitations of the power of the mere and necessary executors are identical. In three and only three cases can they refuse execution, namely, when it is clear that the rescript is invalidated by subreption or obreption, that the conditions in the rescript are not fulfilled, or that the subject seems to be so unworthy of the favor that its granting would prove obnoxious to others in the future:—in these three cases they must refuse execution and in the last case must also notify the Holy See of the status of affairs; in all other cases, they are *obliged to execute* the rescript. To continue when it is clear that the rescript is invalidated by subreption or

[69] De Justis, *De Dispensationibus*, lib. I, cap. VI, n. 286, 506; Reiffenstuel, *Jus Canonicum*, lib. I, tit. III, n. 257; lib. I, tit. XXIX, n. 157; Santi, *Praelectiones*, lib. I, tit. XXIX, n. 9; Bizzari, *Collectanea*, pp. 612, 613.

[70] Can. 6, n. 2.

obreption renders the execution invalid.[71] Only *invalidating* subreption or obreption permits the necessary or mere executors to refuse execution, but since the Code does not distinguish, even the non-fulfillment of *accidental* conditions is sufficient cause for refusal to execute, although the validity of the execution will not be affected unless *essential conditions* are involved.[72] To refuse execution on account of subreption or obreption or the non-fulfilment of the conditions, the executor should be *certain* that the obreption or subreption was invalidating or that the conditions were not fulfilled. In *case of doubt,* the executor must suppose that the petition or conditions were verified and proceed to mandate the rescript to execution.[72a] That Freemasons, persecutors of the Church or of the hierarchy, public sinners, those guilty of public concubinage or public crimes are persons who should be refused rescripts by necessary or mere executors because of their unworthiness to receive papal favors,[73] cannot be accepted as a constant and invariable rule. An accurate list of ineligible or unworthy persons cannot be made—much will depend upon particular circumstances as well as the nature of the favor. The abovementioned persons might very readily be denied execution when the rescripts contain favors that are usually granted on account of the merits of the petitioners, but the same rule would hardly apply, in all cases, to rescripts containing favors that concern the private spiritual good of the petitioners. Because of the somewhat unsettled condition of such cases, and since the same kind of certainty is not required for a refusal that is based upon a judgment that the person is unworthy as for a refusal caused by the existence of subreption or obreption or the non-fulfilment of conditions,[73a] a provision is made by the legislator requiring the executor to notify the Holy See about the refusal

[71] Sanchez, *De Matrimonio,* lib. VIII, disp. XXXIV, n. 21; D'Annibale, *Summula* I, 241.

[72] Vermeersch-Creusen, *Epitome,* I, n. 140; Cicognani, *Commentarium,* p. 252; Ojetti, *Commentarium,* I, p. 257; Michiels, *Normae Generales,* II, p. 275.

[72a] Michiels, *Normae Generales,* II, p. 275.

[73] Augustine, *A Commentary,* I, p. 144, nota (4); Cicognani, *Commentarium,* p. 253; Coronata, *Institutiones,* I, p. 71, nota (6).

[73a] Compare "*videatur*" with "*constet*" and "*manifeste pateat.*"

whenever execution is denied a person because he is deemed unworthy to receive the favor.[73b] If, however, despite his unworthiness, the executor executes a rescript for a person, the rescript would be effective, because there is no nullifying clause in the present canon.[74]

The investigation that falls to the lot of the necessary executor should extend especially to the truthfulness of the petition and the verification of the conditions.[75] An extrajudicial investigation will suffice for rescripts of the external forum; in the internal forum, the petitioner's word may be accepted,[76] unless the executor knows from some other source that the person is not telling the truth. The act would, of course, be invalid if the executor proceeded when he knew that the party was not telling the truth about essential matters.[77] The executor is not bound to make this investigation, if an investigation was made before the petition was sent to the Roman Curia and he is certain that the circumstances of the case have not changed in the meantime,[78] or if certitude can be obtained in some other way than by an investigation.[79] Before the decree of the Holy Office, August 28, 1885,[80] canonists taught that this investigation was necessary for the validity of the execution on account of the clause "*si preces veritate niti reperis*" in the rescript,[81] but since then, the clause "*si preces*

[73b] Michiels, *Normae Generales*, II, p. 276.

[74] Can. 11; Ojetti, *Commentarium*, I, p. 258; Michiels, *Normae Generales*, II, p. 276.

[75] Chelodi, *Jus De Personis*, p. 142, nota (4).

[76] D'Annibale, *Summula*, I, 241; St. Alphonsus, *Theologia Moralis*, VI, n. 1143; De Smet, *De Sponsalibus et Matrimonio*, n. 868; Maroto, *Institutiones*, n. 288.

[77] Sanchez, *De Matrimonio*, lib. VIII, disp. XXXIV, n. 21; Garcia, *De Beneficiis*, VI, II, 250; De Justis, *De Dispensationibus*, lib. I, cap. VI, n. 271; Ojetti, *Commentarium*, I, p. 222.

[78] S. Poenit., 27 Aprilis 1886, ad III—*Coll. de Prop. Fide*, n. 1655; Konings-Putzer, *Commentarium*, n. 74; De Smet, *De Sponsalibus et Matrimonio*, p. 724, nota (4).

[79] Maroto, *Institutiones*, n. 288; Capello, *De Sacramentis*, III, n. 288.

[80] ASS, XXVII (1895-1896), 512.

[81] Sanchez, *De Matrimonio*, lib. VIII, disp. XXIV, n. 26; De Justis, *De Dispensationibus*, lib. I, cap. VI, n. 249; D'Annibale, *Summula*, I, 241.

veritate nitantur" has been substituted, and at present the investigation only affects the lawfulness of the execution.[82]

The *voluntary or free executor* is given the power to grant or deny the favor, and is left to his own prudent judgment and conscience in arriving at his decision. He should use as a guide the style of the Roman Curia, i.e., act as the Curia would act under the circumstances, taking into account the form of the rescript, the directions of the grantor, and the advisability of granting the favor.[83] Unless otherwise stated in the rescript, even the free executor cannot divide the favor and grant only part of what was petitioned, because he is given power merely to grant or to deny the favor,[84] but he can grant one favor without the other when two favors are contained in the same rescript.[85] Finally, the free executor cannot refuse to grant the favor without cause, since his judgment should be prudent and conscientious,[86] but at the same time it must be admitted that refusal on his part would be unfair but not unjust.[86a]

Article IV.—Work of the Executor.

The general rule that governs the work of the executor is contained in the following canon:

Canon 55.—Exsecutor procedere debet ad mandati normam, et nisi conditiones essentiales in litteris appositis impleverit ac substantialem procedendi formam servaverit, irrita est exsecutio.

The executor must always proceed according to the norm of the mandate, i.e., according to the instructions contained in the rescript and the form in which the commission was granted, v.g., whether mere, necessary, or free, and within

---

[82] S. Poenit., 27 Aprilis 1886—*Coll. de Prop. Fide*, n. 1655; D'Annibale, *Summula*, I, 241; Wernz-Vidal, *Jus Canonicum*, V, n. 445.

[83] Can. 54, 2; "*Normae Peculiares*," cap. III, n. 3—AAS, I (1909), 63.

[84] Vermeersch-Creusen, *Epitome*, I, n. 142; Ojetti, *Commentarium*, I, p. 258; Coronata, *Institutiones*, I, n. 77; Michiels, *Normae Generales*, II, p. 277. Contra Maroto, *Institutiones*, n. 288; Ayrinhac, *General Legislation*, p. 159.

[85] Can. 42, §3; Michiels, *Normae Generales*, II, p. 277.

[86] Maroto, *Institutiones*, n. 288.

[86a] Ayrinhac, *General Legislation*, p. 159.

the limitation of time, persons, and conditions prescribed by the mandate. Thus an executor is not permitted to grant less than what is contained in the commission, e.g., temporary secularization for perpetual secularization, nor to divide the favor, e.g., simple benefice for a double benefice, unless permission is contained in the rescript.[87] The execution remains valid, however, unless the essential conditions governing the actions of the executor are not fulfilled, or the substantial form of procedure is not followed.[88] Anything that concerns the mere qualities of an act, e.g., monitions placed in the rescript to help the execution proceed more easily, or that has already been prescribed by common law for the lawfulness of the procedure, does not pertain to the substantial form of execution. To the substantial form of execution belong all acts, not enjoined by common law, that are prescribed in a very strict manner by the rescript,[89] as well as all clauses that limit the forum, e.g., "*in foro interno tantum,*" [90] or are introduced by such words as "*non aliter,*" "*sic, neque alio modo,*" or "*si secus fit, irritum est et inane.*" [91]

The form to be used in the final decree of execution of rescripts pertaining to the *external forum* is prescribed in the following canon:

Canon 56.—Exsecutio rescriptorum quae forum externum respiciunt, scripto facienda est.

Written execution of rescripts for the external forum has always been considered necessary, but some canonists [92] held that the written form was necessary for the validity

---

[87] Vermeersch-Creusen, *Epitome*, I, n. 142; Coronata, *Institutiones*, I, n. 77.

[88] C. 22, X, *de rescriptis*, I, 3; De Angelis, *Praelectiones*, lib. I, tit. III, n. 9. Cf. Part III, chapt. II, article III regarding conditions affecting the execution of rescripts.

[89] Reiffenstuel, *Jus Canonicum*, lib. I, tit. III, n. 146; Chelodi, *Jus De Personis*, n. 80, p. 143, nota (1); Ojetti, *Commentarium*, I, p. 260.

[90] Chelodi, *Jus De Personis*, p. 143, nota (1); Coronata, *Institutiones*, I, n. 77.

[91] Barbosa, *Tractatus Varii, De clausulis*, claus. 81, n. 9; Ojetti, *Commentarium*, I, 260; Michiels, *Normae Generales*, II, p. 279.

[92] Corradus, *Praxis*, lib. I, cap. VI, n. 1; Giovine, *De Dispensationibus*, I, §89.

of the execution, while others[93] insisted that it was only necessary for the lawfulness of the act. Since the Code, authors are agreed[94] that the written form is required for the lawfulness, not for the validity of the execution, since there is no invalidating clause in the present canon.[95] The execution proper, i.e., the decree by which the favor is actually applied to the petitioner, not the preparatory acts, must be put in written form if the executor wishes to fulfill his mandate in a lawful manner. Some reference to the fulfillment of the preparatory acts should, of course, be made in the written decree of execution.[95a] The written form has been adopted by the legislator as the one that is most valuable for the sake of proof; in fact, as the safest and best proof that can be obtained. As a general rule, therefore, rescripts of the external forum must be executed in writing, but circumstances may arise, however, that will permit one to execute a rescript pertaining to the external forum orally, or by telegraph or telephone, or to execute the rescript in writing and then send the information to the party by telegraph or telephone, e.g., some rescripts for religious executed by their Superior General in Rome,[96] but a grave reason is always required to excuse the executor from the written form of execution, and even execution in writing followed by oral or telegraphic, etc., notification can be resorted to only in exceptional cases.

Rescripts granted for the *internal sacramental forum* should ordinarily be executed orally.[97] Regarding rescripts granted for the *internal non-sacramental forum,* the Code[98] merely requires that matrimonial dispensations be recorded in the secret archives of the Diocese. The best way to

[93] Pontius, *De Matrimonio,* lib. VIII, cap. XV, n. 2; D'Annibale, *Summula,* III, 364, nota (23); Gasparri, *De Matrimonio,* n. 396.

[94] Maroto, *Institutiones,* n. 288; Ayrinhac, *General Legislation,* p. 160; Cicognani, *Commentarium,* p. 257; Ojetti, *Commentarium,* I, p. 261; Chelodi, *Jus De Personis,* n. 80; Coronata, *Institutiones,* I, n. 77.

[95] Can. 11.

[95a] Michiels, *Normae Generales,* II, p. 280.

[96] Litt. Encycl, Secret. Stat., 10 Dec. 1891—*Coll. de Prop. Fide,* n. 1775; Augustine, *A Commentary,* I, p. 128; Capello, *De Sacramentis,* III, n. 288; Coronata, *Institutiones,* I, p. 68, nota (1).

[97] Kubelbeck, *The Sacred Penitentiary,* p. 102.

[98] Can. 1047.

proceed in executing such rescripts is to keep the rescript itself, with a note about its execution, in the secret Archives of the Diocese, and the written decree of execution in the secret archives of the parish.[99]

Whether made in writing or done orally, the decree of execution should, as a rule, expressly mention the day of the execution, the mandate of the Holy See, the name of the person to whom the favor is granted, the verification of the petition and the fulfillment of the conditions, and the fact that the favor is granted by the authority of the Holy See.[100] When the written execution is made merely by making a note on the rescript itself, a few words stating that the favor is granted will, of course, suffice. For the validity of the execution, however, it is not necessary in *matrimonial dispensations* to use the word *"dispensamus,"* since such words as *"oratores possunt nuptias inire,"* or *"matrimonium contrahitur"* will suffice; nor is it necessary for the validity of *any* rescript to use the phrase *"auctoritate Apostolica,"* unless the rescript states *"alias dispensationem esse nullam."* As a matter of fact, all that one must really do to execute a rescript validly, is to state that a certain favor is granted to a designated person.[101]

Article V.—Execution through a Substitute

Decretal Law maintained the principle that Papal delegation could be subdelegated when the delegate was selected on account of his office, unless a *mere* or *nudum ministry of execution* was committed to him,[102] but could never be subdelegated when the delegate was chosen on account of his personal qualifications for the work.[103] Canonists

---

[99] Vlaming, *Praelectiones*, n. 503; Capello, *De Sacramentis*, III, n. 288.

[100] De Smet, *De Sponsalibus et Matrimonio*, n. 876; Coronata, *Institutiones*, I, n. 77.

[101] Gasparri, *De Matrimonio*, n. 397; D'Annibale, *Summula*, III, 364, nota (28), (74); Capello, *De Sacramentis*, III, n. 288; Vermeersch-Creusen, *Epitome*, II, n. 324; Coronata, *Institutiones*, I, n. 77; Michiels, *Normae Generales*, II, p. 280.

[102] C. 43, X, *de officio et potestate judicis delegati*, I, 29.

[103] C. 3, X, *de officio et potestate judicis delegati*, I, 29.

agreed [104] that the mere executor could not subdelegate because he received the mere ministry of execution without any jurisdiction; but there was no such agreement about the power of the mixed or necessary executor to subdelegate, some canonists [105] claiming that the necessary executor could subdelegate the power of jurisdiction, i.e., the power of investigation, but not the mere ministry of execution, while others [106] held that he could subdelegate the entire work, even the execution, unless the clause *"per te exequaris"* was contained in the rescript. The clauses of the rescripts helped canonists to determine when the delegate was chosen on account of his personal qualifications for the work and not on account of the office he held. Some clauses stated this explicitly, e.g., *"per se"* or *"personaliter;"* [107] others, implicitly, e.g., *"negotium difficile et arduum committimus;"* [108] while still others were doubtful, e.g., *"conscientiae tuae," "prudentiae tuae," "de qua specialiter confidimus"* or *"de tua industria confidentes."* [109]

The Holy Office on February 20, 1888,[110] declared that the execution of matrimonial dispensations, committed to local Ordinaries or the Ordinaries of the petitioners, could be subdelegated, and on September 5, 1900,[111] decided that the

---

[104] Sanchez, *De Matrimonio*, lib. VIII, disp. XXVII, n. 43; De Justis, *De Dispensationibus*, lib. I, cap. VI, n. 313; De Rosa, *De Executoribus*, pars I, cap. X, n. 36-38; Schmalzgrueber, *Jus Ecclesiasticum*, pars I, tit. XXIX, n. 10; D'Annibale, *Summula*, I, 72, nota (20); Zitelli, *De Dispensationibus*, p. 33.

[105] Sanchez, *De Matrimonio*, lib. VIII, disp. XXVII, n. 43; De Justis, *De Dispensationibus*, lib. I, cap. VI, n. 313; De Rosa, *De Executoribus*, pars. I, cap. X, n. 36-38.

[106] Zitelli, *De Dispensationibus*, p. 33.

[107] Rigantius, *Commentarium*, Reg. 48, n. 20; D'Annibale, *Summula*, I, 72, nota (20).

[108] De Rosa, *De Executoribus*, pars II, cap. V, n. 22; Ferraris, *Bibliotheca*, V. Delegatus, n. 19-21; Wernz, *Jus Decretalium*, II, n. 553.

[109] Sanchez, *De Matrimonio*, lib. VIII, disp. XXVII, n. 43; De Justis, *De Dispensationibus*, lib. I, cap. VI, n. 314; De Rosa, *De Executoribus*, pars I, cap. X, n. 5 add.; Corradus, *Praxis*, lib. IX, cap. V, n. 33; D'Annibale, *Summula*, I, 72, nota (20): denied that such clauses indicated selection on account of personal qualifications. Reiffenstuel, *Jus Canonicum*, lib. I, tit. XXIX, n. 60; Ferraris, *Bibliotheca*, V. Delegatus, n. 19-21; Piat, *Praelectiones*, II, p. 369, nota (1): took the opposite view.

[110] ASS, XX (1887), 543.

[111] ASS, XXXIII (1900-1901), 225.

same would hold for executions of matrimonial dispensations committed to Bishops.

In can. 199, §2, the Code gives the general principle that delegated power can be subdelegated, either habitually or for a single act, unless subdelegation is forbidden or the delegate was selected on account of special qualifications for the work. Application of this principle to rescripts is contained in the following canon:

Canon 57, §1.—Rescriptorum exsecutor potest alium pro suo prudenti arbitrio sibi substituere, nisi substitutio prohibita fuerit, aut substituti persona praefinita.

§2.—Si tamen fuerit electa industria personae, exsecutori non licet alteri committere, nisi actus praeparatorios.

There is no longer any necessity, in discussing the question of the delegation of execution, to distinguish between free, necessary, and mere executors, since the word "*substituere,*" used in the canon, really denotes not only delegation but the whole act of execution, including the actual application of the rescript or the granting of the favor to the designated person, and is sufficiently comprehensive to include the committing to another of the mere ministry of execution, whether the latter alone is granted to the executor, or is connected with the power of investigation.[112] According to the present law, any executor, whether free, necessary, or mere, is allowed to select and substitute another in his place, unless substitution is forbidden, v.g., by the rescript or by law; unless the substitute is designated, e.g., "*te impedito prima Capituli dignitas;*" or unless the executor is selected because of personal qualifications for the task. Although unable to appoint a substitute to perform the entire work of execution, the executor, "*electa industria personae,*" can appoint a delegate to take care of the preparatory acts.

Maroto[113] claims that the preparatory acts can be delegated by the executor even when substitution is forbidden. Such a claim cannot be admitted, however, because one

---

[112] *Cicognani, Commentarium,* p. 260; Ojetti, *Commentarium,* I, p. 262, nota (1); Coronata, *Institutiones,* I, n. 78.

[113] *Institutiones,* n. 288.

must always presume that the legislator expresses and is silent about the things he wishes to express or be silent about. In this particular case, the legislator in §1 states, without qualification, that substitution cannot be freely made when substitution is forbidden or the substitute is designated, and in §2 that only subdelegation of the preparatory acts is allowed when the executor is elected "*industria personae;*" therefore, we must conclude that substitution for the preparatory acts is not permitted, when substitution is forbidden, or when the substitute is named: [114] otherwise, one could not satisfactorily explain why the clause "*si substitutio prohibita fuerit*" was placed in the second paragraph instead of the first; or, if the legislator intended to allow substitution of the preparatory acts in all cases, without exception, why he went to the trouble of dividing the canon in two paragraphs. Surely we cannot presuppose that the legislator distinguishes without meaning and without necessity.

The executor is considered to be "*electa industria personae*" when it is clear that he was selected to perform the work on account of special knowledge, prudence, merit, or influence,[115] or when it is expressed in the canon explicitly by "*per se*" or "*personaliter,*" or implicitly in the statement that a difficult work is committed.[116] The force of the clauses "*conscientiam tuam oneramus,*" etc., is still a controverted question.[117] Certainly, in view of the conflicting opinions of representative canonists before and since the Code, it is extremely doubtful whether such clauses should be interpreted as indicating "*electa industria personae:*" therefore, the law does not bind and, if substitution has been made, "*standum est pro valore actus.*" [118]

---

[114] Ojetti, *Commentarium,* I, p. 261; Michiels, *Normae Generales,* II, p. 283.

[115] Cicognani, *Commentarium,* p. 260; De Meester, *Compendium,* n. 301.

[116] Kearney, *The Principles of Delegation,* p. 85.

[117] Augustine, *A Commentary,* I, p. 142; nota (23); Ojetti, *Commentarium,* I, p. 221: claim that they signify "*electa industria personae.*" Maroto, *Institutiones,* I, p. 846, nota (2); Kearney, *The Principles of Delegation,* p. 85, nota (36): deny the claim.

[118] Can. 15; De Smet, *De Sponsalibus et Matrimonio,* n. 921. De Smet's suggestion that, if time permits, one should recourse to the Holy See, seems too exacting in the light of can. 15.

A person who has been selected on account of his personal qualifications for the work cannot *validly* substitute another except for the preparatory acts,[119] nor can any substitution be *validly* made when substitution is forbidden, nor can any other substitute be *validly* named when the substitute is designated, since in all three cases the law limits the powers of the executors. By *preparatory acts* are meant the acts that precede the actual decree of execution, e.g., recognition of document, investigation and verification of the petition and conditions.[120]

With the exception of the three cases designated by the Code, an executor can validly and lawfully substitute another in his place even when the internal forum is concerned, provided, of course, that the permission has been obtained from the interested party to divulge the secret.[121] The executor must always, however, show prudence in selecting a substitute. Michiels[121a] claims that the *necessary executor,* since his work is not jurisdictional, can substitute one who is not a cleric to do his work unless the grantor of the favor explicitly forbids it in the rescript, or unless the execution of the favor requires the intervention of one who has the power of Orders, but advises the necessary executor to appoint a cleric or even one with ecclesiastical dignity to take his place, and admits that the *voluntary executor* can delegate only one with ecclesiastical jurisdiction, and may even be required to obtain a priest or bishop as substitute, if the nature of the work requires the intervention of one with Sacred Orders. This view, as far as the necessary executor is concerned, is certainly contrary to the teaching of canonists before the Code, who, as has been explained in Article III of the present chapter, always insisted that the work of investigation, performed by the necessary executor, was jurisdictional and, hence, was the distinguishing mark between the necessary and

---

[119] Coronata, *Institutiones,* I, n. 78; Santamaria, *Comentarios,* I, p. 89.

[120] Cicognani, *Commentarium,* p. 261; De Smet, *De Sponsalibus et Matrimonio,* p. 720, nota (3).

[121] Capello, *De Sacramentis,* III, n. 283; De Smet, *De Sponsalibus et Matrimonio,* n. 865.

[121a] *Normae Generales,* II, p. 282.

mere executor. Following the traditional view of the work of the necessary and free executors, it may be admitted that if rescripts are still granted in that form, execution by a mere executor could be performed by a substitute who is not a cleric, and it might even be admitted that the final decree of a necessary execution might be committed to one incapable of receiving jurisdiction, but it must be maintained that the investigation, the jurisdictional part of the necessary executor's work, can be committed only to one who can receive the power of jurisdiction, i.e., a cleric.[121b]

Once the substitution has been made, the power of the original executor ceases entirely, and if the party wishes to contest the decision of the substitute, he must refer to matter to the grantor of the favor, not to the original executor.[122] Moreover, the substitute executor can never subdelegate another to take his place, unless the power to do so is expressly granted to him.[123]

Article VI.—Execution by Successors

Under the influence of the principle of the *"Regulae Juris," "Is qui in jure succedit alterius, eo jure, quo ille, uti debet,"* [124] canonists taught that rescripts that were committed for execution to Bishops, Vicars General, and Deans on account of their office, not because of their personal qualifications, could be executed by their successors because their offices were perpetual (or reputed to be perpetual as in the case of the Vicar General) and did not die with the persons; that rescripts ordinarily granted to Bishops or their Vicars General could not be executed by the Vicar Capitular during the vacancy of the Episcopal See because, according to the style of the Curia, such rescripts, during the Vacancy of the See, were committed for execution to the nearest Bishop, not to the Vicar Capitular, but that the rescripts which were ordinarily granted to the Vicars Capitular could be executed by the Vicar Capitular as suc-

---

121b Can. 118.

122 De Rosa, *De Dispensationibus*, pars II, cap. V, n. 8. 9; D'Annibale, *Summula*, I, 72, nota (20); Coronata, *Institutiones*, I, n. 78.

123 Can. 199, §5.

124 R. J. 46, in VI°.

cessor of the Bishop.[125] This teaching was somewhat modified by an encyclical letter issued by the Holy Office on February 20, 1888,[126] which declared that, whether or not execution had been started, all matrimonial dispensations granted for execution to local *Ordinaries* or Ordinaries of petitioners, that had not been mandated to execution before their death, could be executed by the Vicars Capitular and their Successors, and that all rescripts granted to the Vicar Capitular for execution could be executed by the succeeding Bishop and his Vicar General; and was also modified by another letter issued by the same Office on September 5, 1900,[127] that made a similar provision for matrimonial dispensations granted to *Bishops* for execution. Not long after, this law was extended to the execution of all rescripts of favor.[128] The present law on this matter is contained in the following canon:

Canon 58.—Rescripta quaelibet exsecutioni mandari possunt etiam ab exsecutoris successore in dignitate vel officio, nisi fuerit electa industria personae.

At present, all Rescripts, without exception, whether they contain dispensations, indulgences, privileges, or benefices, etc., that are committed for execution to persons on account of the dignity of office that they hold, can be executed by their successors in the dignity or office, presupposing, of course, that the original executor's power was not terminated by the death of the Pope.[128a] By *dignity* is meant not a mere honorary position, but one with precedence and jurisdiction, since it alone has real succession.[129] Major and minor dignities of chapters are included in this category.[130] *Office* is to be understood here in the

[125] Schmalzgrueber, *Jus Ecclesiasticum*, pars I, tit. III, n. 33.
[126] ASS, XX (1887), 543.
[127] ASS, XXXIII (1900-1901), 225.
[128] Ojetti, *Commentarium*, I, p. 264.
[128a] Cf. Part IV.
[129] Augustine, *A Commentary*, I, p. 147; Blat, *Commentarium*, I, n. 123.
[130] Wernz, *Jus Decretalium*, II, n. 240; Cicognani, *Commentarium*, p. 261.

strict sense of can. 145, §1,[131] because rescripts are ordinarily committed for execution to persons possessing ecclesiastical power of order or of jurisdiction, and only in an office with permanency and stability is succession possible. A successor of a person who had an office or dignity cannot, however, execute the rescripts that were committed to his predecessor on account of the latter's personal qualifications for the work. What has been said in the preceding article in explanation of *"electa industria persona"* need not be repeated here, but as a suggestion of practical importance, it may be added that when in a rescript the executor is designated by the title of his office or dignity, he should not be considered as selected on account of special personal fitness for the work.[132] In executing a rescript committed to his predecessor, a person should always start from the beginning of the execution, acting as though nothing had been done by his predecessor, since the instruction issued by the Sacred Penitentiary on April 3, 1886,[133] is still in force.[134]

Article VII.—Re-execution of Rescripts

Decretal Law [135] declared that the jurisdiction of a delegate ceased after a definite mandate to execution. In applying this principle to the execution of Rescripts of Favor, certain exceptions were admitted by canonists. The general principle stating that all delegation ceased *"finito negotio commisso,"* whether the work was done well or badly, because the *mandatarius* had consumed his jurisdiction,

---

[131] Blat, *Commentarium*, I, n. 123; Cicognani, *Commentarium*, p. 261, 262. Cf. Coronata, *Institutiones*, I, n. 78. Toso, *Commentaria Minora*, I, p. 146; Augustine, *A Commentary*, I, p. 147; Michiels, *Normae Generales*, II, p. 285, for opposite opinion.

[132] Chelodi, *Jus De Personis*, n. 80.

[133] NRT, XIX, p. 48 sq. The instruction stated that even though the execution had already been started, the new Ordinary should execute the rescript as though the Vicar Capitular had done nothing in the matter.

[134] Can. 6, n. 2; De Smet, *De Sponsalibus et Matrimonio*, p. 721, nota (4). Cf. Coronata, *Institutiones*, I, n. 78; Toso, *Commentaria Minora*, I, p. 146; Michiels, *Normae Generales*, II, p. 285, who claim that it is not necessary to repeat the acts performed by the predecessor.

[135] C. 9, X, *de officio et potestate judicis delegati*, I, 29.

when applied to rescripts of favor, was interpreted as meaning that, ordinarily, the work of the executor ceased when the rescript was executed, even though it was executed invalidly.[136] Canonists concluded from this principle that when an executor declared that a rescript of the external forum was subreptious or obreptious his power ceased because by his judgment he consumed his entire jurisdiction, but that his power did not cease either when he declared that a rescript of the Sacred Penitentiary was subreptious or obreptious, because the penitent could go to another confessor for re-execution if the confessor was not designated, or to the same confessor if he was designated, or when he did not observe the form of the mandate or law because *"nihil agit,"* [137] or when a mere executor erred in his work because his work was not jurisdictional and therefore could be corrected.[138] On January 15, 1894, the Sacred Penitentiary,[139] in answer to an inquiry about the proper way to proceed in a marriage case, in which a Bishop, for urgent reasons, had proceeded to execute a rescript before the document had arrived from Rome and had subsequently married a couple who were still in good faith, declared *"Opus esse nova dispensationum executione."* This decision changed the status of invalidly executed matrimonial dispensations, since in accordance with its teaching a matrimonial dispensation, that had been invalidly executed because the rescript had been executed before the executor had received the document and recognized its authenticity and integrity, could be re-executed without any further papal mandate. This rule that was formulated for a particular kind of invalid execution has been extended and generalized by the following canon so as to apply to all invalidations and errors of execution.

---

[136] De Justis, *De Dispensationibus*, lib. I, cap. VI, n. 488; D'Annibale, *Summula*, I, 77, nota (55); Ojetti, *Commentarium*, I, p. 266; Kearney, *The Principles of Delegation*, p. 112.

[137] Sanchez, *De Matrimonio*, lib. VIII, disp. XXVII, n. 39, 40; De Justis, *De Dispensationibus*, lib. I, cap. VI, n. 487, 490, 494; De Rosa, *De Executoribus*, pars I, cap. X, n. 29, 31; Corradus, *Praxis*, lib. VII, cap. IV, n. 55, 56, 73; D'Annibale, *Summula*, I, 77, nota (55); Gasparri, *De Matrimonio*, n. 399.

[138] De Rosa, *De Executoribus*, pars I, cap. X, n. 33.

[139] S. Poenit., 15 Jan. 1894, ad II—*Coll. de Prop. Fide*, n. 1858.

Canon 59, §1.—Exsecutori fas est, si quoquo modo in rescriptorum exsecutione erraverit, iterum eadem exsecutioni mandare.

The present law permits re-execution of all rescripts that were either invalidly executed or, through error, were not executed, whether the invalidation or error was committed knowingly or through ignorance, whether the error or invalidation was caused by subreption or obreption, the non-fulfillment of essential conditions, the non-observance of the substantial form, or by proceeding before the authentic letters or official notification had been received. Maroto,[140] explaining the phrase *"expleto mandato"* of can. 207, §1, in conjunction with can. 59, §1, endeavors to limit the extension of this rule by claiming that after the work is morally speaking complete the delegate cannot, without new delegation, reassume his work. Certainly the words *"quoquo modo"* of the present canon do not permit such a limitation of the power of the executor to re-execute, even when the attempt to execute is morally speaking complete.[141] As a matter of fact, the majority of authors [142] admit that in voluntary jurisdiction a mandate is not fulfilled unless and until the execution is valid. De Meester [143] also attempts to limit the meaning of this canon by stating that the voluntary executor, after he has executed the rescript, whether properly or badly, cannot re-execute because by his work he has discharged his jurisdiction, but there is absolutely nothing in the canon that even suggests such a limitation. The canon does not distinguish between kinds of executors and, therefore, we must conclude that, according to the present law, the power of an executor does not cease until he has validly executed the rescript.[144]

---

140 *Institutiones*, I, p. 856, nota (3).

141 Kearney, *The Principles of Delegation*, p. 112.

142 Chelodi, *Jus De Personis*, n. 129; Coronata, *Institutiones*, I, n. 79, 290; Ayrinhac, *General Legislation*, p. 366; Kearney, *The Principles of Delegation*, p. 112.

143 *Compendium*, I, n. 302, nota (4), p. 320, nota (2).

144 Here concerned only with cessation of power on account of invalid executions. Cf. Part IV where it is explained that the executor's power ceases by lapse of time, revocation, renunciation, etc.

De Smet,[145] while admitting that, according to a response of the Sacred Penitentiary given on June 27, 1885,[146] an executor can re-execute an invalidly executed matrimonial dispensation and then marry the parties although they had previously attempted to contract marriage, advises as a safer rule, if time permits, to recourse in such cases to the grantor for a norm of action, since as a general rule the faculty to dispense for a marriage to be contracted cannot be used to dispense for an invalidly contracted marriage. Such a recourse to the Holy See seems entirely unnecessary, however, not only on account of the answer of the Sacred Penitentiary of 1885, but also on account of the solution given by the Sacred Penitentiary on January 15, 1894,[147] namely, "*Opus est nova dispensationum executione.*" Most authors[148] are of this opinion, stating very definitely that, in case, e.g., a rescript was executed before the presentation of the rescript, and the couple were subsequently married, a new execution of the rescript after the original document is presented, not the execution of a new rescript, is all that is required so that the priest may be able to marry the couple. This conclusion is confirmed by the fact that no law invalidates the first rescript or the first mandate of execution on account of the invalid execution, or even on account of the civil marriage contracted in the meantime.[149]

It is hardly necessary for the executor to have the authentic rescript in his possession at the time of the re-execution, as long as he recognized its authenticity and integrity at the time of its presentation to him;[150] nor does it seem necessary that the investigation be repeated, unless the executor had erred by falsely judging that invalidating subreption or obreption had been committed by the petitioner, or that the essential conditions were not fulfilled, or unless it was probable that the circumstances had

[145] *De Sponsalibus et Matrimonio*, n. 930.

[146] NRT, XIX, p. 57 sq.

[147] *Coll. de Prop. Fide*, n. 1858.

[148] Wernz-Vidal, *Jus Canonicum*, V, n. 445; Capello, *De Sacramentis*, III, n. 288; Chelodi, *Jus Matrimoniale*, p. 52, nota (3).

[149] Wernz-Vidal, *Jus Canonicum*, V, p. 535, nota (147); Feije, *De Impedimentis*, n. 734.

[150] Coronata, *Institutiones*, I, n. 79; Michiels, *Normae Generales*, II, p. 287.

changed in the meantime to such an extent as to endanger the truthfulness of the petition. All that the present canon requires is that the same rescript be mandated to execution, not that the whole process of execution be repeated and, therefore, it is reasonable to conclude that in every case of re-execution it is sufficient to supply what was lacking in the first process and then pass a new decree of execution.[151] Since the same person re-executes the rescript, there is not the same reason for a repetition of the whole process as there is when the rescript is executed by a successor.

Whenever the substitute errs in the execution of a rescript, he, and not the original executor, must re-execute the rescript, because the power to re-execute is given by the present law to the executor, i.e., to the one who actually executed the rescript invalidly and not to the one who was originally commissioned to perform the work.[152] Moreover, if the favored party wishes to change executors, or if the substitute refuses execution, the party must recourse to the Holy See, not to the original executor.[152a]

If it happens that the two-fold power of dispensing from a matrimonial impediment and granting legitimation to the children is conferred upon an executor, and he omits to execute the latter favor, the execution of the other favor is not thereby invalidated:—in such a case, the executor, afterwards, would merely be obliged to execute the favor of legitimation, since a two-fold office was committed to him, and nothing prevents him at any time from granting the latter favor without the former, except when the parties of their own volition refuse to marry.[153]

[151] De Meester, *Compendium*, I, n. 302; Cicognani, *Commentarium*, p. 263.

[152] Michiels, *Normae Generales*, II, p. 286.

[152a] C. 27, X, *de officio et potestate judicis delegati*, I, 29; De Rosa, *De Executoribus*, pars II, cap. V, n. 33; D'Annibale, *Summula*, I, 72, nota (20); Coronata, *Institutiones*, I, n. 79; Michiels, *Normae Generales*, II, p. 286. An exception must be admitted for a party who has received a rescript of the internal sacramental forum that has no designated executor: he can change to any confessor approved by the local Ordinary.

[153] De Justis, *De Dispensationibus*, lib. I, cap. VI, n. 490; Corradus, *Praxis*, lib. VIII, cap. II, n. 27, 33; De Smet, *De Sponsalibus et Matrimonio*, n. 879, p. 737, nota (4).

A different procedure than mere re-execution must be adopted when the rescript itself, and not merely the execution, is invalid. The petitioner or the person who is to be the executor may discover, either *before* or *after* the rescript had been issued by the Roman Curia, that, e.g., the petition was obreptious:—in the former case, the petitioner need only send in another petition adding, correcting, or supplying what was lacking in the first petition, and asking for a decree *"Reformatorium;"* [154] in the latter case, it is necessary to send either for a new dispensation or for a *"Perinde Valere,"* unless for special reasons it is deemed advisable to leave the parties in good faith. The petition for the *"Perinde Valere"* should state substantially what was stated in the first petition together with the reason for the nullity of the first rescript.[155] The *"Perinde Valere"* differs from the ordinary rescript inasmuch as it convalidates the former rescript and, by fiction of law, makes the effects of the second rescript retroactive to the day of the granting of the first rescript. In executing the *"Perinde Valere,"* the first rescript must be declared valid and then re-executed as though it were valid from the beginning; then the second execution will have the same effects as the rescript would have had if it had been validly executed the first time. The rescript *"Perinde Valere"* is, however, generally granted under the express or tacit condition that no other invalidating defect exists except the one mentioned in the second petition. Therefore, if another invalidating defect is later discovered, a petition for a rescript *"Perinde Valere super Perinde Valere"* must be sent to Rome. Upon execution, the rescript *"Perinde Valere super Perine Valere"* will validate the rescript *"Perinde Valere"* and, consequently, produce the same effects as the *"Perinde Valere"* would have produced had it been valid.[155a]

---

[154] Giovine, *De Dispensationibus*, II, §82, n. 4 sq.; Gasparri, *De Matrimonio*, n. 362; Wernz-Vidal, *Jus Canonicum*, V, n. 448.

[155] Giovine, *De Dispensationibus*, II, §82, n. 4 sq.; Gasparri, *De Matrimonio*, n. 362; Feije, *De Impedimentis*, n. 729; Kubelbeck, *The Sacred Penitentiaria*, p. 104; Vlaming, *Praelectiones*, n. 510; De Smet, *De Sponsalibus et Matrimonio*, n. 924, 925, 929.

[155a] Giovine, *De Dispensationibus*, II, §82, n. 6.

Article VIII.—Executorial Taxes

Decretal Law [156] forbade delegates to accept anything from the interested parties except food and drink that could be consumed in a few days, and moderate traveling expenses when it was necessary for them to travel outside their domicile in the interest of people who were not poor. The Roman Pontiffs, during the seventeenth and eighteenth centuries,[157] were very insistent that executors should receive nothing in taxes except the customary food and drink. During the nineteenth century, different papal decisions served to clarify considerably the teaching of the Church on this point:—the Bishop and the Officialis were forbidden to accept anything except what was considered a suitable compensation for the labor incurred by the notary or chancellor in executing dispensations, unless special papal permission to receive more had been granted; [158] moreover, the Bishop and Vicar General were forbidden to receive any money or stipends, even by force of custom, for the execution of rescripts,[159] but the Vicar General was permitted to collect the regular tax for the investigation and other work that preceded the sending of the petition to Rome.[160] In this country, the Third Plenary Council of Baltimore [161] stated very clearly that no money could be received by the executors of rescripts except the alms required by the Holy See and the tax imposed by the Bishop for the sustenance of the Chancery.

Canonists were agreed [162] that executors of rescripts granted by the Sacred Penitentiary for the internal forum could not exact anything for their labor, but should be

---

[156] C. 11, *de rescriptis*, I, 3, in VI°.

[157] Alexander VII, const. "*Inter gravissimas*," 2 Maii, 1656, *Bullarum . . . Taurinensis editio*, XVI, 100; Innocent XII, const. "*Sacerdotalem*," 30 Jan. 1700, *Bullarum . . . Taurinensis editio*, XX, 190.

[158] S. Poenit., 26 Aprilis 1861—NRT, XVIII, p. 411.

[159] S. C. Concil., 22 Junii 1871—*Thesaurus*, vol. 130 (1871), p. 472 sq.; S. C. Concil., 28 Jan. 1882—*Coll. de Prop. Fide*, n. 1562.

[160] S. C. Concil., 18 Aprilis 1885—NRT, XVIII, p. 602.

[161] *Concilii Plenarii Baltimorensis III Acta et Decreta*, n. 134.

[162] Sanchez, *De Matrimonio*, lib. VIII, disp. XXXV, n. 14; De Justis, *De Dispensationibus*, lib. I, cap. VI, n. 241; Giovine, *De Dispensationibus*, II, §55; Gasparri, *De Matrimonio*, n. 403.

compensated for any expenses incurred, and could accept anything that was spontaneously given after the rescripts had been executed. Some canonists [163] maintained that the law of the Church regarding taxes for executors was more severe when matrimonial dispensations were concerned than when other rescripts of the external forum were involved, and, consequently, that the executors of matrimonial dispensations could receive the Chancery tax and remuneration for expenses incurred, but not food and drink that could be consumed in a few days.

Violators of this law that forbade the acceptance or exaction of executorial taxes incurred severe ecclesiastical penalties:—Vicars General incurred excommunication; Bishops, suspension from the exercise of jurisdiction and pontificals, and privation of the returns of their benefice.[164] Some authors [165] claimed that violation of this law invalidated the execution of the rescript, but others [166] insisted that invalidation was incurred only in rescripts granted before 1885 *"in forma pauperum,"* in which the clause *"et nihilominus absolutio et dispensatio a te facienda nullius sit roboris vel momenti"* was inserted.

In 1908, Pius X [167] ordained that the sum of money to be received by the Diocesan Curia for the execution of papal rescripts should be designated in all rescripts by the Officials of the Roman Curia, and should always be less than the tax for the rescripts; moreover, that nothing could be asked for the recognition of rescripts granted *in forma commissoria* except a just compensation for the expenses incurred by the Ordinary, e.g., in investigating the place to be used for a chapel, or in investigating the authenticity of a relic.

---

[163] De Justis, *De Dispensationibus*, lib. I, cap. VI, n. 241; Corradus, *Praxis*, lib. VIII, cap. VI, n. 15; Giovine, *De Dispensationibus*, II, §55. Cf. Sanchez, *De Matrimonio*, lib. VII, disp. XXXV, n. 12 for the opposite view.

[164] Giovine, *De Dispensationibus*, II, §55; Gasparri, *De Matrimonio*, n. 400; Konings-Putzer, *Commentarium*, p. 88.

[165] Konings-Putzer, *Commentarium*, p. 88.

[166] Gasparri, *De Matrimonio*, n. 400.

[167] *"Normae Communes,"* cap. XI, n. 1—AAS, I (1909), 55; *"Normae Peculiares,"* cap. III, n. 5—AAS, I (1909), 64.

The present law regarding executorial taxes is contained in the following canons:

Canon 59, §2.—Quod attinet ad taxas pro rescriptorum exsecutione, servetur praescriptum can. 1507, §1.

Canon 1507, §1.—Salvo praescripto can. 1056 et can. 1234, praefinire taxas . . . pro exsecutione rescriptorum Sedis Apostolicae . . . , in tota ecclesiastica provincia solvendas, est Concilii provincialis aut conventus Episcoporum provinciae; sed nulla vi praefinitio eiusmodi pollet, nisi prius a Sede Apostolica approbata fuerit.

Provincial Councils or Provincial Meetings of Bishops must determine the executorial taxes, but their determination of the taxes will not be valid until the approval of the Holy See has been obtained.[168] According to can. 1056, even a contrary custom will not permit an executor to exact any emolument, except what is necessary for the expenses of the Chancery, for matrimonial rescripts granted "*in forma non-pauperum*," unless the Holy See has expressly granted permission to receive more. Executors who violate this law are bound to restitution. When no tax has been determined for the execution of rescripts by the Provincial Council or Meeting of Bishops, or by a special papal indult, the executorial tax designated in the rescript may be exacted.[169] Finally, the regulation of the "*Normae Peculiares*" regarding taxes for rescripts granted *in forma gratiosa* is still in force.[170]

---

[168] De Meester, *Compendium*, n. 302; Cocchi, *Commentarium*, I, p. 161; Coronata, *Institutiones*, I, n. 80.

[169] De Smet, *De Sponsalibus et Matrimonio*, n. 858; Capello, *De Sacramentis*, III, n. 290.

[170] Blat, *Commentarium*, I, n. 124; Coronata, *Institutiones*, I, p. 76, nota (4).

PART IV

Cessation of Papal Rescripts of Favor

The general principle of the "*Regulae Juris*," "*Decet concessum a principe beneficium esse mansurum*,"[1] admits of limitations and exceptions. Rescripts of favor may be suspended or they may cease entirely: they are suspended when the power of the executor ceases, and cease entirely, indirectly, when the favors contained in or granted by them cease, directly, when they cease as rescripts.

The power of the executor ceases through lapse of the time allotted for the execution; by the total cessation of the cause of the delegation, e.g., if the executor was empowered to dispense a couple and one of them died before the dispensation was granted; by revocation directly intimated to the executor before the execution had been started, either in person, or through a letter or a representative; by renunciation of the office, directly intimated to and accepted by the Holy See; by the Vacancy of the Holy See, when the power had been granted to bestow favors on persons designated in the rescript and "*res integra est*," or when a clause like "*ad beneplacitum nostrum*" appears in the rescript;[2] and by the death of the executor when he was appointed on account of his office or dignity, not on account of his personal qualifications for the work.[3]

Privileges and dispensations that admit of successive applications, e.g., permission to read forbidden books, cease in many different ways. They cease first of all by renunciation that is accepted by the grantor. Private individuals may renounce personal favors, i.e., favors in which they

[1] R. J. 16, in VI.°
[2] Can. 207, §1.
[3] Can. 58.

alone are concerned directly, unless the renunciation would injure the acquired rights of others or the common good, but they cannot renounce privileges or dispensations granted to a community, dignity, or place. A community can renounce the favors granted to the community unless the renunciation would prove detrimental to the Church or to others.[4] Privileges and dispensations that admit of successive applications cease also when the place or thing with which they are connected perish or are destroyed, but real privileges, e.g., privileges granted a community or church will revive if the place is restored within forty years;[5] they cease by non-use or contrary use, if they are burdensome to others and either implicit renunciation is made by the possessors, or legitimate prescription is invoked by the interested parties;[6] and they cease by a change of circumstances which, in the judgment of the Holy See, renders them harmful or their use unlawful, or by lapse of the time for which they were granted.[7] Benefices, personal dispensations and privileges, not real privileges, cease by the death of the petitioners or recipients.[8] Dispensations that admit of successive applications are lost by a certain and total cessation of the motive cause for the granting of the favor.[9] Finally, possessors of dispensations that admit of successive applications may be deprived of favors that they abuse, and in order that persons who abuse papal favors may be punished, provision is made so that grave abuses must be reported by the Ordinary to the Holy See.[10]

Papal Rescripts of Favor cease as rescripts in four different ways:—by the lapse of the determined time for which they were granted, by the fulfilment of a resolutory condition, e.g., "*donec convalueris,*" in the rescript, by revoca-

[4] Can. 72, 86; Reiffenstuel, *Jus Canonicum*, lib. I, tit. III, n. 264, 265, 270; Santi, *Praelectiones*, lib. I, tit. III, n. 37; De Angelis, *Praelectiones*, lib. I, tit. III, n. 11, Wernz, *Jus Decretalium*, I, n. 156. Cf. can. 62.

[5] Can. 75, 86.

[6] Can. 76, 86.

[7] Can. 77, 86.

[8] Can. 74, 86.

[9] Can. 86.

[10] Can. 78, 86.

tion, and by the vacancy of the Holy See.[11] Only the latter two modes of cessation require explanation.

The present canonical teaching about *revocation* is contained in the following canon:

Canon 60, §1.—Rescriptum, per peculiarem Superioris actum revocatum, perdurat usque dum revocatio ei, qui illud obtinuit, significetur.

§2.—Per legem contrarium nulla rescripta revocantur, nisi aliud in ipsa lege caveatur, aut lex lata sit a Superiore ipsius rescribentis.

Decretal law [12] contains an instance of a revocation made by Boniface VIII of all the favors granted by himself and his predecessors. Pre-code canonists [13] maintained that rescripts ceased either by explicit or tacit revocation:—*explicit,* if the grantor clearly and decisively declared that a previous concession was invalid; *tacit,* if the Roman Curia granted a rescript that was to be preferred to a previous rescript, e.g., an actual grant of the favor after a previous grant of an expectative letter for the same favor, or granted a special rescript contrary to a previous general rescript. Many authors [14] claimed, however, that for express revocation to be really effective it had to be made directly to the person to whom the rescript was granted and, therefore, all acts made before the official notification was received would be valid, even though before that time the person had been privately informed that the favor had been recalled.

There can be no doubt about the present law:—it states very clearly and explicitly that the act of revocation has no value unless the notification is official, is made by the authority of the grantor, and is directly intimated to the

[11] Wernz, *Jus Decretalium,* I, n. 156; Chelodi, *Jus De Personis,* n. 81.

[12] C. 15, *de rescriptis,* I, 3, in VI°.

[13] Reiffenstuel, *Jus Canonicum,* lib. I, tit. III, n. 99, 115, 271; De Angelis, *Praelectiones,* lib. I, tit. III, n. 11; Santi, *Praelectiones,* lib. I, tit. III, n. 37, Wernz, *Jus Decretalium,* I, n. 156.

[14] Sanchez, *De Matrimonio,* lib. III, disp. XXXVI, n. 9; Reiffenstuel, *Jus Canonicum,* lib. I, tit. XXXVIII, n. 156; D'Annibale, *Summula,* I, 77, nota (60).

recipient of the rescript, i.e., to the favored party, not the executor.[14a] Any and all acts performed before official notification has been received are valid, even though the acts had been performed after the grantor had manifested before others his intention to revoke the rescript, or after the recipient of the rescript had been privately informed of the action of the grantor.[15] Although denied by Cocchi,[16] tacit revocation still exists in the form of partial revocation of a general rescript by a special rescript, tacit revocation, however, as understood before the Code, namely, in the sense that the special rescript prevails over the general rescript but does not *ipso facto* make it invalid. As a matter of fact, however, this latter kind of revocation is not really tacit revocation but implicit expressed revocation.

The only way in which papal rescripts can be revoked by law is by the express declaration of their revocation by papal laws, since there is no legislator superior to the Pope.

The effect that the *Vacancy of the Holy See* has upon Papal Rescripts of Favor is stated in the following canon:

Canon 61.—Per Apostolicae Sedis aut dioecesis vacationem nullum eiusdem Sedis Apostolicae aut Ordinarii rescriptum perimitur, nisi aliud ex additis clausulis appareat, aut rescriptum contineat potestatem alicui factam concedendi gratiam peculiaribus personis in eodem expressis, et res adhuc integra sit.

The present law has merely retained, without change, the law that existed before the Code. Decretal Law stated very definitely that if a rescript of favor contained the clause *"ad beneplacitum nostrum,"* the favor would cease upon the death of the Pope because the *"beneplacitum"* of a Pope died with him, whereas if it contained the phrase *"ad beneplacitum Apostolicae Sedis,"* the favor would continue to be enjoyed by the recipient of the rescript, because the Holy See itself did not die;[17] that if the matter was

[14a] Michiels, *Normae Generales*, II, p. 296, contra Ojetti, I, p. 268. The one who really *obtains* the rescript is the beneficiary, not the executor.

[15] Coronata, *Institutiones*, I, n. 81.

[16] *Commentarium*, I, p. 161.

[17] C. 5, *de rescriptis*, I, 3, in VI°.

entire *(re integra)*, an executor even after the death of the Pope, could execute a rescript containing a *"gratia facta,"* [18] or exercise a power to grant a certain benefice to a non-designated worthy person, but could not exercise a power a grant a favor to certain designated persons.[19]

Canonists, both before and since the Code,[20] explain that although such clauses in rescripts as *"ad beneplacitum Sedis"* or *"dum revocavero"* are not affected by the Vacancy of the Holy See, because the Holy See does not die, and to revoke a favor presupposes a positive contrary act which cannot be performed after the grantor has died or lost his power, such clauses in the rescript as *"ad beneplacitum nostrum," "donec voluero,"* or *"donec mihi placuerit,"* which presuppose perseverance of the grantor in his original will, cause the favors granted in such rescripts to cease at the Vacancy of the Holy See, because the *"beneplacitum"* of a person ceases with them and no one can juridically will or please or displease when they are physically or juridically dead.

In determining which rescripts could or could not be still executed during the Vacancy of the Holy See, *"re integra,"* pre-Code canonists [21] brought to the fore the Decretal distinction between rescripts *in forma commissoria* that contained a *"gratia facta,"* and those that contained a *"gratia facienda,"* i.e., between rescripts in which the favor had already been granted by the Pope and the executor had merely to apply the rescript to the party, and rescripts in which the favor was really to be granted not by the Pope himself, but by the executor, in virtue of powers received

---

[18] C. 9, *de officio et potestate judicis delegati*, I, 14, in VI°.

[19] C. 36, *de praebendis et dignitatibus*, III, 4, in VI°.

[20] Sanchez, *De Matrimonio*, lib. VIII, disp. XXVIII, n. 49, 50, 52; Reiffenstuel, *Jus Canonicum*, lib. I, tit. III, n. 260-262; De Angelis, *Praelectiones*, lib. I, tit. III, n. 10; Cicognani, *Commentarium*, p. 267; Ojetti, *Commentarium*, I, p. 271.

[21] Sanchez, *De Matrimonio*, lib. VIII, disp. XXVIII, n. 81, 87; Garcia, *De Beneficiis*, VI, II, n. 309-311; Layman, *Theologia Moralis*, lib. I, tract. IV, cap. 23, n. 18; De Justis, *De Dispensationibus*, lib. I, cap. VI, n. 505-506; Reiffenstuel, *Jus Canonicum*, lib. I, tit. III, n. 250-259; Schmalzgrueber, *Jus Ecclesiasticum*, pars I, tit. III, n. 37; De Angelis, *Praelectiones*, lib. I, tit. III, n. 10; Santi, *Praelectiones*, lib. I, tit. III, n. 35; Gasparri, *De Matrimonio*, n. 392; Wernz, *Jus Decretalium*, I, n. 156; D'Annibale, *Summula*, I, 222, nota (6).

from the Pope. They maintained the Decretal principle that, "*re integra*," a rescript containing a "*gratia facta*" did not cease at the Vacancy of the Holy See, because the interested party had an acquired right to the favor, a *jus ad rem*, whereas a rescript containing a "*gratia facienda*" did cease, because the party had no acquired right to the favor, no *jus ad rem*. They explained, moreover, that when a power to absolve was granted to a person or community for the benefit of *non-designated persons*, evidently the favor was given to the person or community and, therefore, was a "*gratia facta*" and even, "*re integra*," did not cease at the physical or juridical death of the grantor. When they treated the question of a power granted to a person in favor of *certain determined persons*, they immediately distinguished between rescripts with a free or voluntary executor, and rescripts with a mixed or necessary executor. The former kind of rescripts, according to their teaching, "*re integra*," ceased at the Vacancy of the Holy See because the favor contained in them was granted not by the Pope but by his delegate and therefore, "*re integra*," the favor was a "*gratia facienda*" and no right has been acquired either by the designated persons, or by the delegate, since the favor was not intended for the delegate; the latter, however, according to canonists, "*re integra*," did not cease at the Vacancy of the Holy See because, due to the fact that the executor had been ordered to grant the favor to the petitioner if he found, upon investigation, that the petition was true, the favor was considered to be a "*gratia facta*," and since the favor was made for the benefit of the petitioner, it bestowed on him a "*jus ad rem*." Apparently, canonists did not discuss the status of rescripts with a mere executor, but on the principles used, they must have considered them, for an "*a fortiori*" *reason*, to be in the same condition as mixed or necessary rescripts. Two decisions of the Holy See during the eighteenth century declared that mixed rescripts could be executed, "*re integra*," even during the Vacancy of the Holy See.[22]

[22] S. C. Ep. et Reg. 15 Julii 1740—Fontes, n. 1857; S. C. Ep. et Reg., 7 Aprilis 1769—Fontes, n. 1877.

Without entering into the distinctions of ancient canonists, the present canon states very clearly and definitely that the only kind of rescripts, "*re integra*," that cease during the Vacancy of the Holy See are rescripts that give power to the executor to grant a favor to specially designated persons, i.e., rescripts of favor that are granted *in forma commissoria* with a *voluntary executor* in favor of specially designated persons, not those that are granted *in forma gratiosa*, nor those granted *in forma commissoria* with a *voluntary executor* that do not designate the beneficiaries, nor any rescript granted with a *necessary* or *mere executor*.[23] Even rescripts granted *in forma commissoria* with a voluntary executor in favor of specially designated persons would not cease at the Vacancy of the Holy See if the matter was not entire, unless a clause like "*ad beneplacitum nostrum*" was inserted in the rescript. Of course, if a clause as "*ad beneplacitum nostrum*," "*donec voluero*," or "*donec mihi placuerit*" were contained in the rescript, *any* rescript would cease at the death of the Pope, whether the *res* was still *integra* or not, just as the favor itself would cease although the rescript had been executed before the Pope died.

The matter is considered to be entire *(re integra)* if the executor has not begun the preparatory acts of the execution;[24] but the matter is not entire after the parties are summoned by the executor to see if the petition is subreptious or obreptious, and very probably not entire after the executor has recognized the integrity and authenticity of the rescript.[25] If, however, the *voluntary* executor acts invalidly during the entire execution of the rescript, "*nihil agit*," and, therefore, the matter is entire.[26] Moreover, the voluntary executor could judge that the matter was not

---

[23] Chelodi, *Jus De Personis*, n. 81; Wernz-Vidal, *Jus Canonicum*, V, n. 444, 447.

[24] D'Annibale, *Summula*, I, 77; Cicognani, *Commentarium*, p. 268; Maroto, *Institutiones*, n. 289; Chelodi, *Jus De Personis*, n. 81.

[25] Coronata, *Institutiones*, I, n. 82; Cicognani, *Commentarium*, p. 261; De Smet, *De Sponsalibus et Matrimonio*, p. 720, nota (3); Michiels, *Normae Generales*, II, p. 302.

[26] Vermeersch-Creusen, *Epitome*, I, n. 148; Cicognani, *Commentarium*, p. 268.

entire and, therefore, could continue to re-execute an invalidly executed or non-executed rescript even during the vacancy of the Holy See, if he at least had validly recognized the authenticity and integrity of the rescript before the death of the Pope, and, e.g., invalidated the execution by not observing the substantial form or the essential conditions, or did not execute because, by mistake, he judged that his power had ceased. This opinion, which at times may be of very practical importance, seems to have a certain degree of probability, since, as already stated,[27] in the re-execution of an invalidly executed rescript it is not necessary to repeat the whole process of execution, but merely to repeat the acts that caused the invalidation and then make a new final decree of execution. It might be well to remember also that if the Vacancy of the Holy See was not commonly known and the executor, in error, proceeded to execution, the favor would be validly received through a right supplied by common error.[28]

Cocchi [29] apparently maintains that consideration should still be given to the Twelfth Rule of the Apostolic Chancery, which says, in effect, that rescripts, granted by the Roman Curia within a year before the death of the Pope, that ceased by the Vacancy of the Holy See because execution had not been started, revive as soon as the Rules of the Chancery go into effect. This view cannot be accepted, however, since the legislative force of the Rules of the Apostolic Chancery ceased when the Code came into existence.[29a]

Even before the Code, it was rather generally admitted that dispensations or favors granted by the Sacred Penitentiary for the internal forum did not cease, even "*re integra,*" during the Vacancy of the Holy See, because the Sacred Penitentiary did not expire with the Pope but re-

---

[27] Part III, Chapt. III, Art. VII.

[28] Can. 209; Sanchez, *De Matrimonio*, lib. III, disp. XXII, n. 59; Reiffenstuel, *Jus Canonicum*, lib. I, tit. III, n. 261; Coronata, *Institutiones*, I, n. 82; Michiels, *Normae Generales*, II, p. 300.

[29] *Commentarium*, I, p. 162.

[29a] Maroto, *Institutiones*, n. 98; De Meester, *Compendium*, n. 602; Vermeersch-Creusen, *Epitome*, I, n. 33; Ojetti, *Commentarium*, I, n. 24.

tained its powers even during the Vacancy of the See.[30] Clement V (1305-1314), in his constitution, "*Ne Romani*," [31] declared that the Sacred Penitentiary did not lose its faculties at the death of the Pope. Centuries later, Benedict XIV, in his constitution "*Pastor bonus*," [32] determined exactly what faculties the Sacred Penitentiary would retain during the Vacancy of the Holy See, namely, all powers for the internal forum that it possessed during the lifetime of the Pope, and even powers for the internal forum that it did not possess while the Pope was alive:—the former powers to be used when the good of souls demanded that the matter should not be delayed until the election of a new Pope; the latter, only when the urgent good of souls or spiritual necessity required an intervention, and ordinarily under the condition that recourse should be made again within a month after the election of the new Pope.[33] Can. 241 states that the Roman Curia has no other powers during the Vacancy of the Holy See than those granted by the constitution "*Vacante Sede Apostolica*," issued by Pius X on December 25, 1904.[34] The Constitution "*Vacante Sede Apostolica*" merely declares that the provisions of Benedict XIV regarding the Sacred Penitentiary are still in force.[35] Since the present law has changed from the old law neither regarding the cessation of rescripts nor the status of the Sacred Penitentiary during the Vacancy of the Holy See, certainly the teaching of pre-Code canonists that rescripts of the Sacred Penitentiary, even "*re integra*," did not cease during the Vacancy of the Holy See, still remains in force.[36] This exception will not, however, have much practical importance for matrimonial dispensations, since matrimonial dispensations granted by the Holy See, whether for the

---

[30] Sanchez, *De Matrimonio*, lib. VIII, disp. XXVIII, n. 92; De Justis, *De Dispensationibus*, lib. I, cap. VI, n. 508; Ballerini-Palmieri, *Opus Theologicum Morale*, VI, n. 1378, 1391; Feije, *De Impedimentis*, n. 734.

[31] C. 2, *de electione et electi potestate*, I, 3, in Clem.

[32] Benedict XIV, const. "*Pastor bonus*," 13 Aprilis 1744, *Bullarii Romani Continuatio*, I, 95.

[33] Capello, *De Curia Romana*, II, pp. 88, 89.

[34] *Codex Juris Canonici*, Documentum I.

[35] *Codex Juris Canonici*, Documentum I, cap. III, n. 16.

[36] Can. 6, n. 2; Coronata, *Institutiones*, I, n. 82.

external or the internal forum, are usually granted *in forma commissoria necessaria,* and, therefore, do not cease at the Vacancy of the Holy See.[37]

Before 1904, the Congregations also retained their ordinary powers during the Vacancy of the Holy See, but only as dormant powers:—only in matters of minor moment, e.g., favors granted by the Secretary without the Signature of the Cardinal Prefect and without the Seal, were they able to exercise their ordinary powers.[38] Pius X, in his constitution "*Vacante Sede Apostolica*"[39] declared that the Roman Congregations, during the Vacancy of the Holy See, would retain their ordinary faculties, i.e., the faculties granted to them by Apostolic letters, but not the extraordinary faculties granted to the Secretaries or Prefects of the Congregations, recognized in rescripts by the clause "*vigore specialium et extraordinariarum facultatum,*" nor the powers that were exercised only "*facto verbo cum SSmo*" or "*ex audientia SSmi;*" and declared, moreover, that they could not freely exercise their ordinary faculties except in matters of minor importance:—in matters of major importance, when the urgency of the case required intervention, the Sacred Congregation of the Cardinals was empowered to commit the affair to the Prefect and other Cardinals of the Congregation to whom the Pope would defer the matter if he were alive. These provisions have been retained by the present law.[40]

Coronata[41] claims that, "*re integra,*" rescripts containing powers to grant favors to designated persons, that are granted by the Congregations in virtue of their ordinary faculties, i.e., powers granted to them by Apostolic letters and especially by the "*Normae Peculiares*" and the Code, can be executed even during the vacancy of the Holy See, because the ordinary powers of the Congregations do not cease when the Holy See becomes vacant. De Smet,[42] on

---

[37] De Smet, *De Sponsalibus et Matrimonio,* n. 865.

[38] Capello, *De Curia Romana,* II, pp. 80-82; Wernz, *Jus Decretalium,* II, p. 654.

[39] *Codex Juris Canonici,* Documentum I, cap. IV, n. 22-25.

[40] Can. 241.

[41] *Institutiones,* I, n. 82.

[42] *De Sponsalibus et Matrimonio,* p. 721, nota (6).

the contrary, denies that such rescripts can be executed, *"re integra."* He admits that the powers remain but contends, because of the general character of the words of canon 61, that the rescripts perish just as similar episcopal rescripts, *vacante dioecesi*, perish despite the fact that the power of the Ordinary continues.

The argument of De Smet is not very convincing, since it is generally admitted that, despite the sweeping statement in can. 61, similar rescripts of the Sacred Penitentiary do not cease during the Vacancy of the Holy See because the Sacred Penitentiary does not lose its powers, and since the present law is not any stricter than the old law under which the exception for rescripts of the Sacred Penitentiary was first admitted. The main difficulty seems to be that, in practice, there is not much difference between the powers that could be exercised by the Congregations before or after the constitution *"Vacante Sede Apostolica"* of 1904. Even before 1904, it was claimed that the Congregations could exercise their ordinary powers in matters of *minor importance* during the Vacancy of the Holy See, and yet no claim was made by canonists that such rescripts could be exercised, *"re integra,"* by the voluntary executor during the Vacancy of the Holy See. Moreover, even at present, the ordinary powers cannot be exercised by the Congregations in matters of *major importance* as they can by the Sacred Penitentiary, since the Sacred Congregation of Cardinals must intervene and commit the matter to the respective Congregation when an urgent case arises. At most, by analogy to the exception made for rescripts of the Sacred Penitentiary, it might be maintained, as a probable opinion, that rescripts granting power to bestow favors of minor importance upon designated persons, that are issued by the Sacred Congregation in virtue of their ordinary faculties, can be executed, *"re integra,"* even during the Vacancy of the Holy See, but such an opinion would not be of much practical importance as it is hardly likely that, according to the style of the Curia, such rescripts would be sent *"in forma commissoria libera."*

BIBLIOGRAPHY

SOURCES

Acta et Decreta Concilii plenarii Baltimorensis tertii, A. D. 1884, Baltimore, 1886.

AAS—*Acta Apostolicae Sedis,* 21 vols., Romae, 1909-1929.

ASS—*Acta Sanctae Sedis,* 41 vols., Romae, 1865-1909.

Bizzari, Andreas, *Collectanea in usum Secretariae Sacrae Congregationis Episcoporum et Regularium edita,* Romae, 1885.

Bullarum Diplomatum et Privilegiorum Sanctorum Romanorum Pontificum, Taurinensis editio . . . auspicante Cardinali Francisco Gaude, 24 vols., Augustae Taurinorum, 1857-1872.

Bullarii Romani Continuatio Summorum Pontificum, 19 vols., Prati, 1756-1883.

Canones et Decreta Concilii Tridentini, Taurini, 1913.

Codex Juris Canonici Pii X Pontificis Maximi iussu digestus Benedicti Papae XV auctoritate promulgatus, Romae, 1917.

Codicis Juris Canonici Fontes cura Emi Petri Card. Gasparri editi, vols. I-IV, Romae, 1923-1926.

Collectanea Sacrae Congregationis de Propoganda Fide, 2 vols., Romae, 1907.

Corpus Juris Canonici, editio Lipsiensis secunda post Aemilii Ludovici Richteri curas ad librorum manu scriptorum et editionis romanae fidem recognovit et adnotatione critica instruxit Aemilius Friedberg, 2 vols., Lipsiae, 1922.

Corpus Juris Civilis: I—*Institutiones, recognovit Paulus Krueger,* D—*Digesta, recognovit Theodorus Mommsen, retractavit Paulus Krueger,* vol. I, *Berolini,* 1922; C—*Codex Justinianus, recognovit et retractavit Paulus Krueger,* vol. II, *Berolini,* 1915; N—*Novellae, recognovit Rudolphus Schoell, opus Schoellii morte interceptum absolvit Gulielmus Kroll,* vol. III, *Berolini,* 1912; C. Th.—*Theodosiani Libri XVI cum Constitutionibus Sirmondianis et Leges Novellae ad Theodosianum Pertinentes Assumpto Apparatu P. Kruegeri Th. Mommsen et Paulus M. Meyer,* 2 vols., Berolini apud Weidmannos, 1905.

Lega, *Coram Lega habitae S. R. Rotae Decisiones sive Sententiae Quas Nempe Emus Cardinalis Michael Lega annis 1904-1914 Ejusdem Sacri Auditorii Decanus Exaravit,* 2. ed., Romae, 1926.

Raccolta di Concordati Su Materie Ecclesiastiche Tra La Santa Sede e le Antorita Civili, Romae, 1919.

Thesaurus Resolutionum Sacrae Congregationis Concilii, 167 vols., Romae, 1718-1908.

REFERENCE WORKS

Aichner, Simon, *Compendium Juris Ecclesiastici*, 2. ed., Brixinae, 1887.

Alphonsus, De Liguori, *Theologia Moralis*, 2 vols., Torino, 1867.

Amort, Eusebius D., *Elementa Juris Canonici Veteris et Moderni*, 3 vols., Ferrariae, 1763.

Augustine, Charles, *A Commentary on the New Code of Canon Law*, 8 vols., St. Louis, 1918-1922.

Ayrinhac, H. A., *Constitution of the Church in the New Code of Canon Law*, New York, 1925.

Ayrinhac, H. A., *General Legislation in the New Code of Canon Law*, New York, 1923.

Ayrinhac, H. A., *Marriage Legislation in the New Code of Canon Law*, New York, 1918.

Baart, Peter A., *The Roman Court*, 4. ed., New York, Cincinnati, 1899.

Badii, Caesar, *Institutiones Juris Canonici*, 3. ed., 2 vols., Florentiae, 1921.

Ballerini-Palmieri, *Opus Theologicum Morale*, 3. ed., 7 vols., Prati, 1898-1901.

Barbosa, Agostinus, *Tractatus Varii*, Lugduni, 1660.

Bargilliat, M., *Praelectiones Juris Canonici*, 37. ed., 2 vols., Parisiis, 1923-1924.

Bartholinus, Joannes Baptista Leonellius, *Tractatus De Subreptione Rescriptorum*, Venetiis, 1601.

Benedictus XIV, *De Synodo Diocesana*, 2 vols., Romae, 1806.

Benedictus XIV, *Institutiones Ecclesiasticae*, 3. ed., 2 vols., Venetiis, 1788.

Blat, Albertus, O. P., *Commentarium Textus Codicis Juris Canonici*, 5 vols., Romae, 1921-1927.

Bonacina, Martinus, *Opera Omnia*, 3 vols., Antverpiae, 1632.

Brys, J., *De Dispensatione in Jure Canonico Praesertim Apud Decretistas et Decretalistas usque ad Medium Saeculum Decimum Quartum*, Brugis-Wetteren, 1925.

Bucceroni, Januarius, *Casus Conscientiae*, 6. ed., 2 vols., Romae, 1901.

Buckland, *Text-Book of Roman Law from Augustus to Justinian*, Cambridge, 1921.

Bury, J. B., Tanner, J. R., Previte-Orton, C. W., Brooke, Z. N., *Cambridge Medieval History*, vols. V, VI, New York, Cambridge, 1929.

Caillaud, L'Abbe, *Manuel des Dispenses, à L'usage du Curé, du Confesseur et de L'official*, 5. ed., Paris, 1875.

Calvinus, Joannes, *Magnum Lexicon Juridicum*, 2 vols., Coloniae Allobrogum, 1759.

Capello, Felix, *De Curia Romana Juxta Reformationem a Pio X Sapientissime Inductam*, 2 vols., Romae, 1911.

Capello, Felix, *Summa Juris Canonici in usum scholarum concinnata*, vol. I, Romae, 1928.

Capello, Felix, *Tractatus Canonico-Moralis de Sacramentis juxta Codicem Juris Canonici*, 3 vols., Taurinorum Augustae, 1927.

Carriere, Josephus, *De Matrimonio*, 2 vols., Parisiis, 1837.

Catholic Encyclopedia, 16 vols., New York, 1907-1912; Supplement, I, 1922.

Celier, L., *Les dataires du XV*[e] *siècle et les Origines de la Daterie Apostolique*, Paris-Fontemoing, 1910.

Chelodi, Joannes, *Jus De Personis juxta Codicem Juris Canonici*, 2. ed., Tridenti, 1927.

Chelodi, Joannes, *Jus Matrimoniale juxta Codicem Juris Canonici*, 3. ed., Tridenti, 1921.

Chelodi, Joannes, *Jus Poenale et Ordo Procedendi in Judiciis criminalibus juxta Codicem Juris Canonici*, Tridenti, 1925.

Cicognani, Hamletus J., *Commentarium ad Librum I Codicis*, Romae, 1925.

Claeys-Bouuaert-Simenon, *Manuale Juris Canonici*, 2. ed., Bandae et Leodii, 1926.

Cocchi, Guidus, *Commentarium in Codicem Juris Canonici ad Usum Scholarum*, 3. ed., 8 vols., Taurinorum Augustae, 1925.

Collet, Pierre, *Theologia Moralis*, 4 vols., Lugduni, 1768.

Collet, Pierre, *Traité des dispenses en général et en particulier*, 5. ed., 3 vols., Louvain, 1700.

Coronata, P. Matthaeus Conte A., O. M. C., *Institutiones Juris Canonici*, vol. I, Taurini, 1928.

Corradus, Pyrrhus, *Praxis Dispensationum Apostolicarum*, Venetiis, 1735.

Coustant, P., et Mopinot, D., *Epistolae Romanorum Pontificum*, Parisiis, 1721.

D'Annibale, Josephus, *Summula Theologiae Moralis*, 3 vols., Romae, 1896.

De Angelis, Philippus, *Praelectiones Juris Canonici*, 4 vols., Romae Parisiis, 1877-1878.

De Becker, I., *De Sponsalibus et Matrimonio Praelectiones Canonicae*, 2. ed., Louvanii, 1903.

De Justis, Vincentius, *De Dispensationibus Matrimonialibus*, Lucae, 1726.

De Meester, A., *Juris Canonici et Juris Canonico-Civilis Compendium*, nova ed., 3 vols. in 4, Brugis, 1921-1928.

Dens, P., *Tractatus de Sponsalibus et Matrimonio*, Mechliniae, 1861.

De Rosa, Thomas, *De Executoribus Litterarum Apostolicarum*, Aschaffenburci, 1747.

De Smet, Aloysius, *De Sponsalibus et Matrimonio*, 4. ed., Brugis, 1927.

Dictionnaire de Théologie Catholique, Paris, 1903 ff.

Duardenus, Franciscus, *Opera Omnia*, 4 vols., Lucae, 1765-1769.

Durieux, *Les Dispenses Matrimoniales—Étude historique, théorique et pratique*, Le Puy, 1913.

Eichmann, Eduard, *Lehrbuch des Katholischen Kirchenrechts*, Paderborn, 1926.

Engel, Ludovicus, *Collegium universi juris canonici,* Venetiis, 1760.

Esmein, A., *Le mariage en droit canonique,* 2 vols., Paris, 1891.

Fanfani, P. Ludovicus J., *De Jure Religiosorum ad Normam Codicis Juris Canonici,* ed. alt., Taurini Romae, 1925.

Feije, Henricus Joannes, *De Impedimentis et Dispensationibus Matrimonialibus,* 3. ed., Louvanii, 1885.

Ferraris, Lucius F., *Bibliotheca Prompta Canonica, Juridica, Moralis, Theologica,* 8 vols., Romae, 1885.

Ferreres, Joannes B., *Compendium Theologiae Moralis ad Normam Codicis Juris Canonici,* 7. ed., 2 vols., Barcinone, 1928.

Ferreres, Joannes B., *La Curia Romana,* Madrid, 1911.

Fournier, Paul, *Yves de chartres et la droit canonique,* Paris, 1898.

Freisen, I., *Geschichte des canonischen Eherechts bis zum Verfall der Glossenlitteratur, Tübingen,* 1888.

Garcia, Nicholas, *Tractatus de beneficiis amplissimus et doctissimus,* Coloniae Allobrogum, 1636.

Gasparri, Petrus, *Tractatus Canonicus de Matrimonio,* 2. ed., 2 vols., Parisiis, 1892.

Genicot, Eduardus, S. J., *Theologiae Moralis Institutiones,* 2 vols., Louvanii, 1896.

Genicot-Salsmans, *Institutiones Theologiae Moralis,* 10. ed., 2 vols., Bruxellis, 1922.

Gennari-Boudinhon, *Consultations de droit canonique,* Paris, 1908.

Giovine, Petrus, *De Dispensationibus Matrimonialibus Consultationes Canonicae,* 2 vols., Neapoli, 1863.

Goeller, Z., *Die Päpstliche Pönitentiarie von ihrem Ursprung bis zu ihrer Umgestaltung unter Pius V,* 2 vols., Rome, 1907.

Golden, Henry Francis, *Parochial Benefices in the New Code,* Washington, D. C., 1921.

Haring, *Grundzüge des Katholischen Kirchenrechts,* Grasz, 1924.

Heiner, Franz, *Katholisches Kirchenrecht,* Paderborn, 1912.

Heiss, M., *De Matrimonio Tractatus Quinque Usui Venerabilis Cleri Americani accomodati appendice adjecta duplice,* Monachii, 1861.

Herinx, Guilelmus, *Summa Theologica Scholastica et Moralis,* Antwerpiae, 1680.

Hilling, Nicholas, *Procedure at the Roman Curia,* New York, 1907.

Hulme, Edward Maslin, *The Middle Ages,* New York, 1929.

Humphrey, William, *Conscience and Law,* London, 1896.

Hunter, William A., *Introduction to Roman Law,* London, 1880.

Hyland, Francis Edward, *Excommunication, Its Nature, Historical Development and Effects,* Washington, D. C., 1928.

Jaffé, Ph., Wattenbach, S., Loewenfeld, F., Kaltenbrumner, F., Ewald, P., *Regesta Pontificum Romanorum,* 2 vols., Lipsiae, 1885-1888.

Kay, Thomas Henry, *Competence in Matrimonial Procedure,* Washington, D. C., 1929.

Kearney, Raymond, *The Principles of Delegation,* Washington, D. C., 1929.

Kilker, Adrian Jerome, *Extreme Unction*, St. Louis-London, 1927.
Konings, A., *Moralis Theologia*, 2 vols., Londoni Tornaci, 1880.
Konings-Putzer, *Commentarium in Facultates Apostolicas*, 5. ed., New York, 1898.
Kubelbeck, William J., *The Sacred Penitentiaria and its Relations to Faculties of Ordinaries and Priests*, Washington, D. C., 1918.
Kugler, *Tractatus de Dispensationibus*, Vratisl, 1727.
Launoi, Joannes, *Opera Omnia*, 5 vols. in 10, Coloniae Allobrogum, 1731.
Laurenius, *Forum Beneficiale*, 2 vols., Augustae Vindelicorum, 1757.
Laurentius, Justinianus, *Opera*, Basiliae Froben, 1560.
Laurin, Franciscus, *Introductio in Corpus Juris Canonici*, Friburgi Brisgoviae et Vindobonae, 1889.
Laymann, Paulus, *Theologia Moralis*, 5 vols. in 1, Lutetiae Parisiorum, 1627.
Leage, R. W., *Roman Private Law*, London, 1924.
Lehmkuhl, Augustinus, *Theologia Moralis*, 5. ed., 2 vols., Friburgi Brisgoviae, 1897.
Leitner, Martin, *Handbuch des katholischen Kirchenrechts auf Grund des neuen Kodex*, 3 vols., Regensburg, 1921-1923.
Leurenius, Petrus, S. J., *Forum Ecclesiasticum de Universo Jure Canonico*, 5 vols., Venetiis, 1729.
Lombardi, C., *Juris Canonici Privati Institutiones*, 2. ed., 3 vols., Romae, 1901.
Mann, Horace K., *The Lives of the Popes in the Middle Ages*, St. Louis, 1910.
Maroto, Philippus, *Institutiones Juris Canonici ad Normam Novi Codicis*, 3. ed., 2 vols., Romae, 1921.
Martin, Michael, *The Roman Curia as it Now Exists*, New York, 1913.
Maschardus, Josephus, *Conclusiones Probationum Omnium*, 3 vols., Venetiis, 1593.
Maschat, Remigius, *Institutiones Canonicae*, 2 vols., Romae, 1757.
Meehan, Andreas B., *Compendium Juris Canonici*, Roffae, 1899.
Menochius, Jacobus, *De Presumptionibus, Conjecturis, Signis et Indiciis Commentaria*, 2 vols., Coloniae Allobrogum, 1684.
Mergentheim, Leo, *Die Quinquennalfakultäten pro Foro Externo. Ihre Erstehung Und Einführung in Deutschen Bistümern*, 2 vols., Stuttgart, 1918.
Merolla, Franciscus, *Disputationum in Universam Theologiam Moralem*, vol. I, III, Neapoli, 1631.
Michiels, P. Gommarus, *Normae Generales Juris Canonici. Commentarius libri I Codicis Juris Canonici*, 2 vols., Lublin Polonia, 1929.
Mollat, G., *Les Papes d'Avignon*, Paris, 1920.
Monin, A., *De Curia Romana, ejus historia ac hodierna disciplina juxta reformationem a Pio X inductam*, Louvanii, 1912.
Monumenta Germanicae historica.

M. P. G.-Migne, J. P., *Patrologia Graeca,* 161 vols., Parisiis, 1858-1864.

M. P. L.-Migne, J. P., *Patrologia Latina,* 221 vols., Parisiis, 1847-1870.

Morey, William C., *Outlines of Roman Law,* 2. ed., New York, London, 1913.

Mothon, Joseph P., *Institutions Canoniques,* vol. III, *Formulaire,* Bruges, 1924.

Munro, Dana Carleton, *The Middle Ages,* New York, 1925.

Noldin, H., S. J., *De Jure Matrimoniali juxta Codicem Juris Canonici,* Lincii, 1919.

Noldin, H., S. J., *De Sacramentis,* 15. ed., Oeniponte, 1923.

Ojetti, B., *Commentarium in Codicem Juris Canonici,* vol. I, Romae, 1927.

Ojetti, B., *De Romana Curia Commentarium in Constitutionem Apostalicam "Sapienti Consilio" seu De Curiae Piana Reformatione,* Romae, 1910.

Ojetti, B., *Synopsis Rerum Moralium et Juris Pontificii,* Romae, 1909.

O'Keeffe, Gerald Michael, *Matrimonial Dispensations, Powers of Bishops, Priests, and Confessors,* Washington, D. C., 1927.

Petrovits, Joseph J. C., *The New Church Law on Matrimony,* 2. ed., Philadelphia, 1926.

Phillips, Georgius, *Kirchenrechts,* 7 vols., Regensburg, 1855-1889.

Piat-Piatus, F., *Praelectiones Juris Regularis,* 3. ed., 2 vols., Tornaci, 1905.

Pighi, Joannes Baptista, *Cursus Theologiae Moralis,* Veronae, 1926.

Pirhing, Enricus, *Jus Canonicum Novo Methodo Explicatum,* ed. novissima, 5 vols., Dilingae, 1722.

Planchard, M. J., *Dispenses Matrimoniales Règles a Suivro pour les Demander les Interpréter les Mettre a Exécution,* Angonleme, 1882.

Pompen, J., *Tractatus De Dispensationibus et De Revalidatione Matrimonii,* Amstelodami, 1897.

Ponsius, Josephus, S. J., *Les Papes d'Avignon,* Paris, 1920.

Pontius, Basilius, *De Sacramento Matrimonii Tractatus,* Bruxellis, 1627.

Prümmer, Dominicus M., *Manuale Juris Canonici in Usum Clericorum Praesertim Illorum qui ad Instituta Religiosa Pertinent,* 3. ed., Friburgi Brisgoviae, 1922.

Radin, Max, *Handbook of Roman Law,* St. Paul, 1927.

Raus, P. J. B., *Institutiones Canonicae,* Lugduni Parisiis, 1923.

Reiffenstuel, Anacletus, *Jus Canonicum Universum,* 4 vols., Venetiis, 1735.

Rigantius, Josephus B., *Commentarium in Regulas, Constitutiones et Ordinationes Cancellariae Apostolicae,* 4 vols. in 2, Coloniae Allobrogum, 1751.

Roelker, Edward D., *Principles of Privilege according to the Code of Canon Law,* Washington, D. C., 1926.

Rosset, Michael, *De Sacramento Matrimonii Tractatus Dogmaticus Moralis Canonicus Liturgicus et Judiciarius*, Parisiis, 1895-1896.

Sabetti-Barrett, *Compendium Theologiae Moralis*, 29. ed., Neo Eboraci Cincinnati, 1920.

Salmaticenses, *Cursus Theologiae Moralis*, Lugduni, 1879.

Sanchez, Thomas, *De Sancto Matrimonii Sacramento Disputationum*, 3 vols., Lugduni, 1669.

Sanguinetti, Sebastianus, *Juris Ecclesiastici Privati Institutiones ad Decretalium Ennarationem Ordinatae*, Romae, 1884.

Santamaria, *Commentarios al Codigo Canonico*, vol. I, Madrid, 1920.

Santi, Franciscus, *Praelectiones Juris Canonici juxta Ordinem Decretalium*, 5 vols. in. 2, Ratisbonae, 1886.

Savigny, Frederich Karl Von-Holloway, William, *System of Roman Law*, vol. I, Madras, 1867.

Scavini, Petrus, *Theologia Moralis Universa ad Mentem S. Alphonsi M. de Ligouri, Pio X, Pontifici M. Dicata*, 11. ed., 4 vols., Madiolani, 1869.

Schäfer, Timotheus P., *Compendium De Religiosis ad Normam Codicis Juris Canonici*, Münster, 1927.

Schenk, Francis J., *The Matrimonial Impediments of Mixed Religion and Disparity of Cult*, Washington, D. C., 1929.

Scherer, Rudolph R. Von, *Handbuch des Kirchenrechts*, 2 vols., Graz und Leipzig, 1898.

Schmalzgrueber, R. P. Franciscus, *Jus Ecclesiasticum Universum*, 12 vols., Romae, 1843-1845.

Schulte, J. F., *Geschichte der Quellen und Literatur des canonischen Rechts*, 3 vols. in 2, Stuttgart, 1875-1880.

Sebastianelli, Guilelmus, *Praelectiones Juris Canonici*, 2. ed., 3 vols., Romae, 1905.

Smith, D. B., *Elements of Ecclesiastical Law*, 9. ed., 2 vols., New York, Cincinnati, Chicago, 1887-1888.

Soglia, Joannes, *Institutiones Juris Publici Ecclesiastici*, Parisiis, 1842.

Sohm, Rudolph-Ledi, J. C., *The Institutes of Roman Law*, Oxford, 1892.

Stiegler, M. A., *Dispensation, Dispensationswesen und Dispensationsrecht im Kirchenrecht geschichtlich dargestellt*, vol. I, Mainz, 1901.

Suarez, F., *Tractatus de Legibus*, Neapoli, 1872.

Tanquerey, Adrianus, *Synopsis Theologiae Moralis et Pastoralis ad mentem S. Thomae et S. Alphonsi Hodiernis Moribus Accomodata*, 8. ed., 3 vols., Romae, 1921.

Thepany, *Traité des dispenses matrimoniales*, Paris, 1889.

Thiel, Andreas, *Epistolae Romanorum Pontificum genuinae et quae ad eos scriptae sunt a S. Hilario ad Pelagium*, Brunsbergae, 1868.

Thomassinus, L., *Vetus et Nova Ecclesiae Disciplina Circa Beneficia et Beneficiarios*, 3 vols., Parisiis, 1688.

Torrubiano Ripoll, J., *Novisimas Instituciones De Derecho Canonico*, Madrid, 1919.

Toso, *Ad Codicem Juris Canonici . . . Commentaria Minora*, Romae, 1921.

Van de Burgt, F. P., *Tractatus de Dispensationibus Matrimonialibus*, Sylvae Ducis, 1885.

Vecchiotti, Septimus M., *Institutiones Canonicae*, 16. ed., 3 vols., Augustae Taurinorum, 1875.

Verani, Cajetanus Felix, *Juris Canonici Universi Commentarius Parititlaris*, Monachii, 1703.

Vermeersch, Arthurus, *De Religiosis Institutis et Personis Tractatus Canonico-Moralis ad Recentissimas Leges Exactus*, 4 ed., tomus alter, Brugis, 1909.

Vermeersch, Arthurus, *Theologiae Moralis Principia, Responsa, Consilia*, 2. ed., 4 vols., Romae, 1926-1928.

Vermeersch-Creusen, *Epitome Juris Canonici cum Commentariis ad Scholas et ad Usum Privatum*, 3. ed., 3 vols., Mechliniae Romae, 1927.

Vlaming, Th. M., *Praelectiones Juris Matrimonii ad Normam Codicis Juris Canonici*, 3. ed., 2 vols., Bussum in Hollandia, 1919-1921.

Wernz, Franciscus Xav., *Jus Decretalium ad Usum Praelectionum in Scholis Textus Canonici sive Juris Decretalium*, vol. I, II, Prati, 1913-1915.

Wernz-Vidal, *Jus Canonicum, auctore P. Francisco Xav. Wernz, S. I. ad Codicis Normam Exactum opera P. Petri Vidal*, vol. II, V, VI, Romae, 1927-1928.

Woywod, Stanislaus, *A Practical Commentary on the Code of Canon Law*, 2 vols., New York, 1925.

Zallinger, J., *Institutiones Juris Ecclesiastici maxime privati, ordine Decretalium*, Romae, 1832.

Zitelli, Zephyrinus, *De Dispensationibus Matrimonialibus*, Romae, 1887.

PERIODICALS

American Ecclesiastical Review, The (AER), Philadelphia, 1889-

Analecta Juris Pontificii, Romae, 1855-1890.

Apollinaris, Romae, 1928-

Archiv für katholisches Kirchenrecht (AkKR), Innsbruck, 1857-

Commentarium pro Religiosis (CpR), Romae, 1920-

Gregorianum, Commentarii de Re Theologica et Philosophica, Romae, 1920-

Il Monitore Ecclesiastico (ME), Romae, 1888-

Irish Ecclesiastical Record, The (IER), Dublin, 1864-

Le Canoniste Contemporain, Paris, 1878-

Nouvelle Revue Théologique (NRT), Paris, 1856-

Periodica, de Re Canonica et Morali, Romae et Brugis, 1905-

Theologisch-Praktische Quartalschrift (LQS), Linz, 1832-

Universitas Catholica Americae

WASHINGTON, D. C.

FACULTAS JURIS CANONICI

1 9 3 0

No. 57

DEUS LUX MEA

TITULI

QUOS

AD DOCTORATUS GRADUM

IN

JURE CANONICO

APUD UNIVERSITATEM CATHOLICAM AMERICAE

CONSEQENDUM

PUBLICE PROPUGNABIT

GULIELMUS H. O'NEILL

SACERDOS DIOECESIS SEATTLENSIS

JURIS CANONICI LICENTIATUS

HORA XI AM DIE XXVIII MAII MCMXXX

TITULI

DE JURE CANONICO

I.	De Dissertatione.	
II.	De Historia Juris Canonici.	
III.	Canones 1-7	De Ambitu Codicis.
IV.	Canones 8-24	De Legibus Ecclesiasticis.
V.	Canones 25-30	De Consuetudine.
VI.	Canones 31-35	De Temporis Supputatione.
VII.	Canones 63-79	De Privilegiis.
VIII.	Canones 80-86	De Dispensationibus.
IX.	Canones 87-107	Generales Notiones de Personis.
X.	Canones 111-117	De Clericorum Adscriptione Alicui Diocesi.
XI.	Canones 118-123	De Juribus et Privilegiis Clericorum.
XII.	Canones 124-144	De Obligationibus Clericorum.
XIII.	Canones 145-195	De Officiis Ecclesiasticis.
XIV.	Canones 196-210	De Potestate Ordinaria et Delegata.
XV.	Canones 211-214	De Reductione Clericorum ad Statum Laicalem.
XVI.	Canones 487-498	De Notione Religionis, et de Erectione et Suppressione Religionis, Provinciae, Domus.
XVII.	Canones 499-537	De Religionum Regimine.
XVIII.	Canones 538-586	De Admissione in Religionem.
XIX.	Canones 587-591	De Ratione Studiorum in Religionibus Clericalibus.
XX.	Canones 592-631	De Obligationibus et Privilegiis Religiosorum.
XXI.	Canones 632-672	De Transitu ad Aliam Religionem, de Egressu e Religione, et de Dimissione Religiosorum.
XXII.	Canones 673-681	De Societatibus sive Virorum sive Mulierum in Communi Viventium Sine Votis.
XXIII.	Canones 1012-1018	De Matrimonio in Genere.
XXIV.	Canones 1019-1034	De Iis quae Matrimonii Celebrationi Praemitti Debent.
XXV.	Canones 1035-1057	De Impedimentis in Genere.
XXVI.	Canones 1058-1066	De Impedimentis Impedientibus.
XXVII.	Canones 1067-1080	De Impedimentis Dirimentibus.

Tituli

XXVIII.	Canones 1081-1093	De Consensu Matrimoniali.
XXIX.	Canones 1552-1568	De Notione Judicii et de Foro Competenti.
XXX.	Canones 1569-1607	De Variis Tribunalium Gradibus et Speciebus.
XXXI.	Canones 1608-1645	De Disciplina in Tribunalibus Servanda.
XXXII.	Canones 1646-1666	De Partibus in Causa.
XXXIII.	Canones 1667-1705	De Actionibus et Exceptionibus.
XXXIV.	Canones 1706-1725	De Causae Introductione.
XXXV.	Canones 1726-1746	De Litis Contestatione, de Litis Instantia, et de Interrogationibus Partibus in Judicio Faciendis.
XXXVI.	Canones 1747-1836	De Probationibus.
XXXVII.	Canones 1837-1857	De Causis Incidentibus.
XXXVIII.	Canones 1858-1877	De Processus Publicatione, de Conclusione in Causa, de Causae Discussione, et de Sententia.
XXXIX.	Canones 2195-2198	De Natura Delicti Ejusque Divisione.
XL.	Canones 2199-2211	De Imputabilitate Delicti, de Causis Illam Aggravantibus vel Minuentibus, et de Juridicis Delicti Effectibus.
XLI.	Canones 2212-2213	De Conatu Delicti.
XLII.	Canones 2214-2240	De Poenis in Genere.
XLIII.	Canones 2241-2285	De Poenis Medicinalibus seu de Censuris.
XLIV.	Canones 2186-2305	De Poenis Vindicativis.
XLV.	Canones 2306-2313	De Remediis Poenalibus et Poenitentiis.
XLVI.	The Periods of Roman Law.	
XLVII.	The Sources of Roman Law.	
XLVIII.	Personality.	
XLIX.	Slavery.	
L.	Citizenship.	
LI.	Patria Potestas.	
LII.	Personae in Manu.	
LIII.	Personae in Mancipio.	
LIV.	Tutela et Cura.	
LV.	Ownership.	
LVI.	De Obligationibus in Genere.	
LVII.	De Obligationibus Extra-Contractualibus.	
LVIII.	Furtum.	
LIX.	Damnum Injuria Datum.	
LX.	Injuria.	

Tituli

Vidit Facultas:
PHILIPPUS BERNARDINI, S.T.D., J.U.D., Decanus.
LUDOVICUS H. MOTRY, S.T.D., J.C.D., a Secretis.
VALENTINUS T. SCHAAF, O.F.M., J.C.D.
FRANCISCUS J. LARDONE, S.T.D., J.U.D.
Vidit Rector Magnificus Universitatis:
JACOBUS HUGO RYAN, Ph.D., S.T.D.

VITA

William H. O'Neill was born in Butte, Montana, on April 11, 1900. He received his elementary education in the Beacon Hill, Immaculate Conception, and Seattle College grammar schools of Seattle, Washington. He graduated from the high-school department of Seattle College in 1916. In the same year he entered St. Patrick's Seminary, Menlo Park, California. He was ordained to the Priesthood on June 14, 1924. He entered the School of Canon Law of the Catholic University of America in 1928, and in 1929 was awarded the degree of Licentiate in Canon Law.

www.ingramcontent.com/pod-product-compliance
Lightning Source LLC
LaVergne TN
LVHW050244080826
844660LV00012B/596

9780813222462